Methodical Programming in COBOL

Ray Welland

Department of Computer Science
University of Strathclyde

Pitman

PITMAN PUBLISHING LIMITED
128 Long Acre, London WC2E 9AN

PITMAN PUBLISHING INC
1020 Plain Street, Marshfield, Massachusetts 02050

Associated Companies
Pitman Publishing Pty Ltd, Melbourne
Pitman Publishing New Zealand Ltd, Wellington
Copp Clark Pitman, Toronto

First published in Great Britain 1983
Reprinted 1984

British Library Cataloguing in Publication Data

Welland, Ray
Methodical programming in COBOL.
1.COBOL (Computer program language)
I.Title
001.64'24 QA76.73.C25

ISBN 0-273-01820-5

Printed and bound in Great Britain by
Biddles Ltd, Guildford, Surrey

Contents

Preface

At the time of writing, the most widely used commercial programming language is COBOL which has been in existence for more than 20 years. Similarly the most widely used scientific programming language is FORTRAN, first formulated in 1957. It has often been claimed that better languages exist for both fields but the difficulty with introducing a new language is the enormous investment in existing software written in both COBOL and FORTRAN. Therefore it seems likely that both these languages will remain with us for a long time yet.

The objective of this book is to try to combine the modern ideas of structured programming with the existing COBOL language to show how good programs can be constructed.

The main targets of this book are students of computing or data processing who may or may not have had previous programming experience. The ideas have been developed while teaching COBOL as a first programming language to accountancy students and teaching COBOL to computing science students already conversant with Pascal.

The approach used in this book is to separate the tasks of program design and coding. Programs are designed using an abstract program design language which can then be translated into COBOL using a defined set of transformations. One attraction of this approach is that students can learn to program without getting overwhelmed by the mass of detail involved in even a simple COBOL program. It would also be possible to design a different set of transformations from the design language into another programming language.

Program designs can be checked by the lecturer, or demonstrator, and discussed before coding commences (and also marked if required). This means that many logical errors can be trapped before the program is actually coded in COBOL.

Use of the book

This book is structured so that the student should be able to design quite substantial programs by the end of Chapter 2. This will enable useful practical work to be undertaken while the fundamental elements of COBOL are explained in Chapters 3 and 4. By the end of Chapter 4 the student should be able to write and run complete, simple COBOL programs.

The next two chapters introduce more features of the language concerned with the handling of input and output, and the expression of more complex algorithms. At the end of Chapter 6 the student has been introduced to all the language elements required to write quite complex COBOL programs. Chapters 7 and 8 are designed to give a 'breathing space' while the student consolidates his understanding by practical experience of COBOL programming.

From Chapter 9 onwards more features of the language are introduced and the student's repertoire of programming techniques is steadily increased.

The Appendices are designed to give summaries of various features of

COBOL for quick reference when writing programs.

Exercises

Programming is essentially a practical subject and to take full advantage of this book the student must actually design and run some programs. Programming is like swimming - one can read all the books available but until one "takes the plunge" one doesn't start really learning.

The exercises are divided into two categories: pencil and paper exercises, to follow up points made in the text, and programming exercises which involve the design, writing and running of complete computer programs. It is recommended that the student should do all of the pencil and paper exercises, and at least one of the programming exercises at the end of each chapter.

Hints on the solutions to the pencil and paper exercises are given at the end of the book.

The COBOL Language

The language used in this book is that defined in the 1974 American National Standard for COBOL, usually called ANS COBOL '74. The definition of ANS COBOL '74 is modular and within each module there are levels of implementation. Therefore what is legitimately described as an ANS COBOL '74 compiler may not have all the features introduced in this book. To assist readers using low-level ANS COBOL compilers, notes are inserted in the text where problems may arise, and Appendix 5 gives some hints on alternative constructs for methodical programming.

Acknowledgements

I would like to thank Charles Clarke and Roy McAllister of the Management Services Division, Strathclyde University, for their help in using the local system to test the COBOL programs in this book. I would also like to acknowledge the strong influence of two ex-colleagues: Bill Findlay and David Watt, of Glasgow University, who taught me much about structured programming.

This book also owes a great deal to another ex-colleague John Jeacocke, of Glasgow University, who encouraged me to use the style of teaching advocated in this book, helped to formulate the design language and made many helpful criticisms of various drafts of the book. Finally, I would like to thank the consulting editor, David Hatter, for his constructive criticisms, and Alfred Waller of Pitmans for his support throughout the writing of this book.

Ray Welland
University of Strathclyde

January 1983

ACKNOWLEDGEMENT

COBOL is an industry language and is not the property of any company or group of companies, or of any organization or group of organizations.

No warranty expressed or implied, is made by any contributor or by the CODASYL Programming Language Committee as to the accuracy and functioning of the programming system and language. Moreover, no responsibility is assumed by any contributor, or by the committee, in connection therewith.

The authors and copyright holders of the copyrighted material used herein:

FLOW-MATIC (trademark of the Sperry-Rand Corporation), Programming for the Univac I and II, Data Automation Systems copyrighted 1958, 1959, Sperry-Rand Corporation; IBM Commercial Translator Form No. F28-8013, copyrighted 1958 by IBM; FACT, DSI 27A5260-2760, copyrighted 1960 by Minneapolis-Honeywell

have specifically authorized the use of this material in whole or in part, in the COBOL specifications. Such authorization extends to the reproduction and use of COBOL specifications in programming manuals or similar publications.

1 Introduction

This chapter includes a very brief history of COBOL and a survey of some of the 'computer basics' which are necessary for this book. However, it is not intended that this book should be read in isolation. Pressure on space dictates that it cannot cover fundamental concepts of computing in any depth while doing justice to its main theme of methodical programming in COBOL. Therefore it will be assumed that the readers are familiar with the basic concepts of computing through attendance at formal classes, from background reading or from using their own home computer.

1.1 History and Objectives of COBOL

In the late 1950s it was recognized that the existing programming languages were inadequate for building large commercial data processing systems. Most programming at that time was being carried out in assembly languages which meant that programs, and skilled staff, were tied to one particular type of computer. Therefore the American Department of Defense, one of the biggest users of computers for inventory control and accounting, pulled together a group of experts with the objective of creating a new high-level programming language suitable for commercial applications of computing. The objectives which this group, called the CODASYL Committee, were given for the design of the language were as follows.

(a) To specify a language independent of any make or model of computer, open-ended and stated in both an English notation and a narrative form.
(b) The language should be extensible so that it could be run on future ranges of machines.
(c) It should be easy to learn so that relatively inexperienced programmers could make a significant contribution.
(d) Programs written in the language should be "self-documenting" and also "readable" by managers and non-technical people.

The committee proposed the language now known as COBOL (COmmon Business Oriented Language) which has been revised regularly since its inception in 1960. The language is reviewed regularly and new proposals published in the COBOL Journal of Development. Various manufacturers have also added their own enhancements to the languages giving rise to a wide range of 'dialects' of the language. In order to maintain the portability of the language, one of its most important advantages, an American National Standard for COBOL was published in 1968 and a new standard in 1974. This book is based on the 1974 standard, commonly called ANS COBOL 74, as this is currently the most widely used version of COBOL. It is expected that a new standard will be agreed in 1983 but this will take some time to become widely implemented and accepted.

Cobol is a very 'rich' and powerful programming language, it has a wide variety of features designed to handle the most complex problems in commercial data processing. A danger for the student is being overwhelmed by this plethora of facilities. This book uses only a minimal useful subset of COBOL initially so that the trainee programmer can grasp the basic principles before learning to use the more advanced features of the language.

1.2 The COBOL Computer

When designing a programming language it is necessary to have a conceptual model of the computer to be used, which is called the abstract machine. For the purposes of this book we shall assume that the model shown in Figure 1.1 is the first approximation to the COBOL abstract machine.

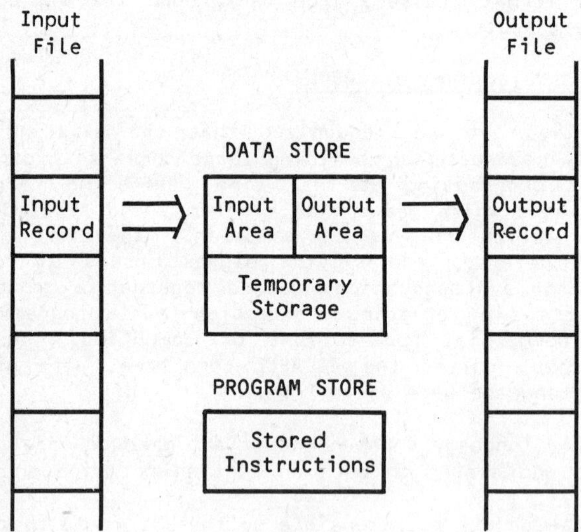

Figure 1.1

The input and output files are divided into records. Each record in a file is in a similar format and usually contains data about one of a group of related 'things'. For example, a file might contain details about a company's employees; each employee would have a record in the file and each record will contain similar data: works number, name, address, national insurance number, salary etc.

A file is accessed in such a way that only one record from a file is available to the program at any given time, the current record. Initially it will be assumed that there is one input file and one output file. The current record of the input file is held in the input area and records are written to the output file via an output area. In a program which does anything useful there will need to be internal storage for intermediate values in calculations, for example. Values held in such temporary storage exist only for the lifetime of a program and if a permanent copy of the values is required they must be sent to the output file. Therefore in the simple model of the COBOL computer the data store is divided into three parts: the input area, output area and temporary storage.

Each of the areas of the data store is divided into a hierarchy of units of storage called records, group-items and elementary-items. At the lowest level, the elementary-item is a named location which can hold a value which can either be a number or a string of characters. Data processing is built around using these stored values in arithmetic operations, transferring them from location to location and making simple decisions based on the values stored in specific locations.

The simple machine will need a number of basic operations which can then be combined to create _programs_. A program is a sequence of instructions which, in the absence of instructions which change the 'flow of control', will be executed in the order they appear in the program store. Obviously there will need to be an operation to get a record from the input file, making it available in the input area, and a complementary operation to put a record, which has been built up in the data store, into the output file. There will also need to be a transfer operation to allow data to be copied from one storage location to another and basic arithmetic operations: add, subtract, multiply and divide, operating on the stored data to create new values.

It would be possible to write a simple computer program consisting only of a sequence of basic operations to be carried out one after the other from the first operation to the last. Such a simple computer program would consist of three parts: initialization, processing and termination. In the majority of programs the processing part will be more complex than a simple sequence of instructions but these three basic parts will still exist.

The initialization will define an _initial state_ for the computer, processing will change the state of the machine by transforming data in some way and termination will tidy up before the program finishes. For example, initialization will define the initial status of the input and output files and the initial values in the data store. At any given time during the processing it may be necessary to find out the _current state_ of the machine, e.g., are there any more input records? Termination in a simple machine might consist of releasing the input and output files and printing some message about the final state of the machine.

Most useful programs, particularly in commercial data processing, will involve repetitions of sequences of instructions. For example, going back to the employee file it should be possible to establish a sequence of operations, called an _algorithm_, for calculating an employee's pay given certain facts such as salary, tax code, superannuation rules etc. This algorithm can then be repeated for each employee's record in the file. Therefore in addition to the basic operations outlined above a special operation to allow _controlled repetition_ of sequences of operations will be required. This implies that a method of recognizing _conditions_ which arise will have to be included in the language. Conditions are formalized questions which can be asked and the result returned will be either _true_ or _false_, a 'Boolean' value.

Many algorithms will involve the choice of alternative courses of action depending on the value of data. Going back to the employee example there might be two different superannuation schemes available to employees, each requiring a special deduction calculation routine. The type of superannuation scheme might be distinguished by a special code 'A' or 'B' in the employee record which needs to be recognized by the program and the appropriate routine used. Therefore in addition to repetition a selection operation is required.

Therefore, to summarize, the basic design language used in this book will have the following operations:

(a) record input/output: get and put,
(b) data transfer, within the data store,
(c) calculation, to perform simple arithmetic,
(d) controlled repetition,
(e) selection.

In addition to these operations there will also have to be facilities for the description of the form of data, and condition tests, to support (d) and (e), above.

These features together with one additional concept called refinement, which is purely a program construction technique, will define the subset of COBOL described in the first part of this book. This subset is powerful enough to write quite complex programs.

1.3 The Real Computer: hardware and software

The machine shown in Figure 1.1 and described in the previous section is called an abstract machine because no such machine actually exists. A program written in COBOL, and designed to run on this abstract machine, will have to be translated into a lower level language which can be run on a real machine. This real machine, or hardware, need not concern the programmer since it can be made to obey the rules for the abstract machine.

In running a COBOL program, there are two distinct phases: compilation and execution. Compilation is the process of translating a COBOL program into a suitable low-level language and is carried out by a special program called a compiler, which is part of the software for a particular computer system. Because this translation process is mechanical, the COBOL program needs to be written in a precise form, according to certain syntactic rules. Therefore part of compilation is checking that the syntax of the program is correct and identifying errors. However, the fact that a program is syntactically correct does not mean that it will do anything useful. In the same way sentences in English can be syntactically correct but meaningless: 'The mat sat on the cat', for example. Once a program has been successfully compiled it needs to be executed and tested with a variety of types of input data to prove that it works. The process of debugging a program is concerned with the location and correction of errors shown to exist by testing. The steps in program development are summarized in Figure 1.2.

Students beginning in programming are often discouraged because their programs do not work at the first attempt. Creating a working program is an iterative process; one frequently takes one step forward and two steps back. The first stage in this process is to design the program and 'desk check' the design by stepping through the design manually. The design can then be translated into COBOL, turned into machine readable form using a computer terminal perhaps, and an attempt made to compile this program. This will almost certainly result in syntax errors, detected by the compiler, which will have to be corrected by the programmer.

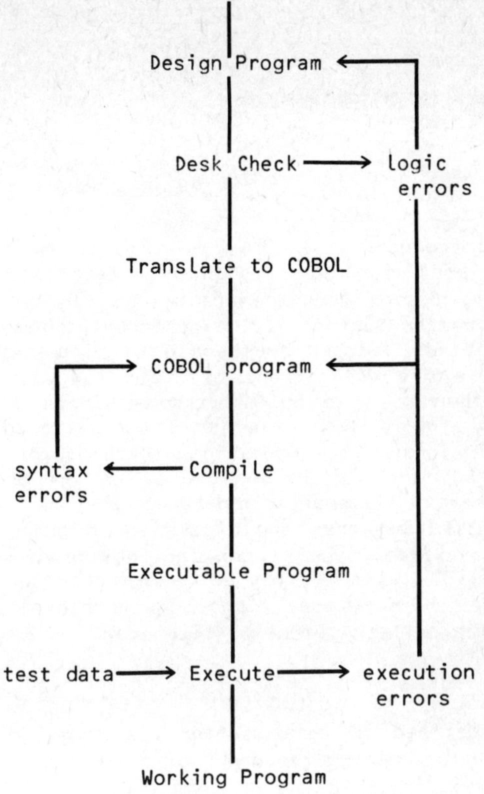

Figure 1.2

Eventually the program will compile, producing an executable program, which can then be executed with an input file of test data. The result of this test will most probably be an execution error. Execution errors can be divided into two categories: run-time errors, where the program stops because some unexpected condition occurs, and logic errors, where the program produces the wrong results. To correct an execution error may involve going back and modifying the COBOL program, possibly modifying the design as well, recompiling the program and then executing it again. Alternatively the execution errors may be caused by incorrect test data which causes unexpected results to be produced by the program. Once the program successfully processes one input file it will then need to be tested with other input files, as a single file of test data is usually insufficient to test all possibilities.

2 The Program Design Language

This chapter introduces the design language which will be used throughout the book for the design of algorithms. Initially the operations of the design language are defined in terms of the 'COBOL computer' described in Section 1.2. These definitions are based on the particular discipline imposed by the use of a specific COBOL program structure and are not definitions of COBOL language constructs. The operations are then used to build up some simple programs which are followed through step by step to illustrate how the operations work.

In the descriptions of the operations anything appearing between the angle brackets '<' and '>' is a thing which the programmer chooses. For example get-next-<filename> indicates that an operation can be defined by substituting the name of a file in place of '<filename>'. Therefore 'get-next-employee' and 'get-next-order-form' could be generated for files called 'employee' and 'order-form', respectively. However, 'get-another-employee' and 'get-employee' could not be generated from the pattern get-next-<filename>.

2.1 Basic Operations

The operations defined in this section are those which carry out a simple task without changing the order of execution of operations.

get-next-<filename>

Attempts to read the next record from the input file, called <filename>, into the input area. If there is no such record then the condition end-of-<filename> is set to true. Initially end-of-<filename> is false and the contents of the input area are undefined.

e.g. get-next-sales
get-next-customer-file

put-<recordname>

Transfers the contents of the area of the data store called <recordname> to the output file, via the output area. After the transfer the area defined by <recordname> is then blanked out. Initially the <recordname> area will be set to all blanks.

e.g. put-details
put-summary-line

transfer <item-1> to <item-2>

Copies the value stored in <item-1> to the location called <item-2>. The contents of <item-1> are unchanged but any existing value in <item-2> is lost. A special case of this operation is:

```
transfer <constant> to <item-2>
```

where <constant> is a fixed value which is to be stored in the location <item-2>.

```
e.g.    transfer total-price to summary-tot-price
        transfer 25 to discount-rate
        transfer "special customer" to details-comment
```

calculate <result-item> = <arithmetic-expression>

The <arithmetic-expression> is evaluated and the result put into the location called <result-name>. The arithmetic expression will be made up of the names of storage locations, constants, arithmetic operators: plus, minus, multiply and divide, and parentheses.

To define the meaning of an arithmetic expression the idea of an 'order of precedence' is required. For example, without a defined order of precedence it is not possible to say whether the result of 2 + 3 *4 is equal to 14 or 20. The order of precedence is defined as:

()	parenthesized expressions
* /	multiply and divide
+ -	add and subtract

If two or more operators at the same level of precedence appear in an expression then they are evaluated from left to right.

This means that expressions in parentheses are evaluated first, followed by multiplications and divisions, and finally additions and subtractions. These rules may need to be applied repeatedly if expressions contain 'nested' parentheses, that is parentheses within parentheses ...

```
e.g.    calculate total-price = sale-price * sale-quantity
        calculate discounted-price =
                      (1 - discount-rate) * total-price
```

It should be noted that the equals sign, in this context, means 'becomes equal to' rather than 'is equal to'. Therefore

```
calculate total-records = total-records + 1
```

is perfectly sensible and means take the value in the data-item total-records, add 1 to it and store the result in total-records.

A sequence of basic operations will be executed in the order written, one after the other from top to bottom. Therefore the sequence:

```
transfer first-item to second-item
transfer second-item to first-item
```

will <u>not</u> exchange the contents of first-item and second-item. The value in first-item will be copied into second-item then this new value will be copied back from second-item to first-item, leaving both locations containing the same value: the original value of first-item.

2.2 Selection and Repetition

Before considering the details of the selection and repetition operations it is necessary to define the conditions which can be used to control these operations.

Conditions

The conditions which will be allowed initially in selection and repetition operations fall into two groups.

The comparative conditions are of the form:

<item-name> <comparison-operator> <compared-value>

where the <comparison-operator> is one of:

<	less than	not <	not less than
>	greater than	not >	not greater than
=	equals	not =	not equal to

and the <compared-value> is either another item-name or a constant.

e.g. sales-quantity < 20
taxable-pay > tax-threshold
employee-super-code not = "A"

Note that the operators '≥' and '≤' are not included but are equivalent to 'not <' and 'not >' respectively.

The file conditions test the current state of the input file and are of the form:

end-of-<filename>   not end-of-<filename>

The condition end-of-<filename> is true if there are no more records available in <filename> because the last get-next-<filename> failed. This condition is false after a successful get-next-<filename> or at the beginning of the program, when no information is available. The condition not end-of-<filename> is simply the converse of end-of-<filename>.

e.g. end-of-sales
not end-of-customer-file

Selection

The selection operation has two forms:

```
if <condition> then
    <procedure-1>
else
    <procedure-2>
endif
```

(a)

```
if <condition> then
    <procedure-3>
endif
```

(b)

The selection operation (a) works as follows:

(1) the <condition> is evaluated to give true or false,
(2) if the <condition> is true then carry out <procedure-1>,
(3) if the <condition> is false carry out <procedure-2>,
(4) after selecting the appropriate procedure continue by carrying out the next operation after endif.

The shortened version of the selection operation, shown in (b) above, works in a similar way except that when the <condition> is false the operation does nothing. Therefore <procedure-3> is executed if and only if the <condition> is true.

The 'procedures' specified can be a sequence of one or more basic operations, or the name of a sequence of operations to be executed (see 2.4) or a mixture of the two.

Examples of selection operations:

```
if taxable-pay not < tax-threshold then
   calculate total-higher-payers = total-higher-payers + 1
   higher-tax-routine
else
   calculate tax-to-pay = taxable-pay * standard-rate
endif

if house-price > stamp-limit then
   add-stamp-duty
endif
```

Repetition

Initially only one repetition operation will be introduced and it has the general form:

```
until <condition> do
    <procedure>
enduntil
```

This operation is defined as follows:

(1) the <condition> is evaluated to true or false,
(2) if the <condition> is true then the operation following enduntil is carried out,
(3) if the <condition> is false then carry out the <procedure> and return to step (1) above.

Informally, the <procedure> is executed repeatedly until the

<condition> becomes true when the operation following enduntil is executed. If the <condition> is true when the until is first executed then this whole operation has no effect and the operation following the enduntil is executed immediately.

The <procedure> specified is similar to that for selection: a sequence of one or more basic operations, or the name of a sequence of operations, or a mixture of the two. For example:

```
until end-of-employee do
    calculate-tax
    get-next-employee
enduntil
```

In this example 'calculate-tax' must be the name of a sequence of operations to be executed.

2.3 Simple Programs

This section discusses some examples of programs to illustrate the material presented in the preceding two sections.

Example 2.1

A very simple but complete program which does something useful is:

```
display-sales-records
    get-next-sales
    until end-of-sales do
        transfer sales-record to printer-line
        put-printer-line
        get-next-sales
    enduntil
```

Here there is an input file called 'sales' which contains records called 'sales-record', and there is an output record called 'printer-line' which is assumed to belong to a lineprinter file. The program starts by attempting to get a record from the sales file. If there are no records in this file then end-of-sales will be true, the until will have no effect and the program will terminate.

If there is at least one record in the sales file then end-of-sales will be false and the operations between until and enduntil will be repeated until end-of-sales becomes true. The operations inside the loop simply transfer the current input record to the output record, transfer the output record to the output file (printing a line in this case) and attempt to get another record from the sales file.

Therefore this simple program will print the entire contents of the sales file on the lineprinter, exactly as they appeared in the input file. In itself this may be occasionally useful but it is important because it forms the basic framework for a large number of programs which read records from an input file, process each record and output the results.

The indentation shown in the example above is not mandatory but it is useful for emphasizing the structure of the program.

Example 2.2

To extend the example above, suppose that each sales record contains the item number of an item sold, 'sales-item-no', the quantity of the item sold, 'sales-quantity', and the price per item, 'sales-price'. Modify Example 2.1 to print the item number, total price charged and quantity discount. The discount is 10% of the total price charged, if the quantity sold is greater than 19 items. Before writing the program design the items of the output record could be defined as:

```
printer-line
   printer-item-no                 item number
   printer-quantity                quantity sold
   printer-price                   price per item
   printer-tot-price               total price charged
   printer-discount                discount given
```

The problem does not require that the values of quantity sold and price per item be printed but it is good practice to print these values to check that they have been correctly input. It is very frustrating to look for a logic error in a program when incorrect data is causing the problem.

The programmer can choose any names for files, records and items, subject to restrictions imposed by the programming language being used. For COBOL, names should commence with a letter and be constructed from letters, digits and hyphens. It is good practice to choose names which have meaning and show the structure of the data e.g. all items belonging to the printer-line have the prefix 'printer-' and names which indicate the content of the item.

A possible program design for the modified problem is:

```
price-and-discount
   get-next-sales
   until end-of-sales do
      calculate total-price = sales-quantity * sales-price
      if sales-quantity > 19 then
         calculate discount = 0.1 * total-price
         calculate total-price = total-price - discount
      else
         transfer 0 to discount
      endif
      transfer sales-item-no to printer-item-no
      transfer sales-quantity to printer-quantity
      transfer sales-price to printer-price
      transfer total-price to printer-tot-price
      transfer discount to printer-discount
      put-printer-line
      get-next-sales
   enduntil
```

To illustrate the action of this program assume that the sales file contains some useful data and that the effect of the initial get-next-sales is to get the following data into the input area:

sales-item	sales-quantity	sales-price
12345	20	6.36

On entering the until loop for the first time the values of the temporary variables total-price and discount will be undefined:

total-price	discount
?	?

After carrying out the operation

    calculate total-price = sales-quantity * sales-price

the temporary storage locations will now contain:

total-price	discount
127.2	?

The next operation is a selection and since the sales-quantity is greater than 19 the procedure selected will start with

    calculate discount = 0.1 * total-price

which has the following effect:

total-price	discount
127.2	12.72

This will be followed by the operation

    calculate total-price = total-price - discount

which takes the current value of total-price subtracts the discount from it and puts the result of this calculation back into the storage location total-price. Therefore the new values in the temporary storage will be:

total-price	discount
114.48	12.72

The next operation to be carried out is the one after endif

    transfer sales-item-no to printer-item-no

this operation and the following four transfers will build up a printer-line of the form:

printer-item-no printer-quantity printer-price

12345		20		6.36

printer-tot-price printer-discount

114.48		12.72

The contents of printer-line will then be transferred to the output file, producing a single line of printed output, possibly:

```
12345    20    6.36    114.48    12.72
```

and an attempt made to get the next record from the sales file.

How the actual format of the input and output are specified is deliberately left vague at the moment - this will be dealt with in Chapter 3, and subsequent chapters.

This program uses temporary storage locations called 'total-price' and 'discount' because these values are required in further calculations. As a general rule if a value to be calculated is required for further computation it should be stored in a temporary storage location, otherwise it can be put into the output record directly. This is because the external representation of the value, in printer-line in this case, will not necessarily be suitable for computation inside the computer.

<u>Example 2.3</u>

To illustrate some other programming techniques and to widen the reader's experience consider the following problem. An estate agent's file of properties contains one record for each property for sale, summarizing the details for that property, including the price called 'property-price'. A program is required to scan the file and count the number of properties for sale at under £25,000 and express this as a percentage of the total number of properties for sale. This is a very simple version of another type of problem, an 'aggregation', which involves processing a file and collecting information about the whole file rather than individual records.

When processing the property file two counters will be required: one for the properties selling at under £25,000, 'cheap-property', and the other for the total number of properties, 'total-property'. The program has three parts: initializing these counters, processing all records in the file and updating the counters, and printing the results of counting. The output from the program will consist of a single line summarizing the information collected:

```
summary-line
    summary-cheap          number of properties
                           priced below £25,000
    summary-total          total number of properties
    summary-percent        percentage of 'cheap' properties
```

Notice that the total number of properties will be printed for checking purposes even though it is not strictly necessary.

A possible program design for this problem is:

```
property-summary
    transfer 0 to cheap-property
    transfer 0 to total-property
    get-next-property
    until end-of-property do
        calculate total-property = total-property + 1
        if property-price < 25000 then
            calculate cheap-property = cheap-property + 1
        endif
        get-next-property
    enduntil
    transfer cheap-property to summary-cheap
    transfer total-property to summary-total
    calculate summary-percent =
                    cheap-property / total-property * 100
    put-summary-line
```

Working through this program in detail is left as an exercise for the reader but there are a number of points about this program design which should be noted. The counters 'cheap-property' and 'total-property' must be given an initial value of zero otherwise they may contain an undefined value when the until loop is first executed. The if operation shows an example of selection without an alternative course of action, if the property-price is less than £25,000 then the 'cheap-property' counter is increased by one otherwise nothing happens at this point. In the final part of this program 'summary-percent' is an example of an item which can be calculated directly for output because its value is not required for further computation.

2.4 Refinement

A small program, such as Example 2.2 given above, can be written down and desk-checked in a matter of a few minutes. The solution can then be translated into a programming language, compiled and tested. If it fails to execute properly then it is usually easy to spot the error, make a quick modification to the program and test the program again, and so on. There are many trivial problems which can be solved by ad hoc methods because the whole problem is small enough to be comprehended as a single unit. However, as the size and complexity of problems grows there is a need to develop a methodical way of creating programs.

Before describing one such methodology it is important to consider what its main aims are. The major requirement of any computer program is that it should be correct that is it produces the expected output for all possible inputs. Therefore the methodology should be designed so that it maximizes the likelihood that programs will be correct. An alternative way of stating the same aim is that the methodology should minimize the possibilities for error by using only 'safe' techniques for program construction.

A very important aspect of commercial data processing is that programs are usually written in the expectation that they will be used for several years. Inevitably programs will need to be modified because of changing circumstances such as amendments to the fiscal laws or revised company policies. In most cases a program will be modified, or 'maintained', by a programmer other than the original author. Many companies have a group of programmers whose sole job is the maintenance of existing software. The fact that a program will probably have to be modified by another programmer demands that it be written in a style which is easy to understand and simple to modify.

It is generally true that if a method is developed to improve specific aspects of a process then there is going to be a 'trade-off' against one or more other problem parameters. The main aims which have been stated are correctness and maintainability and the trade-off is against the efficiency of program execution. The programs written using the methods described in this book will not necessarily be the most efficient solutions to the problem, because it is nearly always possible to speed up the execution of a program by careful 'tuning'. However, the largest part of the cost of a computer project today is associated with the manpower required for the development and maintenance of software and therefore efficiency must be a secondary consideration.

It is not claimed that there is only one methodology fulfilling the above criteria but what is important is that any methodology chosen should be applied consistently. The technique for program development which is described and used throughout this book is called stepwise refinement.

The basic principle of stepwise refinement is that any non-trivial problem can be broken down into a number of sub-problems which can then be solved, if necessary by breaking them down into further sub-problems etc. Applying this idea to programming means that a description of the whole problem is written as a high-level algorithm linking together a number of sub-problems. Each of these sub-problems can then be 'refined' by either writing down the solution to it or writing it as an algorithm in terms of further sub-problems and refining these etc. Therefore the whole process becomes a step by step refinement of the problem from an outline of the program to a complete, detailed program design.

Example 2.4

To illustrate the format of refinement in the program design language consider Example 2.2 again. An alternative approach to the problem would have been to start with an outline program design of the form:

```
price-and-discount-2
    get-next-sales
    until end-of-sales do
        find-price-and-discount
        produce-printer-line
        get-next-sales
    enduntil
```

It should be clear that this program processes each record in the sales file, by analogy with Example 2.1, but the actual processing remains unspecified at this stage.

The refinement names, such as 'find-price-and-discount' and 'produce-printer-line', are invented by the programmer and put into the program design at the current level of development. These refinements will be expanded into sequences of operations or lower level refinements at the next level of development. The link between the two levels of design is provided by the refinement name which will appear, underlined, as a heading for the refinement.

Having decided that 'print-and-discount-2' is the correct basic form of the solution the sub-problems 'find-price-and-discount' and 'produce-printer-line' can now be refined as:

```
find-price-and-discount
   calculate total-price = sales-quantity * sales-price
   if sales-quantity > 19 then
      calculate discount = 0.1 * total-price
      calculate total-price = total-price - discount
   else
      transfer 0 to discount
   endif

produce-printer-line
   transfer sales-item-no to printer-item-no
   transfer sales-quantity to printer-quantity
   transfer sales-price to printer-price
   transfer total-price to printer-tot-price
   transfer discount to printer-discount
   put-printer-line
```

The sequences of operations specified in the refinements, 'find-price-and-discount' and 'produce-printer-line', are the same as those specified in the program design of Example 2.3.

When stepping through a program design which uses refinement the operations specified for each refinement are effectively substituted for the name of the refinement. An alternative way of visualizing this process is that whenever a refinement name is encountered jump to the refinement, carry out the instructions specified in it and return to the next operation after the refinement name. At the end of each refinement there is an implied operation which says go back to the place where this refinement was invoked and carry on processing at that point.

Example 2.5

Example 2.3 can also be reformulated so that the general structure of the program is separated from the detail of the particular problem. Here is an alternative program design:

```
property-summary-2
   initialize-counters
   get-next-property
   until end-of-property do
      update-counters
      get-next-property
   enduntil
   produce-summary

initialize-counters
   transfer 0 to cheap-property
   transfer 0 to total-property
```

```
update-counters
   calculate total-property = total-property + 1
   if property-price < 25000 then
      calculate cheap-property = cheap-property + 1
   endif

produce-summary
   transfer cheap-property to summary-cheap
   transfer total-property to summary-total
   calculate summary-percent =
                cheap-property / total-property * 100
   put-summary-line
```

The sequences of operations contained in the three refinements correspond to those developed in Example 2.3.

2.5 Case Study

The ABC Carpet Company maintains a file of daily orders, where each record contains: an order number, the customer's name and address, the number of square metres of carpet ordered, the price per square metre and the delivery zone. The delivery zone is coded as a single letter either 'A' or 'B', indicating the distance from the warehouse. The company's policy on delivery charges is that the order is delivered free if the cost of the carpet exceeds £200 otherwise there is an additional charge of £5 for zone 'A' and £10 for zone 'B'.

A program is required which will process the orders in the file and calculate the cost of the carpet, the delivery charge, if any, and the total to be charged for each order. After processing all the orders the program should produce totals for carpet sales and delivery charges, and the total amount due.

The input file might be called 'order-file' and the structure of a record in this file will be:

```
order-record
   order-number            order number
   order-customer          customer's name and address
   order-size              size of carpet (square metres)
   order-price             price per square metre
   order-zone              delivery zone 'A' or 'B'
```

and the output record could have the following structure:

```
detail-line
   detail-number            order number
   detail-customer          customer's name and address
   detail-size              size of carpet
   detail-price             price per square metre
   detail-zone              delivery zone
   detail-carpet-charge     charge for carpet
   detail-delivery-charge   delivery charge
   detail-order-charge      total charge for order
```

The amount of output could be reduced by not printing the size, price or zone, but, as recommended previously, these are included for cross-checking.

This output record represents the output required for each order but there is also the need to output the totals, after processing all the orders. In this case it will be assumed that the data-items 'detail-carpet-charge', 'detail-delivery-charge' and 'detail-order-charge' are large enough to hold the totals and therefore the above record can be used for the output of the totals.

This problem requires both the processing of individual records and the accumulation of totals so the structure of the program will be a combination of the structures used in examples 2.2 and 2.3. The overall program structure will therefore be of the form:

```
carpet-orders
    initialize-totals
    get-next-order-file
    until end-of-order-file do
       process-order
       update-totals
       get-next-order-file
    enduntil
    produce-totals
```

There are three totals required but since the total of all orders can be calculated from the sum of the carpet charges plus the sum of the delivery charges, only two counters are necessary. The total charge for carpets will be accumulated in 'total-carpet' and the total charged for delivery in 'total-delivery'. Therefore 'initialize-totals' can be refined as:

```
initialize-totals
    transfer 0 to total-carpet
    transfer 0 to total-delivery
```

It is now necessary to note the names of these temporary data-items and add any other such items to the list as the program is developed.

```
temporary-items
    total-carpet            carpet charges for all customers
    total-delivery          delivery charges for all customers
```

The processing of an individual order, 'process-order', is fairly straightforward and a possible refinement is:

```
process-order
    calculate carpet-charge = order-size * order-price
    if carpet-charge not > 200 then
       find-delivery-charge
    else
       transfer 0 to delivery-charge
    endif
    print-order-details
```

The calculation of the delivery charge is left for further refinement (find-delivery-charge) as is the construction of the output line (print-order-details). Note that 'carpet-charge' and 'delivery-charge' will have to be items in temporary storage as they are both required in further calculations.

The list of temporary data-items needs to be updated:

```
temporary-items
   total-carpet           carpet charges for all customers
   total-delivery         delivery charges for all customers
   carpet-charge          carpet charge for one customer
   delivery-charge        delivery charge for one customer
```

Note that in practice this list can be built up on a separate sheet of paper, rather than repeated.

The refinement of 'update-totals' is now quite simple:

```
update-totals
   calculate total-carpet = total-carpet + carpet-charge
   calculate total-delivery = total-delivery + delivery-charge
```

The last refinement from the overall program design is 'produce-totals'. To distinguish the summary line from the ordinary order lines a suitable message can be put into, say, the customer name and address field, 'detail-customer', leaving the other irrelevant fields blank. The total for all orders can be calculated and output directly as the sum of the two counters 'total-carpet' and 'total-delivery'. Therefore a possible refinement is:

```
produce-totals
   transfer 'Totals' to detail-customer
   transfer total-carpet to detail-carpet-charge
   transfer total-delivery to detail-delivery-charge
   calculate detail-order-charge =
                          total-carpet + total-delivery
   put-detail-line
```

There are now two second level refinements from 'process-order' to be dealt with. The calculation of the delivery charge 'find-delivery-charge' is a straightforward selection of the form:

```
find-delivery-charge
   if order-zone = "A" then
      transfer 5 to delivery-charge
   else
      transfer 10 to delivery-charge
   endif
```

Note that this selection operation assumes that if 'order-zone' is not equal to 'A' then it will be 'B'; in practice this can be a dangerous assumption.

The final refinement required is 'print-order-details' to construct detail-line and this is quite straightforward:

```
print-order-details
    transfer order-number to detail-number
    transfer order-customer to detail-customer
    transfer order-size to detail-size
    transfer order-price to detail-price
    transfer order-zone to detail-zone
    transfer carpet-charge to detail-carpet-charge
    transfer delivery-charge to detail-delivery-charge
    calculate detail-order-charge =
                                carpet-charge + delivery-charge
    put-detail-line
```

The execution of this program is not going to be demonstrated step by step; instead here is an example of an input file:

```
1513 J.Stuart, Flodden             25 15.50 A
1314 R.Bruce, Bannockburn          10  5.60 A
1297 W.Wallace, Stirling Bridge    10 20.00 A
1645 J.Graham, Inverlochy          20 10.01 A
1388 J.Douglas, Otterburn          20 14.40 B
1745 C.Stuart, Prestonpans         15 12.90 B
1689 J.Graham, Killiecrankie       20 10.00 B
```

By following through the operations specified in the program design it should be possible for the reader to show that the output will be of the form:

```
1513 J.Stuart, Flodden             25 15.50 A  387.50  0  387.50
1314 R.Bruce, Bannockburn          10  5.60 A   56.00  5   61.00
1297 W.Wallace, Stirling Bridge    10 20.00 A  200.00  5  205.00
1645 J.Graham, Inverlochy          20 10.01 A  200.20  0  200.20
1388 J.Douglas, Otterburn          20 14.40 B  288.00  0  288.00
1745 C.Stuart, Prestonpans         15 12.90 B  193.50 10  203.50
1689 J.Graham, Killiecrankie       20 10.00 B  200.00 10  210.00
     Totals                                   1525.20 30 1555.20
```

This problem is obviously a simplified version of a real problem and it is unrealistic for a number of reasons. One important assumption, in 'find-delivery-charge', is that the data is correct, this can only be assumed if some previous program has already 'validated' the data, rejecting any incorrect values. The subject of data validation will be dealt with in Chapter 6.

The technique of printing all lines using the same record can only be used if the detail lines and summary line(s) can share exactly the same format. A more general technique, using multiple output records, is discussed in Section 5.5.

The problem is unrealistic because it only deals with one carpet per customer and no allowance is made for the customer who orders two carpets at £150 each and gets charged delivery on both of them. The delivery charge rules are also rather simplistic but an alternative set of charging rules could be 'plugged-in' to the program by replacing 'find-delivery-charge' by a different refinement. This demonstrates one advantage of the stepwise refinement approach; an identifiable sub-problem can be changed without affecting the overall structure of the program.

Exercises 2

2.1. The input to the payroll system of the St. Kilda Puffin Factory consists of employee records which contain the following data-items:

employee number
gross monthly pay
annual tax allowance

All employees pay 5% of their salary to the company pension fund, which is deducted before tax is calculated. They are also liable for tax at 20% of their income after deduction of tax allowances and pension contributions.

Design a payroll program which will calculate and print the pension contribution, tax payable and net pay, per month, for each employee. You may ignore rounding errors resulting from calculating monthly allowances against pay, pension contributions etc.

Desk check your program design using the following data:

Number	Monthly Pay	Tax Allowance
12345	£500	£1200
87654	£260	£2964
23456	£300	£4800

2.2. The data for the 1981 census contains one record for each household and among the items in a record are:

number of people in household
number of living rooms in the house

Design a program to read these records and calculate:

(a) the percentage of households with more than two people,
(b) the percentage of households where the ratio of people to living rooms exceeds 1.5.

2.3. The Rockall Electricity Board runs a simple billing system where the input consists of records containing the following data:

customer account number
tariff code
customer name and address
number of units consumed this quarter

The tariff code is either 'D' for domestic or 'C' for commercial and the rules for calculating the amount to be charged are as follows.

Domestic customers pay a standing charge of £3 per quarter and are charged 10p per unit for the first 100 units and 8p per unit for units used in excess of 100.

Commercial customers are charged 15p per unit for the first 200 units consumed and 5p per unit for units in excess of 200.

Design a billing program which will:

(a) calculate the price charged to each customer account and print this together with details of the account,
(b) print the total units consumed and the total amount due from all customers in the current input file.

3 The COBOL Program

This chapter begins the process of describing COBOL programs. First the overall structure of the program needs to be defined and then there are two major topics: data structures and algorithms. This chapter will deal with the basic program structure and data structures, leaving the algorithms to Chapter 4. By the end of Chapter 4 the reader should be in a position to write a complete simple program and turn it into COBOL.

3.1 Program Structure

A COBOL program is divided into four main units called divisions. The names and functions of these divisions can be summarized as follows.

IDENTIFICATION DIVISION - as the name suggests this is largely documentary and the only important entry is the program name. Documentary material can include: the name of the programmer, the date the program was written or when it was compiled, and introductory remarks on the purpose of the program.

ENVIRONMENT DIVISION - this defines the environment in which the program is to be run. It includes details of the type of computer being used and the names of the actual files being used by the program. This division was designed to be the machine-dependent part of the program; in theory this should be the only part of the program affected if a program is transferred from one computer system to another.

DATA DIVISION - describes all the data structures that are required by the program. The division is divided into two major sections.
FILE SECTION which describes all the input/output files used by the program. This corresponds to the input and output areas of the simple computer model.
WORKING-STORAGE SECTION which contains the descriptions of all the temporary storage items required by the program.

PROCEDURE DIVISION - specifies the operations to be carried out on the data-items defined in the DATA DIVISION. The division is divided into sections and paragraphs, which correspond to the refinements of the program design.

In order to get started it will be assumed that much of the program can be taken as standard and that data structures and algorithms, defined by the reader, can simply be 'plugged-in' to a program skeleton. Once the reader has gained some experience of designing, writing and, it is hoped, running simple COBOL programs, based on this standard program skeleton, more details of the program structure will be discussed.

The format of the standard program skeleton is given in Appendix 1.

The next few chapters will concentrate on the important aspects of the program: the description of data-items and the translation of the program design into procedural statements.

3.2 Reserved Words and User-defined Names

In Chapter 1 the idea of compilation was mentioned. This is the process of translating a COBOL program into a much simpler form suitable for direct execution by a computer. This process of translation is carried out by a compiler which follows a set of syntactic rules to transform the COBOL program into a lower level language. Therefore when writing COBOL programs the programmer has to be aware of these syntactic rules which can at times seem rather arbitrary.

The first set of syntax rules to be considered are those for constructing names in a program. In the data division data-names have to be given to all the data-items to be used for input/output and temporary storage, and in the procedure division all the paragraphs and sections have to be given unique procedure-names. The compiler must be able to distinguish the names chosen by the programmer from those used for standard operations in COBOL and combinations of symbols with special meanings.

There is a list of reserved words in COBOL which have a special meaning to the compiler and may not be used as 'user-defined names', those names chosen by the programmer. The full list of reserved words is given in Appendix 3. This is a very long list and it is doubtful whether any COBOL programmer can remember them all and it is even more doubtful whether anyone knows what they are all for. However, a good "rule of thumb" is that if meaningful names are chosen, constructed from hyphenated words, most of the reserved words will be avoided.

Formally the rules for constructing user-defined names in COBOL are as follows.

(1) The name must not be a reserved word, see Appendix 3.
(2) The characters used to construct the name must come from the set:
    A -> Z
    0 -> 9
    - (hyphen)
(3) A name must not begin or end with a hyphen.
(4) The maximum length of a name is 30 characters.
(5) A data-name must contain at least one letter.

Therefore the following names are valid, though not necessarily meaningful, as both data-names and procedure-names:

```
PRINT-LINE      ADDRESS-LINE-1       1-ADDRESS-PART
A-B-C-D-E       EMPLOYEETAXCODE      1-2-3-4A
```

and names without any alphabetic characters such as:

```
12              1-13                 1-13-2-3
```

would be valid as procedure-names although not recommended as good programming practice.

3.3 The Structure of Data

The rest of this chapter will concentrate on an initial survey of the data division. There are two major aspects of data to be considered: the structure of data and the description, or type of data.

All data-items in COBOL are considered to be part of some data structure and the relationship between data-items is defined by level-numbers. For example, looking back to Example 2.2, a possible structure for the input record would be:

```
01  SALES-RECORD
    05  SALES-ITEM-NO
    05  SALES-QUANTITY
    05  SALES-PRICE
```

This conveys the information that 'SALES-RECORD' is a record description, because it has the level-number 01, and that the following three items are subordinate to (belong to) SALES-RECORD because they have higher level-numbers. The fact that they all have equal level-numbers indicates that there is no further structure in the data and therefore these three items are independent of each other.

The reason for using the level-number 05 for the subordinate data-items is discussed later. The important point at this stage is that changes in level-numbers define structure; the numerical values of level-numbers, apart form 01, are not significant.

One way of visualizing a COBOL data structure is to draw a 'tree', showing the hierarchical relationship between the items, and for the above example the following simple tree results:

```
                 SALES-RECORD
           /          |          \
SALES-ITEM-NO   SALES-QUANTITY   SALES-PRICE
```

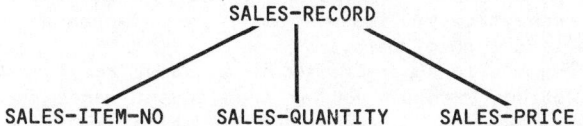

A slightly more complicated record structure is:

```
01  EMPLOYEE-RECORD
    05  EMP-NUMBER
        10  EMP-DIVISION
        10  EMP-SERIAL-NO
    05  EMP-NAME
    05  EMP-DATE-OF-BIRTH
        10  EMP-DOB-DAY
        10  EMP-DOB-MONTH
        10  EMP-DOB-YEAR
```

It can be seen that EMPLOYEE-RECORD is made up of three parts called EMP-NUMBER, EMP-NAME and EMP-DATE-OF-BIRTH. In turn EMP-NUMBER is made up of two components called EMP-DIVISION and EMP-SERIAL-NO, while EMP-DATE-OF-BIRTH is subdivided into three parts: EMP-DOB-DAY, EMP-DOB-MONTH and EMP-DOB-YEAR. The equivalent tree structure summarizes this relationship:

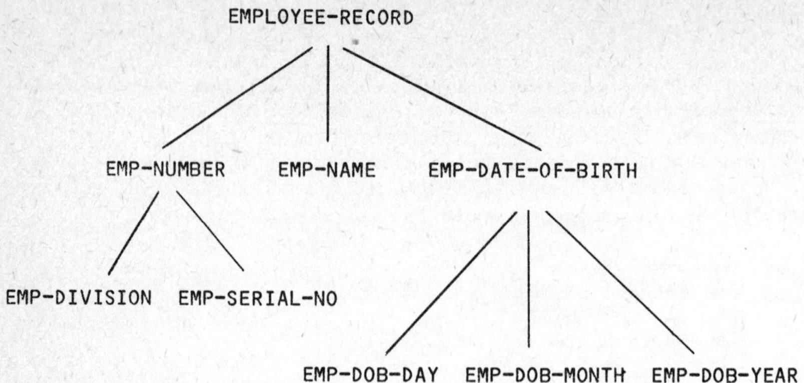

An important piece of terminology needs to be introduced at this point. The items in the tree which have no subordinates are called elementary-items while those which are subdivided are called group-items. In this example the group-items are: EMPLOYEE-RECORD, EMP-NUMBER and EMP-DATE-OF-BIRTH and all the other data-names refer to elementary-items.

The examples given above show good practice regarding the use of level-numbers and indentation. It is always wise to use level-numbers that are not contiguous so that intermediate levels can be introduced if necessary. The only significant level-number is 01 indicating the beginning of a new record and the highest permitted level-number is 49. The EMPLOYEE-RECORD, shown above, would still have the same meaning if the level-numbers were systematically changed to 11 and 21, or 02 and 03, replacing 05 and 10 respectively. Indentation is recommended as a visual aid to showing the structure of data.

It is often useful to be able to ignore parts of an input record or leave blank areas in an output record. Rather than invent names for dummy data-items there is a special data-name FILLER which indicates any item which will never be directly referenced. For example an output record might be defined as follows:

```
01  PRINT-EMP-RECORD
    05  PRINT-WORKS-NO
        10  PRINT-DIVISION
        10  FILLER
        10  PRINT-SERIAL-NO
    05  FILLER
    05  PRINT-NAME
    05  FILLER
    05  PRINT-AGE
```

The FILLERs allow the programmer to describe dummy items which will correspond to blank areas in the output record, which will make it more readable.

3.4 Types of Data

The elementary-items, which are defined as the indivisible elements in the data structure, have to be described by indicating the type of data which they are expected to hold. There are three basic types of data distinguished in COBOL:

Type	Content of data-item
Numeric	0 -> 9 + -
Alphabetic	A -> Z space
Alphanumeric	Any representable character

An elementary-item must belong to only one of these basic types. Every elementary-item is given a picture, abbreviated to PIC, which defines its type and size. The types being coded as: 9 for numeric, A for alphabetic and X for alphanumeric.

The code is repeated to indicate the size of the item so 'PIC 9999' represents four numeric digits and 'PIC AAAAA' indicates five alphabetic characters. A shorthand form of the picture is used to avoid writing out long strings of codes for larger pictures. This consists of the code followed by a repeat count in brackets, e.g. 'PIC 9(6)' is equivalent to 'PIC 999999', a six digit numeric item.

The previous example of the EMPLOYEE-RECORD could be completed by adding pictures as follows:

```
01  EMPLOYEE-RECORD.
    05  EMP-NUMBER.
        10  EMP-DIVISION     PIC AA.
        10  EMP-SERIAL-NO    PIC 9(5).
    05  EMP-NAME             PIC X(25).
    05  EMP-DATE-OF-BIRTH.
        10  EMP-DOB-DAY      PIC 99.
        10  EMP-DOB-MONTH    PIC AAA.
        10  EMP-DOB-YEAR     PIC 99.
```

Note that the group-items are not given pictures explicitly because their type is always alphanumeric and their size defined by the aggregation of their component parts. So in the example above EMP-DIVISION is a two character alphabetic item and EMP-SERIAL-NO is a five digit numeric item; therefore EMP-NUMBER is a seven character alphanumeric item. EMP-NAME is described as a twenty five character alphanumeric item as it may contain characters other than those defined as alphabetic characters e.g. "SCARLET O'HARA", "HARRY S. TRUMAN". EMP-DATE-OF-BIRTH is a seven character alphanumeric item whose component parts are a two digit day, a three letter abbreviation for the month and a two digit year. The size of the EMPLOYEE-RECORD can then be calculated by summing all these components giving a total of 39 characters.

Possible data records corresponding to this description are:

```
AA12345WHITE JOHN                29FEB48
BB00700BOND JAMES                03MAR28
CC874330'NEILL JAMES ALEXANDER   15DEC35
```

Note that the data corresponding to the numeric items have to include leading zeroes as blank is not a legal numeric character.

Going back to PRINT-EMP-RECORD structure defined previously this could now be completed as follows:

```
01  PRINT-EMP-RECORD.
    05  PRINT-WORKS-NO.
        10  PRINT-DIVISION         PIC AA.
        10  FILLER                 PIC X.
        10  PRINT-SERIAL-NO        PIC 9(5).
    05  FILLER                     PIC XXX.
    05  PRINT-NAME                 PIC X(25).
    05  FILLER                     PIC X(6).
    05  PRINT-AGE                  PIC 99.
```

and the output would appear in the following format:

```
AA 12345   WHITE JOHN                        34
BB 00700   BOND JAMES                        54
CC 87433   O'NEILL JAMES ALEXANDER           47
```

Exercises 3

3.1. Which of the following names are valid user-defined names in a COBOL program?

(a) EMPLOYEE-COUNT-1 (b) 1-EMPLOYEE-TOTAL (c) 1.2.3
(d) 1-3-5 (e) 1 (f) PIC
(g) TOTAL-CHARGE-10% (h) -EMP-NO-CONT (i) AAA
(j) TOTAL-CHARGE-LESS-TEN-PERCENT-DISCOUNT

For those names which you think are valid indicate whether they can be used as data-names, procedure-names or both.

3.2. The following record description is taken from a COBOL program. Draw the corresponding tree structure, showing the relationship between the items, and devise a few data records corresponding to this description.

```
01  STUDENT-RECORD.
    05  STUDENT-MATRIC.
        10  STUDENT-MAT-YEAR            PIC 99.
        10  STUDENT-MAT-NUMBER          PIC 9(5).
        10  STUDENT-MAT-CHECK           PIC X.
    05  STUDENT-NAME                    PIC X(30).
    05  STUDENT-SCHOOL.
        10  STUDENT-SCH-AREA.
            15  STUDENT-SCH-REGION      PIC A.
            15  STUDENT-SCH-DISTRICT    PIC XX.
        10  STUDENT-SCH-NO              PIC 999.
    05  FILLER                          PIC XX.
    05  STUDENT-DEGREE-CODE             PIC 999.
```

3.3. Given below is a narrative description of an input record for a stock control system which is to be read by a COBOL program. Turn this description into a COBOL record structure with level-numbers and pictures.

The first part of the record contains the stock number of the part consisting of two components: the manufacturer code and the part serial number. The manufacturer code consists of two letters, followed by three digits and finally a check character. The part serial number is 8 digits. Following the stock number is the part description which does not exceed 30 characters. This is followed by the bin location, consisting of two letters and four digits, a blank area of four characters and the recommended re-order level, three digits.

4 Procedural Statements

This chapter takes a first look at the encoding of algorithms in the Procedure Division of a COBOL program. The primitive operations of the design language, introduced in Chapter 2, can each be turned into a COBOL statement or sequence of statements. The reader is not expected to understand the way in which the primitives are implemented at this stage - this will be explained in Chapter 8.

4.1 The Structure of the Procedure Division

The smallest procedural unit in COBOL is a *statement* which begins with a *verb* followed by one or more *operands*. The names of the verbs were chosen, by the designers of COBOL, to indicate the functions of the corresponding operations. The operand or operands define what is to be manipulated. For example:

```
MOVE PRICE-CHARGED TO PRINT-PRICE
```

is a COBOL statement, MOVE is the verb and PRICE-CHARGED and PRINT-PRICE are operands, while TO is a separator between the operands, required by the syntax of the move statement. COBOL is a very "rich" language with a large number of verbs and only a small subset of these will be considered in this book.

A sequence of statements can be combined to form a *sentence* which is terminated by a period. In order to be able to implement refinement and repetition it is necessary to be able to identify groups of statements forming one or more sentences. Therefore the procedure division is divided into *paragraphs*, each of which has a unique name associated with it. Paragraphs can be collected together into larger units called *sections* but for the present these will not be considered.

4.2 Basic Operations in COBOL

The basic operations of the design language were chosen so that they can be straightforwardly translated into COBOL. However, there are certain rules which must be obeyed and these are outlined below. The translation is assumed to be based on the skeleton program given in Appendix 1.

Get-next operation

The design language operation:

get-next-<filename>

is translated into the procedural statement:

```
PERFORM GET-NEXT-<filename>
```

where the user substitutes the name of the input file for <filename>. The name of the input file must also be substituted throughout the skeleton program given in Appendix 1.

Note that the verb PERFORM is required here and that the hyphenation of the operation name is mandatory.

Put operation

```
put-<recordname>
```

is again straightforwardly translated as:

```
PERFORM PUT-<recordname>
```

where <recordname> is a name, chosen by the user, for an output record. There should be a description for <recordname> in the WORKING-STORAGE SECTION of the DATA DIVISION and the name chosen by the user should be substituted for <recordname> in the skeleton program.

The use of the verb PERFORM and the hyphenation should again be noted.

Constants

A constant in COBOL is either numeric or nonnumeric according to the notation used to represent it. A nonnumeric constant is a string of characters enclosed in quotation marks, for example:

"A" "PITMAN PUBLISHING" "26 RICHMOND ST." "12" "1.2.3"

A numeric constant has no delimiting marks and is simply a number; either a whole number (integer) or a real number with a decimal point. Any numeric constant may be preceded by a sign. Examples of numeric constants are given below.

23 -15 15.5 -2.4 0.672

Note that a real number should always be written with at least one digit before and one after the decimal point, therefore .5 would have to be written as 0.5 and 23. would be illegal in COBOL.

There are also special named constants, called figurative literals, which are used to represent frequently used constants. The most useful of these is SPACES, a nonnumeric constant which represents one or more blank characters. This constant is most frequently used with output records which are to be printed.

Transfer operation

```
transfer <sending-field> to <receiving-field>
```

is translated into COBOL as:

```
MOVE <sending-field> TO <receiving-field>
```

where <sending-field> must be the name of a data-item or a constant and <receiving-field> must be the name of a data-item. The effect of the statement will depend on the size and types of the fields involved in the MOVE. The golden rule is that <sending-field> and <receiving-field> should always be of the same type in which case there are no problems.

If only elementary-items are involved in the MOVE statement then there are two cases to consider:

numeric moves; these rules apply only if <sending-field> and <receiving-field> are both numeric. At this point only integral values will be considered, decimal values will be dealt with in the next chapter. The rule for integers is that digits are copied from rightmost to leftmost until

either <sending-field> is exhausted, in which case any remaining digit positions in <receiving-field> are filled with zeros

or <receiving-field> is exhausted, in which case any remaining digits in <sending-field> are lost.

In the latter case <receiving-field> contains a 'truncated' copy of <sending-field>.

For example consider a data-item defined as follows:

```
INTEGER-RESULT   PIC 999.
```

then the MOVE statements below will have the results indicated.

```
MOVE 35672 TO INTEGER-RESULT  =>  672
MOVE 345 TO INTEGER-RESULT    =>  345
MOVE 3 TO INTEGER-RESULT      =>  003
```

nonnumeric moves; these rules apply only if <sending-field> and <receiving-field> are both of alphanumeric or alphabetic type. The rule here is that characters are copied from leftmost to rightmost until

either <sending-field> is exhausted, in which case any remaining character positions in <receiving-field> are filled with spaces

or <receiving-field> is exhausted, in which case any remaining characters in <sending-field> are lost, another case of truncation.

For example, with a data-item:

```
CHAR-RESULT   PIC X(3).
```

the following MOVE statements will give the results indicated:

```
MOVE "RAYMOND" TO CHAR-RESULT  =>  RAY
MOVE "RCW" TO CHAR-RESULT      =>  RCW
MOVE "R" TO CHAR-RESULT        =>  Rb̸b̸
```

where b̸ is used to represent space.

It is perhaps worth repeating the simple rule: do not mix types in MOVE statements. There are rules governing mixed type moves but for the novice programmer the most sensible thing is move like to like.

It is possible to have a MOVE statement that involves group-items; in this case the group-item, or group-items, will be treated as nonnumeric fields and the appropriate rules given above applied. The major uses for group moves are for making an _exact_ copy of a complex data-item or for _initialization_. An example of initialization is:

```
MOVE SPACES TO PRINT-LINE
```

which simply fills the whole of PRINT-LINE with blanks, regardless of subordinate PIC's in PRINT-LINE.

Calculate operation

```
calculate <result-item> = <arithmetic-expression>
```

translates directly into COBOL as:

```
COMPUTE <result-item> = <arithmetic-expression>
```

and there are only a few simple rules to remember. The <result-item> must be a _numeric_ elementary-item since the <arithmetic-expression> must produce a number when evaluated.

If the value resulting from the evaluation of <arithmetic-expression> is too large to be represented in <result-item> then truncation may occur at the most significant, least significant or both ends of the result. Consider the trivial example:

```
05  RESULT-FIELD        PIC 99.
. . . . .
COMPUTE RESULT-FIELD = 25 * 25
```

the value stored in RESULT-FIELD after this operation will be 25.

There must be spaces around arithmetic operators so that minus and hyphen can be distinguished. For example

```
COMPUTE NET-PAY = GROSS-PAY - DEDUCTIONS
```

is not equivalent to

```
COMPUTE NET-PAY = GROSS-PAY-DEDUCTIONS
```

because of the spacing. The first statement subtracts the value of DEDUCTIONS from the value of GROSS-PAY and stores the result in NET-PAY while the second statement copies the value of an elementary-item called GROSS-PAY-DEDUCTIONS into NET-PAY.

For readers using an ANS COBOL compiler which does not implement the COMPUTE statement an alternative translation of calculate is given in Appendix 5.1.

Refinement

When a refinement is referenced in the program design it is replaced by a COBOL statement of the form:

```
PERFORM <refinement-name>
```

and the translation continues from top to bottom of the program design. The translation of the refinement itself consists of creating a paragraph called <refinement-name> and translating the operations of the refinement into COBOL.

Example

To illustrate the translation of the basic operations into COBOL, suppose that the following is part of a program design:

```
 . . . . .
print-subtotal
get-next-invoice
 . . . . .
   print-subtotal
      transfer 99999 to print-acno
      transfer "subtotal" to print-acname
      calculate print-total-cost = total-sales + total-vat
      put-print-sales
```

then the translation into COBOL would appear as:

```
         . . . . .
         PERFORM PRINT-SUBTOTAL
         PERFORM GET-NEXT-INVOICE
         . . . . .
     PRINT-SUBTOTAL.
         MOVE 99999 TO PRINT-ACNO
         MOVE "SUBTOTAL" TO PRINT-ACNAME
         COMPUTE PRINT-TOTAL-COST = TOTAL-SALES + TOTAL-VAT
         PERFORM PUT-PRINT-SALES.
```

This is, of course, an artificial example being only a fragment of a program to illustrate the translation of the basic operations. A complete example will be given after considering selection and repetition in the next section. The rules for laying out the COBOL statements are given in Appendix 2.

4.3 Selection and Repetition

A vital part of any program is the control structures which modify the straightforward sequential execution of instructions. Refinement is an example of a simple control structure which allows a sequence of instructions to include a reference to another sequence of instructions etc. However, the two most important control structures are those which allow selection among many courses of action and repetition of sequences of statements. In order to implement the selection and repetition operations, introduced in the program design language, it is necessary to consider what conditions can be evaluated as a basis for decision making.

Conditions

A condition is an expression which can be evaluated to give the result true or false. The simple conditions introduced in Section 2.2 were chosen so that they can be translated directly into COBOL and the only problems concern the types of items in the comparison conditions.

In beginners' programs the most common type of comparison is of two numeric items. For example, suppose that a numeric data-item called sales-quantity is to be tested to see if its value is greater than ten. The program design might include the condition:

    sales-quantity > 10

which should be directly translated to:

```
SALES-QUANTITY > 10
```

which compares the value in sales-quantity with a numeric constant, and not:

```
SALES-QUANTITY > "10"
```

which involves a nonnumeric constant and will result in a character comparison taking place. This leads to the apparently stupid result that "5" > "10" is true which can be explained by using the rules for nonnumeric comparisons given below.

The simple rule here is to always compare things of the same type and there should be no problems. In the case of numeric comparisons, the values of the two numbers are compared, using the specified comparator, to produce the result true or false. Therefore the condition

```
SALES-QUANTITY > 10
```

is true if the value stored in sales-quantity is 150 and false if the value stored in sales-quantity is 5 or 10. The condition

```
ACCOUNT-CODE NOT = 12
```

is true for all values of account-code except 12. In a program design it is quite acceptable to write conditions of the form:

    invoice-item-price > £25

but in a COBOL program there are only numeric constants and therefore the equivalent statement would be:

```
INVOICE-ITEM-PRICE > 25
```

and the programmer must implicitly understand the monetary or other units.

If the comparison is nonnumeric then the values stored in the items are compared in the following way.

(a) If the items are of unequal length then the shorter one is extended by adding blanks to the right-hand end to make them of equal length.
(b) The two items are compared character by character from left to right until either two different characters are found or all characters have been compared.
(c) If there are no differences between the values then obviously the two items are equal, otherwise they can be ordered using the relationship between the first pair of different characters found.

Suppose that there is an input data-item defined as

```
EMPLOYEE-SURNAME PIC X(10)
```

then the condition

```
EMPLOYEE-SURNAME = "SMITH"
```

is true if employee-surname contains SMITHbbbbb but false if it contains SMITHSONbb. The condition

```
EMPLOYEE-SURNAME > "M"
```

is true if employee-surname contains THOMASbbbb but false if it contains BRIDGESbbb. This condition is also true if employee-surname contains MAUDSLEYbb because A will be greater than blank in alphabetic ordering. To determine the value of a nonnumeric comparison involving special (non-alphabetic) characters will mean consulting the "collating sequence" of the computer being used.

For the beginning programmer it is probably wisest to use only exact comparisons of nonnumeric items, for example:

```
PART-REF-CODE = "AB"
ACCOUNT-TYPE NOT = "X"
```

where PART-REF-CODE is a two character item, e.g. PIC XX and ACCOUNT-TYPE is a single character item e.g. PIC A.

The file conditions, of the form end-of-<filename>, translate directly into COBOL, provided the standard program structure given in Appendix 1 is used. For example:

```
end-of-sales-file       =>  END-OF-SALES-FILE
not end-of-employee     =>  NOT END-OF-EMPLOYEE
```

A file condition, such as END-OF-SALES-FILE, is implemented using a COBOL condition-name the use of which is explained in Section 6.3.

Some low-level ANS COBOL compilers do not implement condition-names; an alternative translation is given in Appendix 5.2.

Selection

The main problem with the selection operation in COBOL is the termination of a sequence of operations. In the design language the sequences are clearly defined by the use of else and endif but in COBOL the period is used as the sequence terminator in place of endif.

For example, a program design might include:

```
if account-type = "X" then
   transfer "special account" to print-acc-message
   special-account-routine
else
   transfer 0 to discount
   normal-account-routine
endif
put-print-acc
get-next-acc
```

This should be translated into COBOL as:

```
IF ACCOUNT-TYPE = "X"
    MOVE "SPECIAL ACCOUNT" TO PRINT-ACC-MESSAGE
    PERFORM SPECIAL-ACCOUNT-ROUTINE
ELSE
    MOVE 0 TO DISCOUNT
    PERFORM NORMAL-ACCOUNT-ROUTINE.
PERFORM PUT-PRINT-ACC
PERFORM GET-NEXT-ACCOUNT
```

The end of the IF sequence of the selection is recognized by the word ELSE and the end of the ELSE sequence by the period following NORMAL-ACCOUNT-ROUTINE. The indentation is good programming practice and aids visual understanding but is not recognized by the COBOL compiler.

In an analogous way the sequence of operations following an if which does not have an else part is also terminated by a period, representing endif.

For example:

```
if quantity-ordered > 500 then
   calculate discount = discount + 0.01
   transfer "bulk" to discount-reason-1
endif
transfer discount to print-discount
```

should be translated as:

```
IF QUANTITY-ORDERED > 500
    COMPUTE DISCOUNT = DISCOUNT + 0.01
    MOVE "BULK" TO PRINT-DISCOUNT-REASON-1.
TRANSFER DISCOUNT TO PRINT-DISCOUNT
```

Great care should be taken to ensure that periods are correctly placed because they can have a serious effect on the meaning of a program. For example:

```
IF TAXABLE-INCOME > 11000
    PERFORM HIGHER-TAX.
PERFORM GET-NEXT-EMPLOYEE.
```

has a different effect from:

```
IF TAXABLE-INCOME > 11000
    PERFORM HIGHER-TAX
PERFORM GET-NEXT-EMPLOYEE.
```

In the first example PERFORM GET-NEXT-EMPLOYEE is executed whatever the outcome of the selection whereas in the second example it is executed only if the condition is true. The misuse of terminators is one of the most common causes of error among beginners in COBOL programming and often catches out the more experienced programmer as well.

The design of programs and their translation into COBOL is quite straightforward as long as only simple conditions are used and terminators are used correctly. To implement more complex conditions, involving multiple questions, a safe technique is to use simple if statements and refinement.

For example, suppose that a program has to select one of three discount routines depending on a combination of account type and quantity ordered. For records with account type "X" discount one is applied if the quantity ordered exceeds 500 and discount two otherwise; all other account types are processed by discount three.

This could be represented in the program design as follows.

```
        if account-type = "X" then
           account-x-routine
        else
           discount-three
        endif
          . . .
     account-x-routine
        if quantity-ordered > 500 then
           discount-one
        else
           discount-two
        endif
```

The translation to COBOL is quite straightforward, following the rules given previously. Later in the book the use of other techniques for implementing complex conditions, such as 'nested' if statements and compound conditions, will be considered (see Sections 6.4 and 6.5).

Repetition

The translation of the until used in the program design into COBOL uses a variation of the PERFORM statement, already encountered in its simplest form for refinement. The until through to the enduntil is replaced by a PERFORM-UNTIL statement of the form:

```
        PERFORM <loop-body> UNTIL <condition>
```

where <loop-body> is a paragraph name chosen by the programmer when translating the program design into COBOL. The body of the loop, those operations enclosed between do and enduntil, are translated into COBOL as the paragraph <loop-body>.

For example, consider the following overall program structure.

```
Invoice-summary
   get-next-invoice
   until end-of-invoice do
      process-invoice
      get-next-invoice
   enduntil
   print-summary
```

This can be translated into COBOL as follows.

```
INVOICE-SUMMARY.
    PERFORM GET-NEXT-INVOICE
    PERFORM DEAL-WITH-INVOICE UNTIL END-OF-INVOICE
    PERFORM PRINT-SUMMARY.
DEAL-WITH-INVOICE.
    PERFORM PROCESS-INVOICE
    PERFORM GET-NEXT-INVOICE.
```

The name DEAL-WITH-INVOICE does not appear in the program design but is invented at the translation stage to provide a name for the body of the loop.

This additional name is unnecessary if the body of the loop is a single operation or refinement name. For example:

```
find-total-quantity
   transfer 0 to total-quantity
   until item-number = 9999 do
      update-total-quantity
   enduntil
```

can be translated into COBOL as:

```
FIND-TOTAL-QUANTITY.
    MOVE 0 TO TOTAL-QUANTITY
    PERFORM UPDATE-TOTAL-QUANTITY
        UNTIL ITEM-NUMBER = 9999.
```

A very low-level ANS COBOL compiler may not include PERFORM . . . UNTIL and an alternative translation of until is given in Appendix 5.3.

4.4 Case Study

It is now possible to illustrate the complete process of design and construction of a simple COBOL program. Here is a problem.

> A file contains stock records, each of which contain the following data-items:
>
> | | |
> |---|---|
> | stock code | 6 characters |
> | description | 30 characters |
> | quantity on hand | 4 digits |
>
> The stock code consists of a single code letter followed by a code number of five digits.
>
> Write a program to print details of all stock records with a

stock code consisting of either the code letter 'A' followed by a code number less than 100, or a code letter other than 'A' and a code number less than 10. Add a message 'low stock' to the details of any stock record, satisfying the above criteria, where the quantity on hand is less than 25 items.

The process of program design can be started by considering the input and output records. The input file could be called 'stock-file' and each individual record described as:

```
stock-record
   stock-code
      stock-c-letter
      stock-c-number
   stock-description
   stock-quantity
```

The stock-code has to be broken down into its two constituent parts because the letter and number need to be tested separately.

The output record will require four data-items to include the possibility of a message. A possible description is:

```
details
   details-code
   details-description
   details-quantity
   details-message
```

For output, it is probably unnecessary to break down the code into its constituent parts.

The basic format of the program follows that of earlier examples:

```
select-stock
   get-next-stock-file
   until end-of-stock-file do
      process-stock-record
      get-next-stock-file
   enduntil
```

This program will run through the stock records one by one and use 'process-stock-record' to select the records of interest. Therefore the first level of refinement might be:

```
process-stock-record
   if stock-c-letter = "A" then
      check-a-numbers
   else
      check-other-numbers
   endif
```

This divides the stock records into two categories: those with the code letter 'A' and the others. At the next level there are two refinements which could be:

```
check-a-numbers
   if stock-c-number < 100 then
      details-required
   endif

check-other-numbers
   if stock-c-number < 10 then
      details-required
   endif
```

This leaves a single routine 'details-required' to be refined which should construct the output line details, and add the 'low stock' message if necessary. A possible refinement for this is given below.

```
details-required
   transfer stock-code to details-code
   transfer stock-description to details-description
   transfer stock-quantity to details-quantity
   if stock-quantity < 25 then
      transfer "low stock" to details-message
   endif
   put-details
```

This completes the program design. It should be emphasized that there is no single correct solution to any but the most trivial programming problems. The design developed above is not the only possible design and is not necessarily the best design. However, there is a good chance that it will work because of its systematic construction.

At this stage the reader should desk check the program design using a few sample input records. Here are some suggestions for values of code and quantity to check the design:

code	quantity	expected result
A00099	0025	selected
A00250	0003	not selected
A00008	0024	selected, low stock
A12345	1234	not selected
B00009	0004	selected, low stock
Q99999	9999	not selected
X00008	0099	selected
Y00010	0200	not selected

Having desk checked the program design and made any necessary alterations, it can now be translated into COBOL. It doesn't really matter whether translation starts with the data descriptions or procedural statements of the program because in most cases there will be some interaction between them as the program develops.

In this example it is straightforward to write down the descriptions of the input and output records as a starting point.

```
01  STOCK-RECORD.
    05  STOCK-CODE.
        10  STOCK-C-LETTER        PIC A.
        10  STOCK-C-NUMBER        PIC 9(5).
    05  STOCK-DESCRIPTION         PIC X(30).
    05  STOCK-QUANTITY            PIC 9999.

01  DETAILS.
    05  DETAILS-CODE              PIC X(6).
    05  FILLER                    PIC XX.
    05  DETAILS-DESCRIPTION       PIC X(30).
    05  FILLER                    PIC XX.
    05  DETAILS-QUANTITY          PIC 9(4).
    05  FILLER                    PIC X(5).
    05  DETAILS-MESSAGE           PIC X(9).
```

The only item about which there is any choice is 'DETAILS-MESSAGE' which has to be large enough to take any message which has to be printed. In this case the only message is "LOWȸSTOCK" which will fit into a nine character data-item.

It is now possible to work through the program design systematically, coding the successive levels of refinement. Applying the rules given for translating the design language into COBOL the following program fragments are obtained.

```
SELECT-STOCK.
    PERFORM GET-NEXT-STOCK-FILE
    PERFORM STOCK-CHECK UNTIL END-OF-STOCK-FILE.
STOCK-CHECK.
    PERFORM PROCESS-STOCK-RECORD
    PERFORM GET-NEXT-STOCK-FILE.

PROCESS-STOCK-RECORD.
    IF STOCK-C-LETTER = "A"
        PERFORM CHECK-A-NUMBERS
    ELSE
        PERFORM CHECK-OTHER-NUMBERS.

CHECK-A-NUMBERS.
    IF STOCK-C-NUMBER < 100
        PERFORM DETAILS-REQUIRED.

CHECK-OTHER-NUMBERS.
    IF STOCK-C-NUMBER < 10
        PERFORM DETAILS-REQUIRED.

DETAILS-REQUIRED.
    MOVE STOCK-CODE TO DETAILS-CODE
    MOVE STOCK-DESCRIPTION TO DETAILS-DESCRIPTION
    MOVE STOCK-QUANTITY TO DETAILS-QUANTITY
    IF STOCK-QUANTITY < 25
        MOVE "LOW STOCK" TO DETAILS-MESSAGE.
    PERFORM PUT-DETAILS.
```

To complete the program these data descriptions and program fragments have to be incorporated into the program skeleton given in

Appendix 1, and the names for the program, input file and output record systematically inserted. With practice, the translation step and the incorporation into the skeleton can be carried out in one operation.

The complete program is given below, laid out in the correct format as specified in Appendix 2.

```
IDENTIFICATION DIVISION.
PROGRAM-ID. EXAMPLE1.

ENVIRONMENT DIVISION.
CONFIGURATION SECTION.
SOURCE-COMPUTER. <computer-name>.
OBJECT-COMPUTER. <computer-name>.
*    <computer-name> should be replaced by the name
*    of the computer being used to run programs.

INPUT-OUTPUT SECTION.
FILE-CONTROL.
    SELECT STOCK-FILE ASSIGN TO <system-input>.
    SELECT OUTFILE ASSIGN TO <system-output>.
*        <system-input> and <system-output> must conform
*        to the rules for the system being used.

DATA DIVISION.
FILE SECTION.
FD  STOCK-FILE
    LABEL RECORDS OMITTED.
01  STOCK-RECORD.
    05  STOCK-CODE.
        10  STOCK-C-LETTER      PIC A.
        10  STOCK-C-NUMBER      PIC 9(5).
    05  STOCK-DESCRIPTION       PIC X(30).
    05  STOCK-QUANTITY          PIC 9999.
FD  OUTFILE
    LABEL RECORDS OMITTED.
01  OUT-LINE            PIC X(120).

WORKING-STORAGE SECTION.
01  STATE-VECTOR.
    05  END-STOCK-FILE      PIC X.
        88  END-OF-STOCK-FILE   VALUE "E".
01  DETAILS.
    05  DETAILS-CODE            PIC X(6).
    05  FILLER                  PIC XX.
    05  DETAILS-DESCRIPTION     PIC X(30).
    05  FILLER                  PIC XX.
    05  DETAILS-QUANTITY        PIC 9(4).
    05  FILLER                  PIC X(5).
    05  DETAILS-MESSAGE         PIC X(9).
```

```
PROCEDURE DIVISION.
MAIN-PROGRAM.
    PERFORM INIT-STATE
    PERFORM SELECT-STOCK
    PERFORM CLOSE-DOWN.
INIT-STATE.
    MOVE SPACE TO END-STOCK-FILE
    OPEN INPUT STOCK-FILE OUTPUT OUTFILE
    MOVE SPACES TO DETAILS.
CLOSE-DOWN.
    CLOSE STOCK-FILE OUTFILE
    STOP RUN.
GET-NEXT-STOCK-FILE.
    READ STOCK-FILE
        AT END MOVE "E" TO END-STOCK-FILE.
PUT-DETAILS.
    WRITE OUT-LINE FROM DETAILS
    MOVE SPACES TO DETAILS.
SELECT-STOCK.
    PERFORM GET-NEXT-STOCK-FILE
    PERFORM STOCK-CHECK UNTIL END-OF-STOCK-FILE.
STOCK-CHECK.
    PERFORM PROCESS-STOCK-RECORD
    PERFORM GET-NEXT-STOCK-FILE.
PROCESS-STOCK-RECORD.
    IF STOCK-C-LETTER = "A"
        PERFORM CHECK-A-NUMBERS
    ELSE
        PERFORM CHECK-OTHER-NUMBERS.
CHECK-A-NUMBERS.
    IF STOCK-C-NUMBER < 100
        PERFORM DETAILS-REQUIRED.
CHECK-OTHER-NUMBERS.
    IF STOCK-C-NUMBER < 10
        PERFORM DETAILS-REQUIRED.
DETAILS-REQUIRED.
    MOVE STOCK-CODE TO DETAILS-CODE
    MOVE STOCK-DESCRIPTION TO DETAILS-DESCRIPTION
    MOVE STOCK-QUANTITY TO DETAILS-QUANTITY
    IF STOCK-QUANTITY < 25
        MOVE "LOW STOCK" TO DETAILS-MESSAGE.
    PERFORM PUT-DETAILS.
```

The detailed structure of the program skeleton is discussed in Chapter 8 and a summary of the syntax of the individual COBOL statements is given in Appendix 4.

To test the program it will be necessary to construct a file of test data, which could be based on the suggestions given earlier. A possible sample input file is:

```
A00099SELECTED                     0025
A00250NOT SELECTED                 0003
A00008SELECTED - LOW STOCK         0024
A12345NOT SELECTED                 1234
B00009SELECTED - LOW STOCK         0004
Q99999NOT SELECTED                 9999
X00008SELECTED                     0099
Y00010NOT SELECTED                 0200
```

The description field in the stock record is not actually tested in the program, and therefore can be used to indicate the expected results of the test case. Where the combination of stock code and quantity on hand is such that the record should not be printed by the program the description field is 'NOT SELECTED'. If the combination of values means that the record should be printed then the description field is either 'SELECTED' or 'SELECTED - LOW STOCK' when a 'LOW STOCK' message is expected. This is more useful than merely filling the field with spurious data.

If the above file is input to the program 'EXAMPLE1' then the resulting output should be:

```
A00099   SELECTED                      0025
A00008   SELECTED - LOW STOCK          0024     LOW STOCK
B00009   SELECTED - LOW STOCK          0004     LOW STOCK
X00008   SELECTED                      0099
```

If any output description contains the words 'NOT SELECTED' then obviously the program has failed. Similarly if all the items expected to be selected are not included in the output then there is an error. In either of these cases the program will have to be examined, to find the error, modified and executed again to see if correct results are then obtained. This process may go through several cycles and is called debugging. The subject of testing and debugging will be discussed more fully in Chapter 7.

The appearance of the sample output, shown above, could be improved considerably by adding headings to the columns and suppressing the leading zeros in the quantity column. The provision of headings and the 'editing' of output are two of the subjects covered in the next chapter.

Exercises 4

4.1. Suppose that the program given in Section 4.4 was incorrectly entered into the computer and the last three lines of the program were:

```
        IF STOCK-QUANTITY < 25
            MOVE "LOW STOCK" TO DETAILS-MESSAGE
        PERFORM PUT-DETAILS.
```

Show what the output from the program would be for the sample input file given.

This illustrates a typical beginner's error - missing the terminating period at the end of a selection operation. Note that in practice you will be given the erroneous output and be required to infer the coding error which is much more difficult.

4.2. A program design starts with the following top-level structure:

```
get-next-account-file
until end-of-account-file do
   process-account
   get-next-account-file
enduntil
```

Write down the translation of this piece of program design into COBOL.
The above piece of program design is translated into COBOL, by a trainee programmer, as:

```
PERFORM GET-NEXT-ACCOUNT-FILE
PERFORM PROCESS-ACCOUNT UNTIL END-OF-ACCOUNT-FILE
PERFORM GET-NEXT-ACCOUNT-FILE
```

Describe what would happen if this incorrect coding is included in a COBOL program. You may make any reasonable assumptions about the refinement 'process-account'.

Programming Exercises 4

4.3. A file contains records in the following format:

customer identifier	2 letters 6 digits
name of customer	20 characters
date of last transaction	2 digits 3 letters 2 digits
credit limit	5 digits (pounds)

There are no spaces in these records and therefore typical records might be:

```
AA123456PRECISION CASTINGS  03APR8200500
BC980241NUTS AND BOLTS LTD. 22JAN8308000
DD004836A. WASHER(1892) LTD.24DEC8100250
```

A program is required which will produce a listing of these records, with the fields separated by spaces, including separating the two parts of the customer identifier and the three parts of the date. A message 'Low limit' should be added to the details for any customer whose credit limit is less than £500 and a message 'High limit' for those with credit limits exceeding £5000. Therefore the three sample records given above might appear in the following format.

```
AA 123456  PRECISION CASTINGS    03 APR 82  00500
BC 980241  NUTS AND BOLTS LTD.   22 JAN 83  08000  HIGH LIMIT
DD 004836  A. WASHER(1892) LTD.  24 DEC 81  00250  LOW LIMIT
```

The problem can be extended by adding a second message 'No recent orders' for any record which has date of last transaction prior to 1 January 1983.

4.4. A pottery company maintains an outstanding order file in the following format:

item number of item required	6 digits
customer identifier	10 characters
date requested	6 digits
quantity of item required	6 digits

Item numbers with the first three digits between 020 and 070 identify different types of porcelain figurines which require special production techniques. It is only economic to change the production line if the total quantity of figurines required exceeds 100.

Design a program to count the number of outstanding orders for figurines and the total quantity required. The output from the program need only consist of these two numbers. The next chapter will discuss how to add more detail to this output.

5 More Input and Output

Most of the programs written in COBOL will be concerned with money and therefore it is necessary to be able to input, manipulate and output decimal values. These programs will also have to produce reports which are in an acceptable form for people to read and therefore facilities for formatting output are also required.

The input and internal storage of decimal values follow similar conventions and are dealt with first. The output of decimal values is part of the more general topic of the presentation of output which also includes the insertion of currency symbols and zero suppression. When handling financial transactions it must be possible to represent debits as well as credits and therefore signed values need to be considered. To produce readable output it is also necessary to be able to add headings to output and possibly produce several different types of output lines.

5.1 Input and Storage of Decimal Values

The description of a decimal number to be input to a COBOL program includes an implied decimal point. The position of the point is indicated but it is not allocated a character position in the actual input data provided. An implied decimal point is represented by the character 'V' in a picture. For example

```
        10  INVOICE-AMOUNT      PIC 9999V99.
or      10  INVOICE-AMOUNT      PIC 9(4)V99.
```

describes a number occupying six character positions with the decimal point implied between the fourth and fifth digits. Therefore the following inputs would be represented as indicated:

required input value	actual form of input
23.5	002350
1.0	000100
0.03	000003
2172.21	217221

All unused digit positions should be filled with zeros and the numbers aligned so that the decimal point is implied in the correct position.

Any internal storage areas required for decimal numbers should also be described using the implied decimal point descriptor. For example

```
        10  TOT-PRICE       PIC 999V99.
```

describes a data-item which can hold a value between 0 and 999.99. Note that if a value to be stored in this data-item has more digits than can be represented by this picture then the value will be truncated to fit. Truncation often occurs when values are calculated within a program and insufficient space is allocated for the result of the calculation. For example, suppose that there are two data-items

```
05  SALE-QUANTITY        PIC 99.
05  SALE-PRICE           PIC 99V99.
```

and their current values are SALE-QUANTITY = 85 and SALE-PRICE = 28.50. The calculation

```
COMPUTE TOT-PRICE = SALE-QUANTITY * SALE-PRICE
```

will give the result 422.50 in TOT-PRICE because the result is truncated - it should be 2422.50.

It is essential that any data-items used to hold the results of calculations should be large enough to hold the maximum possible value which can be calculated. All too often strange output results are caused not by the "computer going wrong" but by truncation of values due to inadequate provision of storage space.

Truncation of the least significant digits can also occur particularly when calculating fractions of values. For example

```
05  TOT-PRICE       PIC 999V99.
. . . . .
COMPUTE TOT-PRICE = 0.95 * TOT-PRICE
```

would reduce the value in TOT-PRICE by 5%, perhaps representing a special discount. Suppose TOT-PRICE = 125.85 before the calculation then the new value will be 119.55 whereas the correct result is 119.5575 and the least significant digits have been truncated.

Rounded Values

In cases where the least significant digits will be lost in a calculation it is possible to indicate that the result should be rounded to the nearest representable value rather than truncated. In the example given above the statement

```
COMPUTE TOT-PRICE ROUNDED = 0.95 * TOT-PRICE
```

would give the result 119.56 if the original value of TOT-PRICE was 125.85.

The rules for rounding are:

(a) the value calculated is truncated to fit the result data-item,
(b) if the first digit lost is greater than or equal to 5 then the least significant digit of the truncated value is increased by 1, which may carry to other digits,
(c) the value is stored in the result data-item.

These rules also apply to the alternative arithmetic verbs discussed in Appendix 5.1.

5.2 Editing of Output Records

It is desirable for the values printed by a program to be presented in a form acceptable to the recipient of the output. People are used to reading £23.50 rather than 002350, which might be the 'raw' form of this value. The process of converting internal data values into a form more acceptable for human use is called editing. The editing characters which are considered in this section are:

.	decimal point
Z	zero suppression
*	cheque protect
£	currency symbol
,	comma (inserted in large numbers)

To output a decimal value in its correct form the picture must contain an actual decimal point. For example

```
        05  PRINT-INV-AMOUNT        PIC 9999.99.
or      05  PRINT-INV-AMOUNT        PIC 9(4).99.
```

Note the two uses of '.', as a decimal point and as a picture terminator in COBOL syntax. Because of this ambiguity it is important not to leave a space after a decimal point because it will then be treated as a terminator.

Any value transferred to a data-item with this description will be automatically aligned by the position of the decimal point and either truncated or zero filled to fit the description. To illustrate the effect of the above description consider the effect of the following artificial examples, with resulting outputs.

```
MOVE 23 TO PRINT-INV-AMOUNT             =>  0023.00
MOVE 67.5 TO PRINT-INV-AMOUNT           =>  0067.50
MOVE 87653.4 TO PRINT-INV-AMOUNT        =>  7653.40
MOVE 0.5754 TO PRINT-INV-AMOUNT         =>  0000.57
```

Note that there is an inconsistency between the input and output of decimal values - an input data-item which can be represented by six characters, with an implied decimal point, will require at least seven characters to output because of the actual decimal point.

Another important point which cannot be stated too frequently is that an edited data-item is a result item; once a value has been edited no attempt should be made to use that edited value in any further calculations. The data-item PRINT-INV-AMOUNT, defined above, could be used on the left of the equals sign in a COMPUTE statement or as the receiving-field in a MOVE statement. However, it should never appear on the right-hand side of the equals in a COMPUTE statement or as a sending-field in a MOVE statement.

The reader is accustomed to the idea of numbers being written in a free format without the need for leading zeros padding out the number. To achieve this 'natural' format in program output the zero suppression character 'Z' is used in numeric data-items in place of some, or all, of the '9's. For example:

```
05  PRINT-PRICE         PIC ZZZ9.99.
05  PRINT-QUANTITY      PIC Z(4).
```

The 'Z' indicates that if the corresponding position is not filled by a significant digit then it is filled by a space rather than a zero. The following examples, again artificial, illustrate the use of zero suppression.

```
MOVE 23.6 TO PRINT-PRICE          =>  ƀƀ23.60
MOVE 1002.03 TO PRINT-PRICE       =>  1002.03
MOVE 67012.305 TO PRINT-PRICE     =>  7012.30
MOVE 0.05 TO PRINT-PRICE          =>  ƀƀƀ0.05
MOVE 206 TO PRINT-QUANTITY        =>  ƀ206
MOVE 567842 TO PRINT-QUANTITY     =>  7842
MOVE 0 TO PRINT-QUANTITY          =>  ƀƀƀƀ
```

It is good practice to leave one unsuppressed digit in front of the decimal point to produce a leading zero for fractional values, as illustrated by the fourth example above. In most cases, zero suppression symbols to the right of the decimal point have no effect and should be avoided.

The cheque protect symbol '*' works in a similar way to zero suppression except that all unfilled positions are filled by asterisks. This is intended, as the name suggests, for the printing of amounts on cheques where the asterisks prevent the insertion of additional significant digits for fraudulent purposes. Note that zero suppression and cheque protect are mutually exclusive within a given picture.

The currency symbol '£' can be used in two ways as a fixed symbol or a floating symbol. A <u>fixed</u> currency symbol is a single occurrence of the symbol which appears in a fixed position in the output. For example:

```
05  PRINT-TOTAL-SALES        PIC £Z(4)9.99.
```

could be used in the following way:

```
MOVE 123.2 TO PRINT-TOTAL-SALES          =>  £ƀƀ123.20
MOVE 0.5 TO PRINT-TOTAL-SALES            =>  £ƀƀƀƀ0.50
MOVE 656721.458 TO PRINT-TOTAL-SALES     =>  £56721.45
```

The currency symbol remains in its fixed position regardless of zero suppression or truncation.

The position of a <u>floating</u> currency symbol varies within the output field subject to limits defined by the picture. The description:

```
      05  PRINT-TOT-SALES      PIC £££££9.99.
or    05  PRINT-TOT-SALES      PIC £(5)9.99.
```

indicates that the currency symbol can 'float' to any of the positions occupied by a '£' so that it immediately precedes the most significant digit of the value being output. Any unused positions to the left of the currency symbol being printed are filled with spaces. The following examples illustrate the effect of the floating currency symbol.

```
MOVE 621.5 TO PRINT-TOT-SALES          =>  ƀƀ£621.50
MOVE 0.3 TO PRINT-TOT-SALES            =>  ƀƀƀƀ£0.30
MOVE 8265172.831 TO PRINT-TOT-SALES => £65172.83
```

Note that the currency symbol cannot float right out of the field even if this means truncation of the value being printed.

It is not permissible to use floating currency symbols in the same picture as either zero suppression or cheque protect symbols.

The final editing character which will be considered in this section is the comma. Again it is 'natural' to expect large numbers to be written with commas to delineate the thousands, millions, etc. Commas can be inserted into pictures and used in conjunction with other editing symbols. The following pictures give some examples of the use of commas.

```
(a)        05  SUMMARY-SALE-TOTAL  PIC £99,999.99.
(b)        05  SUMMARY-QUANTITY    PIC ZZ,ZZ9.
(c)        05  SUMMARY-VAT-TOTAL   PIC ££££,££9.99.
```

In example (a) the comma will appear regardless of the size of the value to be output. In (b) and (c) the comma will only appear if required - if there is no significant digit to the left of the comma it will be treated as a 'Z' or a '£' respectively. Here are some examples of the use of these data-items.

```
MOVE 23.5 TO SUMMARY-SALE-TOTAL        =>  £00,023.50
MOVE 25 TO SUMMARY-QUANTITY            =>  ƀƀƀƀ25
MOVE 1001 TO SUMMARY-QUANTITY          =>  ƀ1,001
MOVE 528162 TO SUMMARY-QUANTITY        =>  28,162
MOVE 450 TO SUMMARY-VAT-TOTAL          =>  ƀƀƀƀ£450.00
MOVE 18760.23 TO SUMMARY-VAT-TOTAL     =>  ƀ£18,760.23
```

The best way of learning about editing characters is to try to use them in programs. A simple program which reads a few numbers from an input record and transfers them to an output record, containing edited data-items, should help to clarify the ideas discussed in this section.

5.3 Signed Numbers

The exact representation of signed input values is one of the undefined areas in the ANS COBOL '74 standard. The picture notation is clear enough - the symbol 'S' is used to indicate that a value is signed. For example:

```
05  STOCK-MOVEMENT        PIC  S999.
05  STOCK-VALUE           PIC  S999V99.
```

The 'S' indicates that these values should be treated as signed but how the sign is actually represented in the input record is not defined in the standard. A common practice for input from punched cards is to add the sign to the last digit of the number by multi-punching, therefore -325 would appear as 32N if punched for input as STOCK-MOVEMENT. However, if signed input values are to be input to a program the manual for the local system should be consulted.

Any temporary data-items which need to be signed also use the 'S' notation and how the sign is represented need not concern the programmer. All unsigned data-items are assumed to contain positive values and if a negative value is transferred to an unsigned data-item the sign will disappear.

If signed values can be input and held internally then obviously there needs to be a way of representing signs on output. The simplest way is to use a <u>trailing sign</u> appended to a picture which contains any legal combination of editing symbols described in the previous section. This trailing sign can be one of '-', '+', 'CR' or 'DB' and the actions corresponding to these symbols can be summarized as follows:

Sign symbol	Output for Value positive or zero	Value negative
+	+	-
-	space	-
CR	2 spaces	CR
DB	2 spaces	DB

Suppose there is a temporary variable:

```
04  CURRENT-BALANCE      PIC S9(4)V99.
```

then the contents might be output via a data-item of the form:

```
         05  PRINT-BALANCE          PIC ££,££9.99DB.
or       05  CUSTOMER-BALANCE       PIC £*,**9.99-.
```

5.4 Headings on Output

The appearance and usefulness of the output from a computer program can be greatly improved by the addition of headings, especially to tabular output containing columns of figures.

To illustrate the process of designing headings and actually printing them, consider the simple problem introduced in Section 2.3 which subsequently became the program design shown in Example 2.4, reproduced below.

```
price-and-discount-2
    get-next-sales
    until end-of-sales do
        find-price-and-discount
        produce-printer-line
        get-next-sales
    enduntil

find-price-and-discount
    calculate total-price = sales-quantity * sales-price
    if sales-quantity > 19 then
        calculate discount = 0.1 * total-price
        calculate total-price = total-price - discount
    else
        transfer 0 to discount
    endif

produce-printer-line
    transfer sales-item-no to printer-item-no
    transfer sales-quantity to printer-quantity
    transfer sales-price to printer-price
    transfer total-price to printer-tot-price
    transfer discount to printer-discount
    put-printer-line
```

The output from this program consists of five values per line, defined as follows;

```
printer-line
   printer-item-no          item number
   printer-quantity         quantity sold
   printer-price            price per item
   printer-tot-price        total price charged
   printer-discount         discount given
```

It would be useful to be able to produce output of the form shown in Figure 5.1, using editing and adding column headings.

ITEM NO.	QUANTITY	ITEM PRICE	TOTAL PRICE	DISCOUNT
12345	23	20.25	£465.75	£46.57
21876	5	2.50	£7.50	£0.00

Figure 5.1

To do this it has to be possible to define a heading line, describe it in COBOL and output the line at the appropriate point in the program. Assuming that the heading is to appear once at the top of the output, the appropriate place to output the heading is right at the beginning of processing. Therefore the top level of the program design should be modified, as shown below.

```
price-and-discount-3
   put-heading-line
   get-next-sales
   until end-of-sales do
      find-price-and-discount
      produce-printer-line
      get-next-sales
   enduntil
```

The 'put-heading-line' must appear outside the until loop otherwise the heading will be repeated above every line printed.

When translating this program design into COBOL two output records will have to be described - one for the heading and one for the details. These two records will have to be designed so that they are correctly aligned.

In this example the first three values to be output come directly from the input record and are therefore largely defined by the input format. Suppose that the input record is described as:

```
01  SALES-RECORD.
    02  SALES-ITEM-NO        PIC 9(5).
    02  SALES-QUANTITY       PIC 99.
    02  SALES-PRICE          PIC 999V99.
```

then the output data-items could be defined as:

```
    05  PRINTER-ITEM-NO          PIC 9(5).
```

```
05  PRINTER-QUANTITY          PIC Z9.
05  PRINTER-PRICE             PIC ZZ9.99.
```

The other two output data-items are dependent on the values of sales-quantity and sales-price and could therefore be described as:

```
05  PRINTER-TOT-PRICE         PIC £££,££9.99.
05  PRINTER-DISCOUNT          PIC ££££9.99.
```

Now that the format of the output data-items has been decided it is necessary to design the layout of the output. Squared paper is useful for this; putting one character in each square of the paper and positioning the data-items under the headings, remembering to use the maximum possible size of the output data-items. In the example this probably leads to a diagram of the form shown in Figure 5.2.

```
ITEM NO.  QUANTITY  ITEM PRICE  TOTAL PRICE  DISCOUNT

 XXXXX       XX       XXX.XX    XXX,XXX.XX   XXXXX.XX
 XXXXX       XX       XXX.XX    XXX,XXX.XX   XXXXX.XX
```

Figure 5.2

From this layout diagram the sizes of the FILLER data-items can be calculated and the complete output record specified as:

```
01  PRINTER-LINE.
    05  FILLER                PIC X.
    05  PRINTER-ITEM-NO       PIC 9(5).
    05  FILLER                PIC X(7).
    05  PRINTER-QUANTITY      PIC Z9.
    05  FILLER                PIC X(7).
    05  PRINTER-PRICE         PIC ZZ9.99.
    05  FILLER                PIC XXXX.
    05  PRINTER-TOT-PRICE     PIC £££,££9.99.
    05  FILLER                PIC XXX.
    05  PRINTER-DISCOUNT      PIC ££££9.99.
```

Now the corresponding heading line has to be created and this requires the introduction of a new idea - the 'VALUE clause'.

Value Clauses

Any temporary data-item can be given an initial value using the VALUE clause of COBOL. For example:

```
05  REPORT-HEADING      PIC X(15)
    VALUE "PROFIT AND LOSS".
```

This assigns the value "PROFIT AND LOSS" to the data-item called REPORT-HEADING. This will be its value at the beginning of the execution of the program and this value will remain until changed by a statement such as:

```
MOVE "BALANCE SHEET" TO REPORT-HEADING
```

This statement will change the value in REPORT-HEADING and the original value is lost. A data-item can also be assigned an initial value of blanks by using the constant 'SPACES'. For example:

```
05  FILLER  PIC X(10) VALUE SPACES.
```

would create a data-item with the special name FILLER containing ten blank characters. This could not be accessed independently but could usefully form part of a larger data structure.

In the special case of a heading line, it is not going to need to be changed. Therefore all the data-items forming the heading can be called FILLER, as individual parts of the heading will not need to be accessed.

It would be possible, using the VALUE clause, to create a single monolithic constant for the whole heading line. However, experience has shown that this leads to problems if apparently minor adjustments need to be made to headings. Therefore it is recommended that all headings should be broken down into small units which can be individually modified. A possible description for the heading of the example is given below.

```
01  HEADING-LINE.
    02  FILLER      PIC X(8)  VALUE "ITEM NO.".
    02  FILLER      PIC XX    VALUE SPACES.
    02  FILLER      PIC X(8)  VALUE "QUANTITY".
    02  FILLER      PIC XX    VALUE SPACES.
    02  FILLER      PIC X(10) VALUE "ITEM PRICE".
    02  FILLER      PIC XX    VALUE SPACES.
    02  FILLER      PIC X(11) VALUE "TOTAL PRICE".
    02  FILLER      PIC XX    VALUE SPACES.
    02  FILLER      PIC X(8)  VALUE "DISCOUNT".
```

The layout diagram, shown in Figure 5.1, indicates that HEADING-LINE and PRINTER-LINE should be the same length, 53 characters. A count of the number of characters in each of these records shows that they both total 53 characters. If the totals do not agree then the descriptions should be checked against the layout diagram and the sizes of the data-items adjusted.

Once the program starts producing output minor changes in the relative positioning of headings and data-items will become apparent. However, the effort put into the initial design of the output is usually more than compensated for by a reduction in the number of such modifications required when the program is being tested.

Having designed and described the heading line it still has to be output to the printer at the appropriate point in the program. In the program design there is the operation:

```
put-heading-line
```

and this can be translated into COBOL as:

```
PERFORM PUT-HEADING-LINE
```

A specification for PUT-HEADING-LINE then has to be added after PUT-

PRINTER-LINE in the program skeleton.

```
PUT-PRINTER-LINE.
    WRITE OUT-LINE FROM PRINTER-LINE
    MOVE SPACES TO PRINTER-LINE.
PUT-HEADING-LINE.
    WRITE OUT-LINE FROM HEADING-LINE.
```

Note the difference between the two put operations. The general format of a put operation for a constant output line is:

```
PUT-<constant-line>.
    WRITE OUT-LINE FROM <constant-line>.
```

This is because the <constant-line> does not need to be blanked out for re-use later.

The record OUT-LINE is the output-area for the program and must be described, as part of the output file description, in the FILE SECTION of the DATA DIVISION. A description of OUT-LINE is included in the program skeleton in Appendix 1. The records PRINTER-LINE and HEADING-LINE must be described in the WORKING-STORAGE SECTION of the program.

It is often useful to be able to introduce blank lines into output reports to improve the readability of the output. This could be done by defining a <constant-line> of the form:

```
01  BLANK-LINE      PIC X VALUE SPACE.
```

The corresponding put operation would then be defined as:

```
PUT-BLANK-LINE.
    WRITE OUT-LINE FROM BLANK-LINE.
```

Then whenever a blank line is required in the output all that is required is:

```
    PERFORM PUT-BLANK-LINE.
```

Note that all output records which are to be printed will have their length restricted by the number of characters in the printer's line. The most common line length is 120 characters, which is assumed in all the examples in this book. Records containing less than the maximum number of characters available are padded with blanks in the course of the put-operation (cf nonnumeric move). This is why BLANK-LINE can be defined as a constant containing only one space.

5.5 Multiple Output Records

The output of headings, described in the previous section, is a special case of the problem of defining multiple output records for a given output file. In general there are three types of output records, which can be identified by their content:

(a) variable data only, such as the typical detail lines used in previous examples,
(b) constant data only, such as headings or blank lines,
(c) a mixture of constant and variable data, such as a heading with a

page number.

In this section a set of simple rules will be developed for using an output file which requires a mixture of any number of these record types.

For records which contain only variable data, <u>each</u> record described should have an associated put-<record-name> operation defined for it. This should follow the format shown in Appendix 1:

```
PUT-<record-name>.
    WRITE OUT-LINE FROM <record-name>
    MOVE SPACES TO <record-name>.
```

This construction ensures that the contents of <record-name> are always blanked out ready for the next line to be constructed.

To ensure that the initial state of each record is correct, <u>each</u> record should be set to spaces at the end of the paragraph INIT-STATE in the standard program skeleton.

For example, suppose that a program needed to output two different detail lines called called 'report-line-1' and 'report-line-2'. Part of the program design might be:

```
Example 5.1
   if cust-type < 10 then
      print-line-1
   else
      print-line-2
   endif
 . . .
print-line-1
   . . .
   put-report-line-1

print-line-2
   . . .
   put-report-line-2
```

The corresponding COBOL program would contain descriptions for REPORT-LINE-1 and REPORT-LINE-2 and the program skeleton should be modified as follows:

```
PROCEDURE DIVISION.
MAIN-PROGRAM.
    PERFORM INIT-STATE
    PERFORM <main-process>
    PERFORM CLOSE-DOWN.
INIT-STATE.
    MOVE SPACE TO END-<input-file-name>
    OPEN INPUT <input-file-name> OUTPUT OUTFILE
    MOVE SPACES TO REPORT-LINE-1 REPORT-LINE-2.
CLOSE-DOWN.
    CLOSE <input-file-name> OUTFILE
    STOP RUN.
```

```
GET-NEXT-<input-file-name>.
    READ <input-file-name>
        AT END MOVE "E" TO END-<input-file-name>.
PUT-REPORT-LINE-1.
    WRITE OUT-LINE FROM REPORT-LINE-1
    MOVE SPACES TO REPORT-LINE-1.
PUT-REPORT-LINE-2.
    WRITE OUT-LINE FROM REPORT-LINE-2
    MOVE SPACES TO REPORT-LINE-2.
```

The program design fragment, shown in Example 5.1, could then be translated into COBOL as follows:

```
EXAMPLE-5-1.
    IF CUST-TYPE < 10
        PERFORM PRINT-LINE-1
    ELSE
        PERFORM PRINT-LINE-2.
. . .
PRINT-LINE-1.
    . . .
    PERFORM PUT-REPORT-LINE-1.
PRINT-LINE-2.
    . . .
    PERFORM PUT-REPORT-LINE-2.
```

In another program, there might be two report lines required to be output together and the program design might contain:

Example 5.2

```
fill-report-lines
put-report-line-1
put-report-line-2
```

In this example 'fill-report-lines' is assumed to transfer data to both 'report-line-1' and 'report-line-2'. Translating this design fragment into COBOL would give:

```
EXAMPLE-5-2.
    PERFORM FILL-REPORT-LINES
    PERFORM PUT-REPORT-LINE-1
    PERFORM PUT-REPORT-LINE-2
```

Since REPORT-LINE-1 and REPORT-LINE-2 are independent they can filled at the same time and then output in sequence.

The rules for records containing only constant data were given in the previous section. There is no need to modify INIT-STATE and the put-<constant-line> operation is defined as:

```
PUT-<constant-line>.
    WRITE OUT-LINE FROM <constant-line>.
```

When dealing with records which contain both constant and variable data, these are treated as a special case of the constant line. However, the important point to remember is that the programmer is responsible for ensuring that all variable parts of the record are correctly initialized and reset each time the record is used.

For example, consider the following record description for a page heading.

```
01  MAIN-HEADING.
    02  FILLER          PIC X(47) VALUE SPACES.
    02  FILLER          PIC X(23)
        VALUE "PROFIT AND LOSS ACCOUNT".
    02  FILLER          PIC X(47) VALUE SPACES.
    02  MAIN-PAGE-NO    PIC ZZ9.
```

The put-main-heading operation should be defined as:

```
PUT-MAIN-HEADING.
    WRITE OUT-LINE FROM MAIN-HEADING.
```

Whenever this operation is used a value must always be assigned to MAIN-PAGE-NO, for example:

```
PRINT-HEADING.
    MOVE PAGE-COUNT TO MAIN-PAGE-NO
    PERFORM PUT-MAIN-HEADING.
```

5.6 Case Study

It is now possible to write the complete COBOL program for the case study introduced in Section 2.5. The specification for the program was:

> The ABC Carpet Company maintains a file of daily orders, where each record contains: an order number, the customer's name and address, the number of square metres of carpet ordered, the price per square metre and the delivery zone. The delivery zone is coded as a single letter either 'A' or 'B', indicating the distance from the warehouse. The company's policy on delivery charges is that the order is delivered free if the cost of the carpet exceeds £200 otherwise there is an additional charge of £5 for zone 'A' and £10 for zone 'B'.
>
> A program is required which will process the orders in the file and calculate the cost of the carpet, the delivery charge, if any, and the total to be charged for each order. After processing all the orders the program should produce totals for carpet sales and delivery charges, and the total amount due.

The program design developed in Section 2.5 is going to be slightly modified as it is now possible to include headings for the output and to print a separate record containing the totals.

To include headings a reference to a refinement called 'print-headings' is inserted at the top level of the program design, <u>outside</u> the main processing loop. The top level of the design then becomes:

```
carpet-orders
   initialize-totals
   print-headings
   get-next-order-file
   until end-of-order-file do
      process-order
      update-totals
      get-next-order-file
   enduntil
   produce-totals
```

In this case it might be appropriate to have a page heading giving the name of the company and the column headings for the output details. If these are to be separated by blank lines then the refinement of 'print-headings' would be:

```
print-headings
   put-page-heading
   put-blank-line
   put-col-headings
   put-blank-line
```

In the data division of the COBOL program it will then be necessary to give descriptions for 'page-heading', 'col-headings' and 'blank-line', and the corresponding put operations will need to be added to the procedure division.

At this stage, it will be assumed that there is only one set of headings and that the output will not require a continuation page with new headings. The problems of pagination will be discussed in Chapter 8.

The original version of 'produce-totals', given in Section 2.5, assumed that the summary was to be output using the same output record as the detail lines. In this section a separate output record, called 'summary-line', is used to output the totals. This record will contain a mixture of constant and variable data; the constant part being a suitable message and the variable part the values of the three totals to be output.

Therefore the new output record could be:

```
summary-line
   TOTALS FOR ALL ORDERS          fixed message
   summary-carpet-charges         total of charges for carpets
   summary-delivery-charges       total of all delivery charges
   summary-order-charges          total of all charges
```

It would also improve the appearance of the output to separate the summary information from the details by a blank line. Therefore the new refinement of 'produce-totals' is:

```
produce-totals
   put-blank-line
   transfer total-carpet to summary-carpet-charges
   transfer total-delivery to summary-delivery-charges
   calculate summary-order-charges =
                              total-carpet + total-delivery
   put-summary-line
```

A 'put-summary-line' paragraph will have to be added to the procedure division of the COBOL program remembering that this is a record containing both constant and variable data.

The complete program design with these modifications follows.

```
carpet-orders
    initialize-totals
    print-headings
    get-next-order-file
    until end-of-order-file do
       process-order
       update-totals
       get-next-order-file
    enduntil
    produce-totals

initialize-totals
    transfer 0 to total-carpet
    transfer 0 to total-delivery

print-headings
    put-page-heading
    put-blank-line
    put-col-headings
    put-blank-line

process-order
    calculate carpet-charge = order-size * order-price
    if carpet-charge not > 200 then
       find-delivery-charge
    else
       transfer 0 to delivery-charge
    endif
    print-order-details

update-totals
    calculate total-carpet = total-carpet + carpet-charge
    calculate total-delivery = total-delivery + delivery-charge

produce-totals
    put-blank-line
    transfer total-carpet to summary-carpet-charges
    transfer total-delivery to summary-delivery-charges
    calculate summary-order-charges =
                                total-carpet + total-delivery
    put-summary-line

find-delivery-charge
    if order-zone = "A" then
       transfer 5 to delivery-charge
    else
       transfer 10 to delivery-charge
    endif
```

```
print-order-details
   transfer order-number to detail-number
   transfer order-customer to detail-customer
   transfer order-size to detail-size
   transfer order-price to detail-price
   transfer order-zone to detail-zone
   transfer carpet-charge to detail-carpet-charge
   transfer delivery-charge to detail-delivery-charge
   calculate detail-order-charge =
                         carpet-charge + delivery-charge
   put-detail-line
```

Before attempting to translate this design into COBOL the format of the input record needs to be defined. A possible definition for this record is given below.

Order number	4 digits
Customer name and address	30 characters
Carpet size (sq. metres)	2 digits
Price per square metre	4 digits (pence)
Delivery zone	1 letter ('A' or 'B')

The complete program corresponding to this design can now be developed.

```
       IDENTIFICATION DIVISION.
       PROGRAM-ID. CARPETS.

       ENVIRONMENT DIVISION.
       CONFIGURATION SECTION.
       SOURCE-COMPUTER. <computer-name>.
       OBJECT-COMPUTER. <computer-name>.
      *    <computer-name> should be replaced by the name
      *    of the computer being used to run programs.

       INPUT-OUTPUT SECTION.
       FILE-CONTROL.
           SELECT ORDER-FILE ASSIGN TO <system-input>.
           SELECT OUTFILE ASSIGN TO <system-output>.
      *        <system-input> and <system-output> must conform
      *        to the rules for the system being used.

       DATA DIVISION.
       FILE SECTION.
       FD  ORDER-FILE
           LABEL RECORDS OMITTED.
       01  ORDER-RECORD.
           05  ORDER-NUMBER          PIC 9999.
           05  ORDER-CUSTOMER        PIC X(30).
           05  ORDER-SIZE            PIC 99.
           05  ORDER-PRICE           PIC 99V99.
           05  ORDER-ZONE            PIC A.
       FD  OUTFILE
           LABEL RECORDS OMITTED.
       01  OUT-LINE          PIC X(120).
```

```
WORKING-STORAGE SECTION.
01  STATE-VECTOR.
    05  END-ORDER-FILE       PIC X.
        88  END-OF-ORDER-FILE    VALUE "E".

01  TEMPORARY-ITEMS.
    05  TOTAL-CARPET             PIC 9(6)V99.
    05  TOTAL-DELIVERY           PIC 999.
    05  DELIVERY-CHARGE          PIC 99.
    05  CARPET-CHARGE            PIC 9(4)V99.

01  PAGE-HEADING.
    05  FILLER       PIC X(36)   VALUE SPACES.
    05  FILLER       PIC X(18)   VALUE "ABC CARPET COMPANY".

01  BLANK-LINE       PIC X       VALUE SPACE.

01  COL-HEADINGS.
    05  FILLER       PIC X(6)    VALUE "NUMBER".
    05  FILLER       PIC XXXX    VALUE SPACES.
    05  FILLER       PIC X(25)   VALUE
        "CUSTOMER NAME AND ADDRESS".
    05  FILLER       PIC X(5)    VALUE SPACES.
    05  FILLER       PIC XXXX    VALUE "SIZE".
    05  FILLER       PIC XX      VALUE SPACES.
    05  FILLER       PIC X(5)    VALUE "PRICE".
    05  FILLER       PIC XX      VALUE SPACES.
    05  FILLER       PIC XXXX    VALUE "ZONE".
    05  FILLER       PIC X(5)    VALUE SPACES.
    05  FILLER       PIC X(7)    VALUE "CARPETS".
    05  FILLER       PIC XX  VALUE SPACES.
    05  FILLER       PIC X(6)    VALUE "DELIV.".
    05  FILLER       PIC X(7)    VALUE SPACES.
    05  FILLER       PIC X(5)    VALUE "TOTAL".

01  DETAIL-LINE.
    05  FILLER                   PIC X.
    05  DETAIL-NUMBER            PIC 9(4).
    05  FILLER                   PIC XXX.
    05  DETAIL-CUSTOMER          PIC X(30).
    05  FILLER                   PIC XXX.
    05  DETAIL-SIZE              PIC Z9.
    05  FILLER                   PIC XXX.
    05  DETAIL-PRICE             PIC Z9.99.
    05  FILLER                   PIC XXX.
    05  DETAIL-ZONE              PIC A.
    05  FILLER                   PIC X(6).
    05  DETAIL-CARPET-CHARGE     PIC ££££9.99.
    05  FILLER                   PIC XXX.
    05  DETAIL-DELIVERY-CHARGE   PIC ££9.
    05  FILLER                   PIC X(6).
    05  DETAIL-ORDER-CHARGE      PIC £(5)9.99.
```

```
01  SUMMARY-LINE.
    05  FILLER            PIC X(18)   VALUE SPACES.
    05  FILLER            PIC X(21)   VALUE
        "TOTALS FOR ALL ORDERS".
    05  FILLER            PIC X(19)   VALUE SPACES.
    05  SUMMARY-CARPET-CHARGES        PIC ££££,££9.99.
    05  FILLER            PIC XX      VALUE SPACES.
    05  SUMMARY-DELIVERY-CHARGES      PIC £££9.
    05  FILLER            PIC XXXX    VALUE SPACES.
    05  SUMMARY-ORDER-CHARGES         PIC ££££,££9.99.

PROCEDURE DIVISION.
MAIN-PROGRAM.
    PERFORM INIT-STATE
    PERFORM CARPET-ORDERS
    PERFORM CLOSE-DOWN.
INIT-STATE.
    MOVE SPACE TO END-ORDER-FILE
    OPEN INPUT ORDER-FILE OUTPUT OUTFILE
    MOVE SPACES TO DETAIL-LINE.
CLOSE-DOWN.
    CLOSE ORDER-FILE OUTFILE
    STOP RUN.
GET-NEXT-ORDER-FILE.
    READ ORDER-FILE
        AT END MOVE "E" TO END-ORDER-FILE.
PUT-DETAIL-LINE.
    WRITE OUT-LINE FROM DETAIL-LINE
    MOVE SPACES TO DETAIL-LINE.
PUT-PAGE-HEADING.
    WRITE OUT-LINE FROM PAGE-HEADING.
PUT-BLANK-LINE.
    WRITE OUT-LINE FROM BLANK-LINE.
PUT-COL-HEADINGS.
    WRITE OUT-LINE FROM COL-HEADINGS.
PUT-SUMMARY-LINE.
    WRITE OUT-LINE FROM SUMMARY-LINE.
CARPET-ORDERS.
    PERFORM INITIALIZE-TOTALS
    PERFORM PRINT-HEADINGS
    PERFORM GET-NEXT-ORDER-FILE
    PERFORM DEAL-WITH-ORDER UNTIL END-OF-ORDER-FILE
    PERFORM PRODUCE-TOTALS.
INITIALIZE-TOTALS.
    MOVE 0 TO TOTAL-CARPET
    MOVE 0 TO TOTAL-DELIVERY.
PRINT-HEADINGS.
    PERFORM PUT-PAGE-HEADING
    PERFORM PUT-BLANK-LINE
    PERFORM PUT-COL-HEADINGS
    PERFORM PUT-BLANK-LINE.
DEAL-WITH-ORDER.
    PERFORM PROCESS-ORDER
    PERFORM UPDATE-TOTALS
    PERFORM GET-NEXT-ORDER-FILE.
```

```
PROCESS-ORDER.
    COMPUTE CARPET-CHARGE = ORDER-SIZE * ORDER-PRICE
    IF CARPET-CHARGE NOT > 200
        PERFORM FIND-DELIVERY-CHARGE
    ELSE
        MOVE 0 TO DELIVERY-CHARGE.
    PERFORM PRINT-ORDER-DETAILS.
UPDATE-TOTALS.
    COMPUTE TOTAL-CARPET = TOTAL-CARPET + CARPET-CHARGE
    COMPUTE TOTAL-DELIVERY = TOTAL-DELIVERY + DELIVERY-CHARGE.
PRODUCE-TOTALS.
    PERFORM PUT-BLANK-LINE
    MOVE TOTAL-CARPET TO SUMMARY-CARPET-CHARGES
    MOVE TOTAL-DELIVERY TO SUMMARY-DELIVERY-CHARGES
    COMPUTE SUMMARY-ORDER-CHARGES =
            TOTAL-CARPET + TOTAL-DELIVERY
    PERFORM PUT-SUMMARY-LINE.
FIND-DELIVERY-CHARGE.
    IF ORDER-ZONE = "A"
        MOVE 5 TO DELIVERY-CHARGE
    ELSE
        MOVE 10 TO DELIVERY-CHARGE.
PRINT-ORDER-DETAILS.
    MOVE ORDER-NUMBER TO DETAIL-NUMBER
    MOVE ORDER-CUSTOMER TO DETAIL-CUSTOMER
    MOVE ORDER-SIZE TO DETAIL-SIZE
    MOVE ORDER-PRICE TO DETAIL-PRICE
    MOVE ORDER-ZONE TO DETAIL-ZONE
    MOVE CARPET-CHARGE TO DETAIL-CARPET-CHARGE
    MOVE DELIVERY-CHARGE TO DETAIL-DELIVERY-CHARGE
    COMPUTE DETAIL-ORDER-CHARGE =
            CARPET-CHARGE + DELIVERY-CHARGE
    PERFORM PUT-DETAIL-LINE.
```

An example of the output from this program is shown in Figure 5.3.

Exercises 5

5.1. The input record for a COBOL program contains the following data-item:

```
05  MONTHLY-HIRE-CHARGE     PIC 9(4)V99.
```

Write down the form in which you would input each of the following values to this data-item: 23, 27.5, 133.42 and 2,125.

ABC CARPET COMPANY

NUMBER	CUSTOMER NAME AND ADDRESS	SIZE	PRICE	ZONE	CARPETS	DELIV.	TOTAL
1514	J.STUART, FLODDEN	25	15.50	A	£387.50	£0	£387.50
1314	R.BRUCE, BANNOCKBURN	10	5.60	A	£56.00	£5	£61.00
1297	W.WALLACE, STIRLING BRIDGE	10	20.00	A	£200.00	£5	£205.00
1645	J.GRAHAM, INVERLOCHY	20	10.01	A	£200.20	£0	£200.20
1388	J.DOUGLAS, OTTERBURN	20	14.40	B	£288.00	£0	£288.00
1745	C.STUART, PRESTONPANS	15	12.90	B	£193.50	£10	£203.50
1689	J.GRAHAM, KILLIECRANKIE	20	10.00	B	£200.00	£10	£210.00
	TOTALS FOR ALL ORDERS				£1,525.20	£30	£1,555.20

Figure 5.3

5.2. A program includes the following data descriptions:

```
01  TEMPORARY-ITEMS.
    05  DISCOUNT-GIVEN   PIC 99V99.
    05  FULL-PRICE       PIC 9(4)V99.
    05  FINAL-PRICE      PIC 9(4)V99.
```

and the following statements appear in the procedure division of the same program:

```
COMPUTE DISCOUNT-GIVEN = 0.155 * FULL-PRICE
COMPUTE FINAL-PRICE = FULL-PRICE - DISCOUNT
```

For each of the following values of FULL-PRICE:
10.00 20.50 37.25 1500.00
calculate the corresponding values of DISCOUNT-GIVEN and FINAL-PRICE.

5.3. Explain the effect of the following pictures:

```
05  EDITED-ITEM-1   PIC  Z(5)9.
05  EDITED-ITEM-2   PIC  £(5)9.99.
05  EDITED-ITEM-3   PIC  £**,***.99.
05  EDITED-ITEM-4   PIC  £££,££9.99DB.
05  EDITED-ITEM-5   PIC  ZZ,ZZ9+.
```

by showing the output which will be produced if each of the following values is moved to each of the above data-items: 87654321, 0.756 and -253.

Programming Exercises 5

5.4. The input to the payroll system of the St. Kilda Puffin Factory consists of employee records which contain the following data-items:

employee number	2 letters followed by 4 digits
gross monthly pay	5 digits (pence)
annual tax allowance	4 digits (pounds)

All employees pay 5% of their salary to the company pension fund, which is deducted before tax is calculated. They are also liable for tax at 20% of their income after deduction of tax allowances and pension contributions.

Design a payroll program which will calculate and print the pension contribution, tax payable and net pay, per month, for each employee. The output should appear in the following format:

THE ST. KILDA PUFFIN FACTORY

EMP. NO.	ALLOW.	GROSS PAY	PENSION	TAX	NET PAY
AA1023	£1,200	£500.00	£25.00	£75.00	£400.00
BC2048	£2,321	£482.96	£24.14	£50.08	£408.74

Investigate the effect of truncation and rounding in the calculation of the pension contribution, the taxable pay and the net pay.

[Problem 5.4 first appeared in the exercises for Chapter 2. It should also be possible to implement the other two exercises given for Chapter 2, if further ideas for programs are required.]

5.5. The National Savings Bank of Ruritania summarizes the state of each of its customer's accounts at the end of each month by producing a record in the form:

account number	8 digits
account name	25 characters
opening balance	6 digits (pence, signed)
total amount of debits	5 digits (pence)
total amount of credits	5 digits (pence)

The bank's policy regarding service charges is:

> If the closing balance is in credit and greater than £25 then the customer's account is credited with 1% interest on the closing balance. If the closing balance is in debt then the customer pays a service charge of 2% interest on the closing balance. For accounts in credit between zero and twenty-five pounds no charge is made nor interest paid.

Write a program to read the account records, calculate the closing balance of each account and print the charge made or interest added, if any. The output should include suitable headings and properly edited currency fields.

6 Developing Algorithms

This chapter is concerned with increasing the number of techniques which are available to solve problems with more complex conditions than those examples explored so far.

The repertoire of conditions available is increased by introducing class conditions, to check the contents of data-items, and condition names, which allow a single condition to be associated with a set of values. Both class conditions and condition names are very useful in the group of problems concerned with data validation - the checking of raw input for errors before processing it.

Complex conditions can be implemented by combining simple conditions in some way, two possibilities will be considered: 'nested' if statements and creating compound conditions within a single if statement.

As programs become more complex the need for more state variables often becomes apparent and how these can be implemented is explained. Finally a small case study, on the validation of input data, is included to illustrate the use of some of the constructs described.

6.1 Data Validation

COBOL is a language designed for commercial data processing and this implies that at least some programs in a system will have to handle raw input from some form of man/machine interface. Some errors will occur in the input data regardless of what method is used for the transcription of raw data into machine-readable form. In a commercial programming environment it is essential that as many errors as possible should be detected before the input data is processed.

Failure to detect errors sometimes leads to the sort of error which the daily newspapers love, for example when an old age pensioner receives a gas bill for £6,000,000. It is also desirable that errors should be detected before they cause a program to stop with an execution error. It is not very good policy for a program processing 10,000 input records to fail after 9,000 have been processed because of a simple typing error.

Some error detection can be done by the use of simple conditions to check ranges of values or provide 'reasonableness' checks. For example, under normal circumstances the number of units of electricity consumed by a domestic household might be expected to be less than, say, 3000 units per billing period. Therefore the billing program could include a check of the form:

```
if units-used not > 3000 then
   normal-billing
else
   query-units-used
endif
```

The procedure 'query-units-used' might construct a report on all customers whose use of units is 'abnormal'. The input can then be checked to see whether there is an error in transcribing the original data or whether the meter is being wound backwards. In practice the program will also have to provide an override facility to allow processing of a genuine abnormal bill.

To assist the detection of errors in data COBOL provides two additional types of conditions called class conditions and condition-names.

6.2 Class Conditions and Redefinition

A class condition is used to establish whether the current contents of a particular data-item are of a given type. One of the commonest requirements is to ensure that the contents of a data-item are numeric before it is used in an arithmetic operation. Using a nonnumeric value in an arithmetic operation will normally result in an execution error.

The two class conditions provided in COBOL are alphabetic and numeric and they take the form:

<data-item> numeric   <data-item> not numeric
<data-item> alphabetic   <data-item> not alphabetic

The condition '<data-item> numeric' is true if <data-item> contains only characters from the set defined for numeric type items, that is the digits 0 to 9 and operational signs, and false otherwise. A data-item containing spaces or an explicit decimal point is not numeric. The condition '<data-item> not numeric' is simply the converse of the numeric condition.

The condition '<data-item> alphabetic' is true if <data-item> contains only characters from the set defined for alphabetic type items, that is the letters A to Z and space. Note that a data-item containing punctuation is not alphabetic.

The translation of these conditions into COBOL is quite straightforward, for example:

if sale-price not numeric then
if tariff-code alphabetic then

become:

```
IF SALE-PRICE NOT NUMERIC
IF TARIFF-CODE ALPHABETIC
```

Considering the problem of erroneous data leads on to the connected problem of the output of invalid values for numeric data-items. This is a slight digression from the main theme of this chapter but can usefully be discussed at this point.

Suppose that an output data-item has been described as:

```
05  PRINT-ITEM-PRICE    PIC £££9.99.
```

It is intended to be used to output the value of a data-item in the input record described as:

```
05  SALE-ITEM-PRICE PIC 999V99.
```

The effect of the statement:

```
MOVE SALE-ITEM-PRICE TO PRINT-ITEM-PRICE
```

is clearly defined if the value of SALE-ITEM-PRICE is numeric. However, if the input record contains 'ABCDE' what does the editing mean? Some COBOL systems may attempt to perform the editing resulting in the production of a mutilated version of the original data which may even appear to indicate that the original value was numeric. Other COBOL systems will give an execution error at this point and the program will fail. Neither of these alternatives is acceptable.

There are two straightforward solutions to this problem: either have two output records, one for the 'normal' lines and the other for error lines, or allow alternative descriptions to be given for a particular output data-item. The first solution is preferable but is best implemented using two output files and will be considered in Chapter 9. The second, less satisfactory, solution can be implemented using the REDEFINES clause of COBOL which will be explained here and used in the case study at the end of this chapter.

Redefines Clauses

The REDEFINES clause allows the programmer to give two names and descriptions for the same part of an input or output record. The two alternatives used must define data-items of exactly the same length. In the example given previously it would be possible to write:

```
05  SALE-ITEM-PRICE     PIC 999V99.
05  SALE-PRICE-ERROR REDEFINES SALE-ITEM-PRICE
                        PIC X(5).
. . . . .
05  PRINT-ITEM-PRICE    PIC £££9.99.
05  PRINT-PRICE-ERROR REDEFINES PRINT-ITEM-PRICE
                        PIC X(7).
```

At the program design level the use of redefinition can be indicated by connecting the alternative names for the same area by the special symbol '=='. For example:

```
sale-item-price == sale-price-error
print-item-price == print-item-error
```

The program design could then include the refinement:

```
produce-item-price
   if sale-item-price numeric then
      transfer sale-item-price to print-item-price
   else
      transfer sale-price-error to print-price-error
   endif
```

The corresponding part of the procedure division of the program would then be:

```
PRODUCE-ITEM-PRICE.
    IF SALE-ITEM-PRICE NUMERIC
        MOVE SALE-ITEM-PRICE TO PRINT-ITEM-PRICE
    ELSE
        MOVE SALE-PRICE-ERROR TO PRINT-PRICE-ERROR.
```

If the value in SALE-ITEM-PRICE is numeric then it will be edited for output otherwise, if it is invalid, it will be output in its 'raw' form so that it can be inspected and corrected for subsequent re-input to the program.

In practice the separation of the valid and invalid data will probably include the setting of an error flag and the production of an error message which will lead to a more complex structure than that shown in the above example.

The rules for using redefinition can be summarized as follows:

(a) the alternative description (the redefining item) must be the first data-item with the same level-number following the data-item being redefined (the redefined item),
(b) the redefined and redefining items must be of the same length,
(c) the two data-items are linked by the REDEFINES clause of the form:
<redefining-name> REDEFINES <redefined-name>

It is possible for either the redefined or redefining items to be a group data-item. This is most useful for the alignment of output columns. In the example given because the erroneous data is transferred using a nonnumeric move the invalid values will be space filled and will not be aligned with the valid values. For example, using PRODUCE-ITEM-PRICE, a mixture of valid and invalid values might appear as:

```
. . .    £23.26      . . .
. . .   ABCDE        . . .
. . .     £0.65      . . .
. . .   £123.20      . . .
. . .   )%%))        . . .
```

Some people would argue that this is quite acceptable as it emphasizes the invalid values while others will argue that it 'spoils the appearance of the output'.

The alignment problem can be overcome by making the redefining item a group item, for example:

```
05  PRINT-ITEM-PRICE    PIC £££9.99.
05  PRINT-INVALID-PRICE REDEFINES PRINT-ITEM-PRICE.
    10  FILLER        PIC XX.
    10  PRINT-PRICE-ERROR   PIC X(5).
```

Now because SALE-ITEM-PRICE and PRINT-PRICE-ERROR are the same size there will be no space filling - the spaces will be absorbed by the FILLER. Using PRODUCE-ITEM-PRICE with the mixture of valid and invalid values used as an example previously the output will now appear as follows:

```
. . .      £23.26          . . .
. . .       ABCDE          . . .
. . .       £0.65          . . .
. . .     £123.20          . . .
. . .       )%%))          . . .
```

Note that the second rule for REDEFINES clauses still holds in this case - the total length of PRINT-INVALID-PRICE (seven characters) is exactly the same as that of PRINT-ITEM-PRICE.

6.3 Condition-names

A condition-name allows a set of values to be associated with a particular data-item. Suppose that a legal account number in some organization must be a number between 1000 and 4000, these might be the only numbers which have been allocated perhaps. It would be useful to be able to write in a program design:

<u>if</u> correct-acc-no <u>then</u>

The condition 'correct-acc-no' could then be defined such that it is <u>true</u> if the account number is legal and <u>false</u> otherwise. This can be done in COBOL by using a <u>condition-name</u> associated with a data-item. The description of the appropriate data structure in this case would be:

```
05  ACC-NO          PIC 9999.
    88  CORRECT-ACC-NO  VALUE 1000 THRU 4000.
```

This defines a condition-name CORRECT-ACC-NO which is <u>true</u> if the value of the associated data-item ACC-NO lies within the range 1000 to 4000 (inclusive) and <u>false</u> otherwise. In the procedure division of the COBOL program it is then possible to write:

```
IF CORRECT-ACC-NO
```

This example may seem trivial as it would be possible to achieve the same effect using a combination of simple conditions, for example:

```
IF ACC-NO NOT < 1000 AND ACC-NO NOT > 4000
```

(Combinations of simple conditions will be discussed in Sections 6.4 and 6.5.) However, the set of values associated with a condition-name can be any combination of ranges of values and single values. The more complex the set of values the more attractive the use of condition-names becomes. Another advantage of condition-names is that the definition of the condition can be easily changed by modifying the 88 level in the data division rather than the algorithmic part of the program.

In the example a special value of ACC-NO = 9999 might be added to the set of legal values, in which case the data description becomes:

```
05  ACC-NO          PIC 9999.
    88  CORRECT-ACC-NO  VALUE 1000 THRU 4000, 9999.
```

Later it might be decided to add a further range of values, say 5000 to

6500, and again the description can be modified to:

```
05  ACC-NO       PIC 9999.
    88  CORRECT-ACC-NO  VALUE 1000 THRU 4000, 9999,
                              5000 THRU 6500.
```

In this latter example the equivalent combination of simple conditions is not so easy to write.

The commas between the values, or ranges of values, are not strictly necessary but can be included to improve readability.

As another example of the use of a condition-name, suppose that part of an identifier is a code letter, the legal values of which are A to H, J to N, P, R to T and V to X (all ranges inclusive of end points). Then in the program design it is possible to write a condition of the form:

<u>if</u> valid-code-letter <u>then</u>

The condition 'valid-code-letter' is to be <u>true</u> if code-letter contains one of the values listed above and <u>false</u> otherwise. To implement this the appropriate data description is:

```
05  CODE-LETTER     PIC A.
    88  VALID-CODE-LETTER
        VALUE "A" THRU "H", "J" THRU "N", "P"
               "R" THRU "T", "V" THRU "X".
```

And it will now be possible to write in the procedure division of the program:

```
IF VALID-CODE-LETTER
```

A data-item may have more than one condition-name associated with it. For example:

```
05  C-SURNAME.
    10  C-SURNAME-FIRST      PIC A.
        88  C-SURNAME-GROUP-1        VALUE "A" THRU "K".
        88  C-SURNAME-GROUP-2        VALUE "L" THRU "N".
        88  C-SURNAME-GROUP-3        VALUE "O" THRU "Z".
    10  C-SURNAME-REST       PIC X(29).
```

In this example it is possible to write in the procedure division of the program any of the conditions:

```
C-SURNAME-GROUP-1      NOT SURNAME-GROUP-1
C-SURNAME-GROUP-2      NOT SURNAME-GROUP-2
C-SURNAME-GROUP-3      NOT SURNAME-GROUP-3
```

or to use these conditions as parts of compound conditions, to be discussed in Section 6.5.

Some ANS COBOL compilers may not implement condition-names; alternative translations are discussed in Appendix 5.2.

6.4 <u>Nested IF Statements</u>

An <u>if</u> operation which appears between the <u>if</u> and the <u>endif</u> of another <u>if</u> operation is said to be 'nested' within that <u>if</u> operation. In theory, _if_ operations can be nested to any depth (_if_ within _if_ within _if_ ...) but in practice too many levels of nesting obscure the meaning of a program. It is recommended that no more than three levels of nesting should be used in a program.

The way in which nested IF statements are interpreted in COBOL involves the understanding of a simple rule about the matching of IFs and ELSEs. Once this rule has been established, guidelines for translating _if_ structures from the design level into COBOL can be formulated. Consider the following extract from a COBOL program:

```
EXAMPLE-6-1.
    IF QUANTITY-ORDERED NOT > QUANTITY-LIMIT
        IF ACCOUNT-TYPE = "W"
            PERFORM PREPARE-INVOICE
    ELSE
        PERFORM LARGE-QUANTITY.
```

This piece of COBOL can be interpreted in two ways as shown in Examples 6.1 and 6.2.

```
Example 6.1
if  quantity-ordered not > quantity-limit then
   if account-type = "W" then
      prepare-invoice
   else
      large-quantity
   endif
endif
```

```
Example 6.2
if  quantity-ordered not > quantity-limit then
   if account-type = "W" then
      prepare-invoice
   endif
else
   large-quantity
endif
```

The piece of COBOL, shown in EXAMPLE-6-1, will be interpreted as shown in Example 6.1 because the rule in COBOL is "an ELSE is matched with the immediately preceding unmatched IF". Therefore the ELSE in the example will be made to match IF ACCOUNT-TYPE ... and _not_ IF QUANTITY-ORDERED ... in spite of the indentation. To translate the design fragment shown in Example 6.2 into COBOL would require the use of refinement. The corresponding piece of COBOL should be:

```
EXAMPLE-6-2.
    IF QUANTITY-ORDERED NOT > QUANTITY-LIMIT
        PERFORM CHECK-ACCOUNT-TYPE
    ELSE
        PERFORM LARGE-QUANTITY.
CHECK-ACCOUNT-TYPE.
    IF ACCOUNT-TYPE = "W"
        PERFORM PREPARE-INVOICE.
```

Consider the following piece of design:

```
Example 6.3
if customer-type = "W" then
   if quantity-ordered > 100 then
      bulk-discount
   else
      trade-discount
   endif
else
   non-trade-customer
endif
```

This can be translated directly into COBOL because all ifs have elses and therefore no ambiguities in matching ELSEs with IFs can occur. The translation into COBOL could be:

```
EXAMPLE-6-3.
    IF CUSTOMER-TYPE = "W"
        IF QUANTITY-ORDERED > 100
            PERFORM BULK-DISCOUNT
        ELSE
            PERFORM TRADE-DISCOUNT
    ELSE
        PERFORM RETAIL-CUSTOMER.
```

Some nested if structures which contain ifs without elses can be translated into COBOL directly. For example:

```
Example 6.4
if taxable-pay > higher-threshold then
   higher-tax-deduction
else
   if taxable-pay > 0 then
      normal-tax-deduction
   endif
endif
```

This can be translated into COBOL as:

```
EXAMPLE-6-4.
    IF TAXABLE-PAY > HIGHER-THRESHOLD
        PERFORM HIGHER-TAX-DEDUCTION
    ELSE
        IF TAXABLE-PAY > 0
            PERFORM NORMAL-TAX-DEDUCTION.
```

There is only one ELSE and this clearly matches the only IF which precedes it, therefore the translation is correct and unambiguous.

By studying these examples a set of guidelines can be established for the translation of if structures into COBOL. There are three cases to consider.

(a) All if operations are complete, that is all ifs have corresponding elses: the structure can be translated directly into COBOL.
(b) The only incomplete if operations are at the end of the structure,

in such a way that two or more endifs come together: the structure can be translated directly into COBOL.

(c) There are incomplete if operations in the middle of the structure: each incomplete if operation should be replaced by a reference to a paragraph where that if operation can be developed.

Finally an extra guideline: If in any doubt about nested IF statements use refinement to make things absolutely clear. For example, Example 6.3 could equally well be translated as:

```
EXAMPLE-6-3A.
    IF CUSTOMER-TYPE = "W"
        PERFORM CHECK-QUANTITY
    ELSE
        PERFORM RETAIL-CUSTOMER.
    . . . . .
CHECK-QUANTITY.
    IF QUANTITY-ORDERED > 100
        PERFORM BULK-DISCOUNT
    ELSE
        PERFORM TRADE-DISCOUNT.
```

The nested IF statement is considered a higher level feature of ANS COBOL '74 and therefore may not be implemented in some low-level ANS COBOL compilers. In this case the translation of a nested if in the design language will always require the use of refinement as shown in Example 6.3 and its translation EXAMPLE-6-3A.

A low-level implementation of ANS COBOL which does not include nested IF statements will probably not include compound conditions either (see next section) and this means that the only selection mechanism will be the simple IF statement with refinement.

6.5 Compound Conditions

Initially only simple conditions were introduced into the design language and these are sufficient for many problems. However, many problems have actions which are dependent on a combination of two or more conditions. One way of dealing with combinations of conditions is to use nested IF statements as was discussed in Section 6.4.

An alternative approach is to build compound conditions by combining simple conditions using the logical operators and and or, together with parentheses if necessary. Combinations of conditions can be also be negated using the not operator but this is rarely necessary.

The and operator combines two conditions in such a way that the compound condition is true only if both the connected conditions are true. For example:

```
Example 6.5
if account-type = "C" and account-no < 9000 then
    special-customer-account
endif
```

In this structure the refinement 'special-customer-account' is executed if and only if both the simple conditions are true. The translation to COBOL is quite straightforward:

```
EXAMPLE-6-5.
    IF ACCOUNT-TYPE = "C" AND ACCOUNT-NO < 9000
        PERFORM SPECIAL-CUSTOMER-ACCOUNT.
```

Because the translation is so straightforward further examples will be discussed using only the design language.

The example shown in Example 6.5 is equivalent to the nested _if_ structure shown in Example 6.6.

Example 6.6

```
if account-type = "C" then
   if account-no < 9000 then
      special-customer-account
   endif
endif
```

If an _else_ is added to Example 6.5 then the operations specified in the else part will be carried out for all combinations of conditions which cause the compound condition to be _false_. For example:

Example 6.7

```
if account-type = "C" and account-no < 9000 then
   special-customer-account
else
   all-other-accounts
endif
```

The structure shown in Example 6.7 is equivalent to the nested _if_ structure shown in Example 6.8.

Example 6.8

```
if account-type = "C" then
   if account-number < 9000 then
      special-customer-account
   else
      all-other-accounts
   endif
else
   if account-no < 9000 then
      all-other-accounts
   else
      all-other-accounts
   endif
endif
```

The third _if_ operation is obviously redundant and can be replaced by a straightforward reference to 'all-other-accounts', giving the structure shown in Example 6.9.

Example 6.9

```
if account-type = "C" then
   if account-no < 9000 then
      special-customer-account
   else
      all-other-accounts
   endif
else
   all-other-accounts
endif
```

Looking at examples 6.7, 6.8 and 6.9 gives an indication of why both nested if structures and compound conditions are useful. A slight change to Example 6.9 is shown in Example 6.10 - how can this be reformulated starting with a compound condition?

Example 6.10

```
if account-type = "C" then
   if account-no < 9000 then
      special-customer-account
   else
      special-transfer-account
   endif
else
   all-other-accounts
endif
```

To express the logic of Example 6.10 starting with a compound condition gives rise to the rather clumsy structure shown in Example 6.11.

Example 6.11

```
if account-type = "C" and account-no < 9000 then
   special-account-customer
else
   if account-type = "C" and account-no not < 9000 then
      special-transfer-account
   else
      all-other-accounts
   endif
endif
```

Therefore in this case the nested if structure is more appropriate. This is because the selection is not a choice between alternatives but a choice from three courses of action.

A simple guideline is that if a combination of conditions leads to a choice from only two courses of action (one of which may be do nothing) then a compound condition is appropriate otherwise a nested if structure will be better.

Having dealt with and at some length, similar comments apply to the use of the logical operator or. If two conditions are combined using or then the compound condition is true if either of the connected conditions is true or both of them are true. This is called the 'inclusive or'. Examples 6.12 and 6.13 illustrate the use of or.

Example 6.12

```
if stock-level < reorder-level or stock-status = "X" then
   place-order
endif
```

Example 6.13

```
if month-no < 1 or month-no > 12 then
   error-in-month
else
   check-days
endif
```

Formally and and or can be defined as shown in the 'truth table' of Figure 6.1.

c1	c2	c1 and c2	c1 or c2
true	true	true	true
true	false	false	true
false	true	false	true
false	false	false	false

Figure 6.1

Readers using a low-level ANS COBOL compiler which does not implement compound conditions will need to express all compound conditions using nested IF statements or Boolean data-items (see Appendix 5.4).

Testability of Compound Conditions

A problem arises with compound conditions if two, or more, simple conditions being combined are not independently testable. In evaluating the condition:

c1 and c2

if c1 is evaluated to false then obviously there is no need to evaluate c2 since the result must be false. Similarly, in evaluating:

c1 or c2

if c1 is true then there is no need to evaluate c2. However, some compilers do not take advantage of these optimisations and may still evaluate c2, which can lead to problems.

For example, consider:

```
if sales-price numeric and sales-price < 500 then
```

In the case where sales-price is not numeric, the condition 'sales-price < 500' is still evaluated and this may cause an execution error because this condition is not defined for nonnumeric values of sales-price. Therefore in a compound condition it is advisable to only combine independently testable simple conditions.

The example shown above would be better written as a nested if structure:

```
if sales-price numeric then
```

```
if sales-price < 500 then
```

This ensures that the condition 'sales-price < 500' is only evaluated if sales-price is numeric.

All the examples used have shown the use of compound conditions in if operations but it is also possible to use them with until loops as well. Problems with the testability of conditions can also arise in until loops. A common trap is to write an until loop of the form:

```
until trans-code = 2 or end-of-transactions do
```

where 'trans-code' is part of the input record for the file 'transactions'. The program will fail, at this point, when 'end-of-transactions' is true because the condition 'trans-code = 2' is undefined (there is no input record to test). Even reversing the order of the conditions may not be sufficient to solve the problem because, as already explained, some compilers do not optimise condition evaluation but evaluate all simple conditions in a compound condition. A solution to this type of problem will be discussed in Section 6.6.

Evaluation of Compound Conditions

It is possible to create compound conditions by combining more than two simple conditions using and and or in which case rules for the evaluation of compound conditions have to be formulated. This is a similar problem to defining an order of precedence for arithmetic operators.

Example 6.14

```
if stock-level < reorder-level and reorder-flag = "R"
   or stock-level = 0 then
```

The compound condition shown in Example 6.14 can be interpreted in two ways by either evaluating the and before the or or vice-versa. The rule in COBOL is that ands are evaluated before ors. So the compound condition in Example 6.14 is interpreted by evaluating

```
stock-level < reorder-level and reorder-flag = "R"
```

to true or false and then combining this result with the value of stock-level = 0 using the or operator. To change the order of evaluation of a compound condition parentheses can be used, again paralleling the practice in arithmetic expressions. Therefore

```
if c1 and c2 or c3 then
```

is equivalent to:

```
if (c1 and c2) or c3 then
```

but not equivalent to:

```
if c1 and (c2 or c3) then
```

A simple guideline is that if in doubt use parentheses to make the meaning clear.

As with nested if structures it is possible to build compound conditions of great complexity but in practice highly complex compound conditions tend to obscure the meaning of programs and indicate poor program design.

The use of the logical operator not also often indicates poor program design. This logical operator can be used to negate a simple condition or a compound condition. Here are three bad examples of the use of the not operator:

```
if not (customer = "A") then
if not (stock-level > 0 and stock-status = "X") then
if not (customer-type = "W" or quantity-ordered > 100) then
```

These three examples can be rewritten more clearly as:

```
if customer-type not = "A" then
if stock-level not > 0 or stock-status not = "X" then
if customer-type not = "W" and quantity-ordered not > 100 then
```

The second and third examples illustrate the use of De Morgan's Laws which can be formally stated as:

```
not (c1 and c2)  =  not c1 or  not c2
not (c1 or  c2)  =  not c1 and not c2
```

To summarize this section the following simple guidelines are suggested.

(a) Compound conditions can be used when a two way selection is required, based on a complex condition.
(b) The simple conditions forming a compound condition should all be independently testable.
(c) The use of more than two logical operators in a compound condition obscures the meaning of a program and indicates poor program design.
(d) The use of the logical operator not is usually unnecessary and again makes a program more difficult to understand.

6.6 Boolean Data-items

As algorithms become more complex a point is reached where combinations of conditions and nested if structures are inadequate for expressing the structure of a problem. What often happens is that a number of conditions need to be tested, and consequent actions taken, and then later in the program it is necessary to 'remember' what the values of conditions were.

Many programming languages have a special type called Boolean (or logical) which can be used for this purpose. A data-item of type Boolean is one which can only hold the values true and false and therefore can be set to indicate that 'this happened' or 'this didn't happen'.

In COBOL there is no explicit data type corresponding to Boolean but the basic idea can be simulated using condition-names. In a program design statements of the following form can be written:

```
transfer true to <Boolean-item>
transfer false to <Boolean-item>
if <Boolean-item> then
if not <Boolean-item> then
until <Boolean-item> do
```

The last one of these constructs should look familiar, it strongly resembles:

<u>until</u> end-of-<filename> <u>do</u>

The condition end-of-<filename> is an example of a pseudo Boolean data-item. Looking at the standard program skeleton gives an example of how to implement the type Boolean in COBOL.

In general to implement a Boolean data-item in COBOL:

(a) choose a name for a data-item, different from the name of the Boolean data-item but preferably related to it.
(b) choose a value for <u>true</u> and, using the name of the Boolean data-item as a condition-name, append this to the data-item chosen in (a).
(c) Add this structure to STATE-VECTOR.

For example, suppose that a Boolean data-item called VALID-RECORD is to be implemented then the following structure would be appropriate:

```
05  RECORD-VALIDITY      PIC X.
    88  VALID-RECORD     VALUE "T".
```

To set or reset the Boolean data-item a value must be moved to the data-item with which the Boolean data-item is associated. Therefore:

transfer <u>true</u> to valid-record

becomes:

```
MOVE "T" TO RECORD-VALIDITY
```

because the value "T" has been chosen to represent <u>true</u>. To reset the value of valid-record:

transfer <u>false</u> to valid-record

becomes:

```
MOVE "F" TO RECORD-VALIDITY
```

Note that, in this implementation, any legal value other than "T" can be used to reset VALID-RECORD to false.

To test the value of a Boolean data-item all that is necessary is to use its name, as this is a condition-name. Therefore, in the example used above, it is possible to write:

```
IF VALID-RECORD
IF NOT VALID-RECORD
```

in the PROCEDURE DIVISION of the program. An example of the use of a Boolean data-item is given in the next section.

A Boolean data-item can be used to solve the problem of related conditions in an <u>until</u> loop discussed in the previous section under "Testability of Compound Conditions". The structure:

```
until trans-code = 2 or end-of-transactions do
   process-transaction
   get-next-transactions
enduntil
```

is unsafe because the condition 'trans-code = 2' is not testable when 'end-of-transactions' is true. A safe testing sequence can be ensured by introducing a Boolean data-item, say 'group-complete', as follows:

```
set-group-complete
until group-complete do
   process-transaction
   get-next-transactions
   set-group-complete
enduntil
 . . . . .
set-group-complete
   if end-of-transactions then
      transfer true to group-complete
   else
      if trans-code = 2 then
         transfer true to group-complete
      else
         transfer false to group-complete
      endif
   endif
```

An example of the use of the above method is given in the case study of Section 8.7. This technique can also be used, as an alternative to compound conditions, to implement any loop where termination depends on two or more conditions.

Boolean data-items are very useful but are only one restricted type of a more general class of <u>state variables</u>. Since a number of condition names can be associated with a single data-item in COBOL it is possible to define a state-variable with three or more identifiable states. An example of the use of more general state-variables is given in Exercises 8.2.

6.7 Case Study

This case study is intended to draw together some of the ideas discussed in this chapter. Here is a problem concerned with data validation and some simple processing.

> The telephone billing system of the Rockall Telecom Corporation receives input records in the following format:
>
> | | |
> |---|---|
> | Area code | 3 characters (see below) |
> | Telephone number | 6 digits |
> | Customer name and address | 40 characters |
> | Rental charge | 4 digits (pence) |
> | Dialled units | 4 digits |
> | Operator-connected units | 3 digits |
>
> The area code consists of <u>either</u> two letters followed by a digit <u>or</u> a single letter followed by two digits.

A program is required to check the validity of this data and to process the valid records, calculating the amount to be charged for each customer. The following validity checks should be carried out on the records:

(a) the area code is in the correct format,
(b) the rental charge, dialled units and operator-connected units are all valid numbers,
(c) the rental charge is not less than the minimum of £8.50.

If any of these checks fails the details of the record should be printed together with a suitable error message or messages.

For each valid record calculate the amount to be charged by adding the following elements:

(a) the rental charge,
(b) charge for units used; dialled units at 2p each and operator-connected at 3p each,
(c) VAT at 12.5%.

The output from the program should consist of a tabular summary of the details of each record together with either the amount to be charged or any relevant error messages.

The general structure of the solution might be:

```
validate and bill
   print-headings
   get-next-phone-file
   until end-of-phone-file do
      transfer false to errors-present
      check-record
      if not errors-present then
         calculate-charge
      endif
      print-billing-line
      get-next-phone-file
   enduntil
```

The general strategy in this solution is to:
- assume that there are no errors in the current record by setting the Boolean data-item 'errors-present' to <u>false</u>;
- check the validity of the record setting the Boolean data-item 'errors-present' to <u>true</u> if one or more errors are detected;
- test the value of the 'errors-present' and if no errors have been detected calculate the charge;
- print the details of the current record and move on to the next record.

There are then four refinements to consider: print-headings, check-record, calculate-charge and print-billing-line. The refinement of 'print-headings' will be a straightforward procedure similar to that for the previous case study (Section 5.6). For example:

```
print-headings
    put-page-heading
    put-blank-line
    put-col-headings
    put-blank-line
```

The most complex of the refinements is 'check-record' and it can be broken down into four smaller tasks:

```
check-record
    check-area-code
    check-rental
    check-dialled-units
    check-op-units
```

Before proceeding to refine 'calculate-charge' it is necessary to decide on names for the data-items in the input record. The following structure will be used in this solution:

```
phone-record
    phone-area              area code
    phone-number            telephone number
    phone-customer          customer name and address
    phone-rental            rental charge (pence)
    phone-dialled           dialled units
    phone-op-units          operator-connected units
```

The processing of the valid records in calculate-charge is quite straightforward:

```
calculate-charge
    calculate basic-charge =
       phone-rental + 0.02 * phone-dialled + 0.03 * phone-op-units
    calculate billing-charge = 1.125 * basic-charge
```

Where basic-charge is assumed to be a temporary data-item and billing-charge is part of the output record. At this point it is necessary to start building up the list of temporary data-items:

```
temporary-items
    basic-charge            customer charge before VAT added
```

To refine 'print-billing-line' it will be necessary to make a first attempt at defining the structure of the output record - this will need to be extended as error messages will need to added in the checking process. Assuming that all input data is to be printed, for checking, the basic structure of the output record could be:

```
billing-line
    billing-area            area code
    billing-number          telephone number
    billing-customer        customer name and address
    billing-rental          rental charge (edited, pounds.pence)
    billing-dialled         dialled units (edited)
    billing-op-units        operator-connected units (edited)
    billing-charge          total charge with VAT added
```

The refinement of print-billing-line then appears to be quite obvious:

```
print-billing-line
   transfer phone-area to billing-area
   transfer phone-number to billing-number
   transfer phone-customer to billing-customer
   transfer phone-rental to billing-rental
   transfer phone-dialled to billing-dialled
   transfer phone-op-units to billing-op-units
   put-billing-line
```

It is now necessary to return to the checking procedure and refine the four procedures: check-area-code, check-rental, check-dialled-units and check-op-units.

Looking first at 'check-area-code', this will be required to check the individual characters of the area code and so the input record description will need to be expanded to allow for this. The data-item 'phone-area' will have to be a group-item consisting of three elementary items, say: phone-area-1, phone-area-2 and phone-area-3. Therefore the input record 'phone-record' will become:

```
phone-record
   phone-area
      phone-area-1
      phone-area-2
      phone-area-3
   phone-number
    . . .
```

Informally, the refinement of 'check-area-code' should be of the form:

```
check-area-code
   if phone-area-1 invalid then
      area-error
   else
      if phone-area-2 invalid then
         area-error
      else
         if phone-area-3 invalid then
            area-error
         endif
      endif
   endif
```

Where 'area-error' is a refinement which will define the appropriate action for an invalid value of area-code.

The tests are linked together into a single structure since once one part of the area code is found to be invalid there seems to be little point in testing the rest of the code.

From the description of area code it can be deduced that phone-area-1 must be alphabetic, phone-area-2 can be either alphabetic or numeric and phone-area-3 must be numeric. Therefore the informal condition 'phone-area-1 invalid' can be written as 'phone-area-1 <u>not alphabetic</u>' and the informal condition 'phone-area-3 invalid' can be written as 'phone-area-3 <u>not</u> <u>numeric</u>'.

However, the informal construction:

```
if phone-area-2 invalid then
   area-error
```

represents a compound condition and can be written in several equivalent ways, for example:

```
(a)  if phone-area-2 not alphabetic
           and phone-area-2 not numeric then
        area-error

(b)  if not (phone-area-2 alphabetic or phone-area-2 numeric) then
        area-error

(c)  if phone-area-2 not alphabetic then
        if phone-area-2 not numeric then
           area-error
        endif
```

Based on the guidelines given at the end of Section 6.5, the first of these possibilities would be chosen. Therefore, a possible refinement of check-area-code is:

```
check-area-code
   if phone-area-1 not alphabetic then
      area-error
   else
      if phone-area-2 not alphabetic
            and phone-area-2 not numeric then
         area-error
      else
         if phone-area-3 not numeric then
            area-error
         endif
      endif
   endif
```

The first approximation to the refinement of 'area-error' is:

```
area-error
   transfer true to errors-present
```

Setting 'errors-present' to true will ensure that after all the checks have been completed no attempt will be made to calculate a charge for this erroneous record. If a record contains several errors then 'errors-present' may be set to true in more than one refinement. This does not matter as it is only necessary to distinguish between no errors and any errors - the actual number of errors is irrelevant.

The refinement of 'check-rental' illustrates the point about related conditions (see 6.5). The data-item 'phone-rental' needs to be checked to see whether its contents are numeric and also to check that it exceeds the minimum permitted value of £8.50. The second condition is only testable if the first is true. Therefore the basic form of the refinement should be:

```
check-rental
   if phone-rental not numeric then
      transfer true to errors-present
   else
      if phone-rental < 8.5 then
         transfer true to errors-present
      endif
   endif
```

A first approximation to the refinements of 'check-dialled-units' and 'check-op-units' is quite straightforward:

```
check-dialled-units
   if phone-dialled not numeric then
      transfer true to errors-present
   endif

check-op-units
   if phone-op-units not numeric then
      transfer true to errors-present
   endif
```

Having decided on the basic structure of the program design there are two further points to be considered: the construction of error messages and the printing of nonnumeric data occurring in supposedly numeric data-items.

The simplest way to deal with the error messages is to add four separate data-items to 'billing-line' to hold error messages relating to each of the four data-items being checked: phone-area, phone-rental, phone-dialled and phone-op-units. These might be called: billing-area-message, billing-rental-message, billing-dialled-message and billing-op-units-message respectively. Now the relevant refinements need to be modified to fill these data-items when necessary.

The first refinement which needs to be modified is 'check-rental' where two error messages can be added:

```
check-rental
   if phone-rental not numeric then
      transfer true to errors-present
      transfer "rental invalid" to billing-rental-message
   else
      if phone-rental < 8.5 then
         transfer true to errors-present
         transfer "rental too low" to billing-rental-message
      endif
   endif
```

The modifications to the other refinements affected are quite straightforward:

```
check-dialled-units
   if phone-dialled not numeric then
      transfer true to errors-present
      transfer "dialled invalid" to billing-dialled-message
   endif
```

```
check-op-units
   if phone-op-units not numeric then
      transfer true to errors-present
      transfer "op. units invalid" to billing-op-units-message
   endif

area-error
   transfer true to errors-present
   transfer "area invalid" to billing-area-message
```

Finally to complete the program design it is necessary to decide which supposedly numeric data-items, whose output would normally be edited, need to have alternative output data-items.

In this example there are three such data-items: phone-rental, phone-dialled and phone-op-units. Three alternative input data-items can be defined: phone-rental-error, phone-dialled-error and phone-op-units-error; together with three corresponding alternative output data-items: billing-rental-error, billing-dialled-error and billing-op-units-error. The program design will then need to be modified so that these alternative data-items are correctly referenced.

```
check-rental
   if phone-rental not numeric then
      transfer true to errors-present
      transfer "rental invalid" to billing-rental-message
      transfer phone-rental-error to billing-rental-error
   else
      transfer phone-rental to billing-rental
      if phone-rental < 8.5 then
         transfer true to errors-present
         transfer "rental too low" to billing-rental-message
      endif
   endif

check-dialled-units
   if phone-dialled not numeric then
      transfer true to errors-present
      transfer "dialled invalid" to billing-dialled-message
      transfer phone-dialled-error to billing-dialled-error
   else
      transfer phone-dialled to billing-dialled
   endif

check-op-units
   if phone-op-units not numeric then
      transfer true to errors-present
      transfer "op. units invalid" to billing-op-units-message
      transfer phone-op-units-error to billing-op-units-error
   else
      transfer phone-op-units to billing-op-units
   endif
```

Having made these modifications the refinement 'print-billing-line' can be reduced to:

```
print-billing-line
   transfer phone-area to billing-area
   transfer phone-number to billing-number
   transfer phone-customer to billing-customer
   put-billing-line
```

The process of developing the program design has been shown in a number of stages to emphasize and discuss certain points. In practice, the complete program design can be built up without the need to work through all these intermediate steps explicitly.

Before showing the COBOL program for this problem, it will probably be helpful to draw together all the final versions of the refinements into a single program design, which can then be studied and checked as an entity.

The final version of the input record is:

```
phone-record
   phone-area
      phone-area-1
      phone-area-2
      phone-area-3
   phone-number
   phone-customer
   phone-rental == phone-rental-error
   phone-dialled == phone-dialled-error
   phone-op-units == phone-op-units-error
```

The complete description of the output record is:

```
billing-line
   billing-area
   billing-number
   billing-customer
   billing-rental == billing-rental-error
   billing-dialled == billing-dialled-error
   billing-op-units == billing-op-units-error
   billing-charge
   billing-area-message
   billing-rental-message
   billing-dialled-message
   billing-op-units-message
```

Only one temporary data-item was noted during the program design:

```
temporary-items
   basic-charge
```

The final version of the complete program design is given below.

```
validate-and-bill
   print-headings
   get-next-phone-file
   until end-of-phone-file do
      transfer false to errors-present
      check-record
      if not errors-present then
         calculate-charge
      endif
      print-billing-line
      get-next-phone-file
   enduntil

print-headings
   put-page-heading
   put-blank-line
   put-col-headings
   put-blank-line

check-record
   check-area-code
   check-rental
   check-dialled-units
   check-op-units

calculate-charge
   calculate basic-charge =
      phone-rental + 0.02 * phone-dialled + 0.03 * phone-op-units
   calculate billing-charge = 1.125 * basic-charge

print-billing-line
   transfer phone-area to billing-area
   transfer phone-number to billing-number
   transfer phone-customer to billing-customer
   put-billing-line

check-area-code
   if phone-area-1 not alphabetic then
      area-error
   else
      if phone-area-2 not alphabetic
            and phone-area-2 not numeric then
         area-error
      else
         if phone-area-3 not numeric then
            area-error
         endif
      endif
   endif

area-error
   transfer true to errors-present
   transfer "area invalid" to billing-area-message
```

```
check-rental
   if phone-rental not numeric then
      transfer true to errors-present
      transfer "rental invalid" to billing-rental-message
      transfer phone-rental-error to billing-rental-error
   else
      transfer phone-rental to billing-rental
      if phone-rental < 8.5 then
         transfer true to errors-present
         transfer "rental too low" to billing-rental-message
      endif
   endif

check-dialled-units
   if phone-dialled not numeric then
      transfer true to errors-present
      transfer "dialled invalid" to billing-dialled-message
      transfer phone-dialled-error to billing-dialled-error
   else
      transfer phone-dialled to billing-dialled
   endif

check-op-units
   if phone-op-units not numeric then
      transfer true to errors-present
      transfer "op. units invalid" to billing-op-units-message
      transfer phone-op-units-error to billing-op-units-error
   else
      transfer phone-op-units to billing-op-units
   endif
```

The next stage in the process of program development is to describe the input and output records. In the course of describing the output record and headings for this example, it rapidly becomes obvious that, as specified, there is too much information to fit into one lineprinter line of 120 characters. The solution suggested is to shorten the messages and use a double line of column headings to squeeze more information into the page. Any solution which requires the actual data lines to be split over two output lines leads to unreadable output.

The messages are shortened by replacing "xxxxxx invalid" by "invalid" and "rental too low" by "too low". The type of error is then included in the headings for the message data-items. The 'put-col-headings' in the design has to be further refined to:

```
put-col-headings
   put-col-headings-1
   put-col-headings-2
```

to output the two column heading lines.

The final version of the program is given below and sample output is shown in Figure 6.2, following the program.

```
       IDENTIFICATION DIVISION.
       PROGRAM-ID. TELEBILL.
```

```
 ENVIRONMENT DIVISION.
 CONFIGURATION SECTION.
 SOURCE-COMPUTER. <computer-name>.
 OBJECT-COMPUTER. <computer-name>.
*    <computer-name> should be replaced by the name
*    of the computer being used to run programs.

 INPUT-OUTPUT SECTION.
 FILE-CONTROL.
     SELECT PHONE-FILE ASSIGN TO <system-input>.
     SELECT OUTFILE ASSIGN TO <system-output>.
*        <system-input> and <system-output> must conform
*        to the rules for the system being used.

 DATA DIVISION.
 FILE SECTION.
 FD  PHONE-FILE
     LABEL RECORDS OMITTED.
 01  PHONE-RECORD.
     05  PHONE-AREA.
         10  PHONE-AREA-1        PIC X.
         10  PHONE-AREA-2        PIC X.
         10  PHONE-AREA-3        PIC X.
     05  PHONE-NUMBER            PIC 9(6).
     05  PHONE-CUSTOMER          PIC X(40).
     05  PHONE-RENTAL            PIC 99V99.
     05  PHONE-RENTAL-ERROR REDEFINES PHONE-RENTAL
                                 PIC XXXX.
     05  PHONE-DIALLED           PIC 9999.
     05  PHONE-DIALLED-ERROR REDEFINES PHONE-DIALLED
                                 PIC XXXX.
     05  PHONE-OP-UNITS          PIC 999.
     05  PHONE-OP-UNITS-ERROR REDEFINES PHONE-OP-UNITS
                                 PIC XXX.
 FD  OUTFILE
     LABEL RECORDS OMITTED.
 01  OUT-LINE           PIC X(120).

 WORKING-STORAGE SECTION.
 01  STATE-VECTOR.
     05  END-PHONE-FILE       PIC X.
         88  END-OF-PHONE-FILE   VALUE "E".
     05  ERROR-FLAG       PIC X.
         88  ERRORS-PRESENT      VALUE "T".

 01  TEMPORARY-ITEMS.
     05  BASIC-CHARGE         PIC 999V99.

 01  PAGE-HEADING.
     05  FILLER        PIC X(46)   VALUE SPACES.
     05  FILLER        PIC X(28)   VALUE
         "ROCKALL TELECOM. CORPORATION".

 01  BLANK-LINE        PIC X       VALUE SPACES.
```

```
01   COL-HEADINGS-1.
     05   FILLER   PIC X(63)    VALUE SPACES.
     05   FILLER   PIC X(5)     VALUE "UNITS".
     05   FILLER   PIC X        VALUE SPACE.
     05   FILLER   PIC X(5)     VALUE "UNITS".
     05   FILLER   PIC X(11)    VALUE SPACES.
     05   FILLER   PIC X(35)    VALUE
          "<———— ERRORS DETECTED ————>".

01   COL-HEADINGS-2.
     05   FILLER   PIC XXXX     VALUE "AREA".
     05   FILLER   PIC XX       VALUE SPACES.
     05   FILLER   PIC X(6)     VALUE "NUMBER".
     05   FILLER   PIC X(9)     VALUE SPACES.
     05   FILLER   PIC X(25)    VALUE
          "CUSTOMER NAME AND ADDRESS".
     05   FILLER   PIC X(10)    VALUE SPACES.
     05   FILLER   PIC X(6)     VALUE "RENTAL".
     05   FILLER   PIC XX       VALUE SPACES.
     05   FILLER   PIC XXXX     VALUE "DIAL".
     05   FILLER   PIC XX       VALUE SPACES.
     05   FILLER   PIC XXX      VALUE "OP.".
     05   FILLER   PIC XXX      VALUE SPACES.
     05   FILLER   PIC X(6)     VALUE "CHARGE".
     05   FILLER   PIC XXXX     VALUE SPACES.
     05   FILLER   PIC XXXX     VALUE "AREA".
     05   FILLER   PIC X(5)     VALUE SPACES.
     05   FILLER   PIC X(6)     VALUE "RENTAL".
     05   FILLER   PIC XX       VALUE SPACES.
     05   FILLER   PIC X(7)     VALUE "DIALLED".
     05   FILLER   PIC XX       VALUE SPACES.
     05   FILLER   PIC X(8)     VALUE "OPERATOR".

01   BILLING-LINE.
     05   FILLER                          PIC X.
     05   BILLING-AREA                    PIC XXX.
     05   FILLER                          PIC XX.
     05   BILLING-NUMBER                  PIC 9(6).
     05   FILLER                          PIC XX.
     05   BILLING-CUSTOMER                PIC X(40).
     05   FILLER                          PIC XX.
     05   BILLING-RENTAL                  PIC ££9.99.
     05   BILLING-RENTAL-WRONG REDEFINES BILLING-RENTAL.
          10   FILLER                     PIC XX.
          10   BILLING-RENTAL-ERROR       PIC XXXX.
     05   FILLER                          PIC XX.
     05   BILLING-DIALLED                 PIC ZZZ9.
     05   BILLING-DIALLED-ERROR REDEFINES BILLING-DIALLED
                                          PIC XXXX.
     05   FILLER                          PIC XX.
     05   BILLING-OP-UNITS                PIC ZZ9.
     05   BILLING-OP-UNITS-ERROR REDEFINES BILLING-OP-UNITS
                                          PIC XXX.
     05   FILLER                          PIC XX.
     05   BILLING-CHARGE                  PIC £££9.99.
     05   FILLER                          PIC XXX.
```

```
    05  BILLING-AREA-MESSAGE        PIC X(7).
    05  FILLER                      PIC XX.
    05  BILLING-RENTAL-MESSAGE      PIC X(7).
    05  FILLER                      PIC XX.
    05  BILLING-DIALLED-MESSAGE     PIC X(7).
    05  FILLER                      PIC XX.
    05  BILLING-OP-UNITS-MESSAGE    PIC X(7).

PROCEDURE DIVISION.
MAIN-PROGRAM.
    PERFORM INIT-STATE
    PERFORM VALIDATE-AND-BILL
    PERFORM CLOSE-DOWN.
INIT-STATE.
    MOVE SPACE TO END-PHONE-FILE
    OPEN INPUT PHONE-FILE OUTPUT OUTFILE
    MOVE SPACES TO BILLING-LINE.
CLOSE-DOWN.
    CLOSE PHONE-FILE OUTFILE
    STOP RUN.
GET-NEXT-PHONE-FILE.
    READ PHONE-FILE
        AT END MOVE "E" TO END-PHONE-FILE.
PUT-BILLING-LINE.
    WRITE OUT-LINE FROM BILLING-LINE
    MOVE SPACES TO BILLING-LINE.
PUT-PAGE-HEADING.
    WRITE OUT-LINE FROM PAGE-HEADING.
PUT-BLANK-LINE.
    WRITE OUT-LINE FROM BLANK-LINE.
PUT-COL-HEADINGS-1.
    WRITE OUT-LINE FROM COL-HEADINGS-1.
PUT-COL-HEADINGS-2.
    WRITE OUT-LINE FROM COL-HEADINGS-2.
VALIDATE-AND-BILL.
    PERFORM PRINT-HEADINGS
    PERFORM GET-NEXT-PHONE-FILE
    PERFORM CHECK-AND-PRINT UNTIL END-OF-PHONE-FILE.
PRINT-HEADINGS.
    PERFORM PUT-PAGE-HEADING
    PERFORM PUT-BLANK-LINE
    PERFORM PUT-COL-HEADINGS
    PERFORM PUT-BLANK-LINE.
PUT-COL-HEADINGS.
    PERFORM PUT-COL-HEADINGS-1
    PERFORM PUT-COL-HEADINGS-2.
CHECK-AND-PRINT.
    MOVE "F" TO ERROR-FLAG
    PERFORM CHECK-RECORD
    IF NOT ERRORS-PRESENT
        PERFORM CALCULATE-CHARGE.
    PERFORM PRINT-BILLING-LINE
    PERFORM GET-NEXT-PHONE-FILE.
```

```
CHECK-RECORD.
    PERFORM CHECK-AREA-CODE
    PERFORM CHECK-RENTAL
    PERFORM CHECK-DIALLED-UNITS
    PERFORM CHECK-OP-UNITS.
CALCULATE-CHARGE.
    COMPUTE BASIC-CHARGE = PHONE-RENTAL
        + 0.02 * PHONE-DIALLED + 0.03 * PHONE-OP-UNITS
    COMPUTE BILLING-CHARGE = 1.125 * BASIC-CHARGE.
PRINT-BILLING-LINE.
    MOVE PHONE-AREA TO BILLING-AREA
    MOVE PHONE-NUMBER TO BILLING-NUMBER
    MOVE PHONE-CUSTOMER TO BILLING-CUSTOMER
    PERFORM PUT-BILLING-LINE.
CHECK-AREA-CODE.
    IF PHONE-AREA-1 NOT ALPHABETIC
        PERFORM AREA-ERROR
    ELSE
        IF PHONE-AREA-2 NOT ALPHABETIC
                AND PHONE-AREA-2 NOT NUMERIC
            PERFORM AREA-ERROR
        ELSE
            IF PHONE-AREA-3 NOT NUMERIC
                PERFORM AREA-ERROR.
AREA-ERROR.
    MOVE "T" TO ERROR-FLAG
    MOVE "INVALID" TO BILLING-AREA-MESSAGE.
CHECK-RENTAL.
    IF PHONE-RENTAL NOT NUMERIC
        MOVE "T" TO ERROR-FLAG
        MOVE "INVALID" TO BILLING-RENTAL-MESSAGE
        MOVE PHONE-RENTAL-ERROR TO BILLING-RENTAL-ERROR
    ELSE
        MOVE PHONE-RENTAL TO BILLING-RENTAL
        IF PHONE-RENTAL < 8.5
            MOVE "T" TO ERROR-FLAG
            MOVE "TOO LOW" TO BILLING-RENTAL-MESSAGE.
CHECK-DIALLED-UNITS.
    IF PHONE-DIALLED NOT NUMERIC
        MOVE "T" TO ERROR-FLAG
        MOVE "INVALID" TO BILLING-DIALLED-MESSAGE
        MOVE PHONE-DIALLED-ERROR TO BILLING-DIALLED-ERROR
    ELSE
        MOVE PHONE-DIALLED TO BILLING-DIALLED.
CHECK-OP-UNITS.
    IF PHONE-OP-UNITS NOT NUMERIC
        MOVE "T" TO ERROR-FLAG
        MOVE "INVALID" TO BILLING-OP-UNITS-MESSAGE
        MOVE PHONE-OP-UNITS-ERROR TO BILLING-OP-UNITS-ERROR
    ELSE
        MOVE PHONE-OP-UNITS TO BILLING-OP-UNITS.
```

An example of the output from this program is shown in Figure 6.2.

ROCKALL TELECOM. CORPORATION

				UNITS	UNITS		<--------	ERRORS	DETECTED	-------->
AREA	NUMBER	CUSTOMER NAME AND ADDRESS	RENTAL	DIAL	OP.	CHARGE	AREA	RENTAL	DIALLED	OPERATOR
9BC	123458	FIRST AREA CODE INVALID	£12.50	75	50		INVALID			
A*3	123457	SECOND AREA CODE INVALID	£12.50	50	5		INVALID			
ABC	123456	THIRD AREA CODE INVALID	£12.50	25	0		INVALID			
AR1	234567	RENTAL NOT NUMERIC	))!)	100	75			INVALID		
AR2	234568	RENTAL TOO LOW	£8.49	125	100			TOO LOW		
AD1	345678	DIALLED NOT NUMERIC	£9.50	ABCD	150				INVALID	
A01	345679	OPERATOR UNITS NOT NUMERIC	£15.65	1000	)*)					INVALID
ZZ9	999999	MAXIMUM VALUES IN ALL DATA-ITEMS--------	£99.99	9999	999	£371.18				
VA1	567893	MINIMUM RENTAL	£8.50	1	1	£9.61				
VA2	567890	NO DIALLED OR OPERATOR UNITS	£9.50	0	0	£10.68				
VA3	567891	NO OPERATOR UNITS	£18.15	150	0	£23.79				
VA4	567892	ALL DATA-ITEMS USED IN CALCULATION	£19.14	1212	115	£52.68				
3*A	456789	ALL DATA-ITEMS INVALID	ABCD	EFGH	IJK		INVALID	INVALID	INVALID	INVALID

Figure 6.2

Exercises 6

6.1. The following construct appears in a program design:

```
if model-stocked then
   check-part-available
endif
```

The value of the condition-name 'model-stocked' should be true for the following values of its associated data-item 'part-model-id':

4 to 9 (inclusive), 12 to 16 (inclusive), 20 and 24

(a) Write data descriptions for 'part-model-id' and 'model-stocked', and the translation of the above design fragment into COBOL.
(b) Show how the above design fragment could be expressed using nested ifs, compound ifs and refinement if condition-names were not available. Translate this new design fragment into COBOL.

6.2. An input record, for a COBOL program, contains a single character item called ACCOUNT-TYPE which should contain either 'W' (wholesale) or 'R' (retail). At some point in processing a record, different routines are required to deal with records relating to wholesale, retail and erroneous account types. The following paragraph, extracted from a COBOL program, is supposed to perform the routine appropriate to the value of ACCOUNT-TYPE.

```
PROCESS-AC-TYPE.
    IF ACCOUNT-TYPE = "W"
        PERFORM WHOLESALE-ROUTINE
    IF ACCOUNT-TYPE = "R"
        PERFORM RETAIL-ROUTINE
    IF (ACCOUNT-TYPE NOT = "W")
            OR (ACCOUNT-TYPE NOT = "R")
        PERFORM AC-TYPE-ERROR.
```

Explain what this piece of COBOL coding actually does when executed for various values of ACCOUNT-TYPE. Give an equivalent program design fragment for the above piece of COBOL. Construct a correct form of the program design and code this in COBOL, using nested IF statements.

Programming Exercises 6

6.3. The Picardy Rose Company despatches bushes to customers throughout the British Isles and needs a simple computerised system for invoicing. The input to the invoicing program will consist of records in the following format:

customer number	6 digits
customer designation	1 letter (see below)
distance code	1 letter
quantity ordered	5 digits
price per bush	4 digits (pence)

The program is required to validate the records by applying the following checks:

(a) the customer designation is either 'W' (wholesale) or 'R' (retail),
(b) the distance code is either 'A', 'B' or 'C',
(c) the quantity ordered is a valid number and is not less than the minimum permitted order of 5 bushes,
(d) the price is a valid number.

If any of these checks fails then the details of the record should be printed together with a suitable error message or messages, if more than one error is detected.

For each valid record, calculate the amount to be charged to the customer's account by applying the following rules:

(a) a discount of 7% of the purchase price is given for a delivery distance code 'A' and 3.5% for delivery code 'B',
(b) an additional discount of 4% of the purchase price is given for any quantity ordered which exceeds 100, regardless of distance,
(c) a retail customer has to have VAT at 15% added to the amount charged.

The output from the program should consist of a listing of the details of each record together with either any appropriate error messages or the amount charged. All output fields should be edited and the report should include a company heading and suitable headings for the columns of output.

6.4. The Instant Death (Agriculture) Company hires out crop-spraying equipment to farmers on a daily basis and also sells the necessary chemicals for spraying.

Input to the company's customer account program consists of records in the following format:

equipment code	1 letter and 3 digits
hire charge per day	6 digits (pence)
spray price per litre	4 digits (pence)
customer number	2 letters and 3 digits
number of days hired	3 digits
litres of spray used	5 digits

The equipment code consists of two parts: a code letter indicating the type of equipment, and a serial number of three digits. Equipment is grouped into three categories, according to code letter,

category one: 'A', 'B' and 'C';
category two: 'F' and 'G';
category three 'W', 'X', 'Y' and 'Z'.

These nine code letters are the only code letters allowed.

The following validity checks should be carried out on the records:

(a) the customer number is valid,
(b) the equipment code letter is one of the nine allowed,
(c) the number of days hired and litres of spray used are valid numbers.

If any of these checks fails the details of the record should be printed together with relevant error messages.

For each valid record, calculate the amount to be paid by the customer by adding the following elements:

(a) the basic hire charge, less a discount of 5% if the hire was for more than ten days,
(b) an insurance charge dependent on the type of equipment: category one at £5 per day, category two at £7 per day and category three at £11 per day,
(c) a charge for the amount of spray used.

The output from the program should consist of a listing of the details of each order together with the amount to be charged or relevant error messages. The report should include suitable headings and editing of data-items.

7 Errors and Testing

The student working steadily through this book will have had quite a lot of ideas on programming and the COBOL language 'thrown at him' by the time he reaches this chapter. It is hoped that he will also have attempted to design, code and run some COBOL programs, or be in the process of developing one or more programs.

The objective of this chapter is to provide a 'breathing space' for him to consolidate his programming experience. Some ideas on how to develop programs are introduced here but not much additional material on COBOL is included. However, this does not mean that this chapter is an optional extra!

Having designed a program, checked the design and translated it into COBOL, the next stage in the development process is to try to compile the program (see Section 1.3). For the beginning programmer the first compilation usually produces a multitude of syntax errors. These have to be sorted out, corrections made and the program resubmitted for compilation. Gradually the number of syntax errors is reduced until a 'clean' compilation is achieved. It is very difficult to formulate rules for dealing with syntax errors - experience is the best teacher. However, some general guidelines on finding syntax errors are given in the first section of this chapter.

When a program has been successfully compiled it needs to be debugged. A bug in a program is an error which causes the program to fail or produce the wrong results. Debugging is the process of locating bugs in a program, attempting to correct them and testing to see if they have been corrected. This process may go through many cycles. Therefore some hints on how to debug programs are given in the next section.

In association with debugging there is the problem of testing. The execution of a program needs to be tested by using a variety of sets of test data and the results produced by the program compared with those expected. The third section of this chapter discusses how to design test data so as to increase the likelihood of showing up bugs in the program.

7.1 Syntax Errors

The object of compilation is to translate a program from COBOL, a high-level language, into a lower level language which can be executed by the computer. This translation process is mechanical and depends on the COBOL program being syntactically correct, that is written according to the syntax rules for COBOL summarized in Appendix 4. If the programmer fails to obey these syntax rules then the compiler will produce an error message or messages attempting to identify the error. The compiler will then try to 'recover' from the error and continue with the compilation of the program.

It is impossible to produce a set of rules for identifying and correcting syntax errors but some general guidelines can be given to assist the novice. The biggest problem which often faces the programmer is that a multitude of error messages may result from a single error in the program. For example, here is an extract from a COBOL program listing:

```
154        PERFORM CHECK-AREA-RECORD
      . . .
167     CHECK AREA RECORD.
```

The numbers on the left are line numbers added to the compilation listing by the compiler, in order to reference the lines of the program. In this particular case, line 167 will probably produce a number of error messages of the form:

(a) CHECK should be followed by a full stop,
(b) AREA is a reserved word used illegally,
(c) RECORD is also a reserved word used illegally.

Additionally there may be other error messages depending on how confused the compiler is by the time it gets to the end of this line.

At the end of the program there will be another error message indicating that the paragraph-name CHECK-AREA-RECORD referenced in line 154 has not been defined. All of these messages have come from the one error - lack of hyphenation.

It is quite easy to get a lot of error messages for a single error in COBOL and experience will help in sorting out which ones are significant. Another common problem which causes a cascade of errors is a missing or defective division header. For example, failure to put a full stop after the last entry in the ENVIRONMENT DIVISION may cause the DATA DIVISION header to 'disappear' with chaotic results, as every DATA DIVISION entry will be treated as if belonging to the ENVIRONMENT DIVISION. Similar disasters can be caused by failure to spell environment or procedure correctly.

Other points which, in the author's experience, have quite often caused problems are concerned with right-hand margins and the line number associated with an error message. Many COBOL compilers were written for punched-card systems and therefore the right-hand margin is set on the assumption that the program is in 'card-image' format. This means that the length of a line is restricted to a maximum of eighty characters. When typing a program at an on-line terminal the same physical limitations do not apply and longer lines may be typed. Unfortunately, if the compiler assumes that there is a right-hand margin, this may result in the ends of lines being lost. In the worst compilers the full line may be listed but only part of it analyzed by the compiler.

Another common problem is that students often appear with an error message associated with a particular line in their program and say "but there's nothing wrong with that line". The error usually turns out to be caused by an error in the preceding line or lines which has caused the line flagged to be wrongly interpreted. For example:

```
201        COMPUTE DISCOUNT-DUE
202            = 0.05 * (SALE-PRICE * (SALE-QUANTITY - 10)
203        PERFORM PRINT-DETAILS
```

The compiler will probably flag line 203 as an error, perhaps with a message about a missing arithmetic operator or, less helpfully, that PERFORM has been used illegally. The fault lies in the preceding line, 202, where the omission of the closing parenthesis has caused the compiler to continue searching for the components of an arithmetic expression.

To complete this section here are some general guidelines which should help in the avoidance of syntax errors.

(a) Check spelling of reserved words, data-names and paragraph-names. For example, it is very easy to write:

```
05  SUMMARY-VAT-CHARGES . . .
```

in the DATA DIVISION and in the PROCEDURE DIVISION:

```
COMPUTE SUMMARY-VAT-CHARGE = . . .
```

(b) Check that hyphens have been inserted where required and that hyphenation has been used consistently. For example the paragraph:

```
TOTAL-PERCENTS.
```

must not be referenced as follows:

```
PERFORM TOTAL-PER-CENTS
```

(c) Ensure that reserved words are not used as data-names or paragraph-names. Use of well-hyphenated names usually avoids this problem.

(d) Be careful to insert full stops where required and only where required. This is particularly important in IF statements. For example:

```
210         IF VALID-RECORD
211             PERFORM CALCULATE-PRICE.
212             PERFORM PRINT-BILL
213         ELSE
```

The full stop at the end of line 211 terminates the IF statement and so the ELSE in line 213 will be flagged as an error.

Missing full stops in certain critical positions may cause a cascade of errors, as already described.

(e) Spacing is important, particularly around arithmetic and relational operators. For example:

```
IF CUST-AC-CODE NOT= "A"
```

will cause an error because there is no space between NOT and '='.

However, as already stated, there is no substitute for experience. Attempting to compile some programs will teach one more than reading a whole book of good advice on how to avoid syntax errors.

7.2 Debugging

Debugging is a cyclic process consisting of the following steps:

(a) Execute the compiled program with test data.
(b) Inspect the results obtained and identify the errors, if there are no errors check if more test cases are required (see Section 7.3).
(c) Locate the bugs in the program, or data, which are causing the errors.
(d) Amend the program or data, to try to remove the bugs, and return to step (a).

Before dealing with techniques for locating errors some general observations on debugging may be helpful. The first point is that debugging is not easy - it often requires considerable mental effort to find bugs. It is also worth noting that it is estimated that in removing one bug there is a 50-50 chance of introducing another one. Therefore the beginner should not be discouraged if at times it seems that each step forward is accompanied by an apparent step backwards.

Two major causes of bugs in programs are logic errors and errors in the test data. To reduce the number of logic errors it is recommended that the program design should be checked carefully before translation into COBOL. This can be done by manually 'executing' the design with different data values. If a COBOL program does fail with a logic error the design should be checked to see whether the error is in the design or the translation process. Any significant change to the program should be made at the design level, and carefully checked, before changing the corresponding COBOL program. This is a hard discipline to accept, especially for small programs, as there is an understandable desire to 'get the program working'. However, it is an excellent habit to establish from the beginning.

The data used to test a program should also be checked carefully because an error in the data is often the cause of a puzzling error in the results. Any student who comes to the author for advice and claims that his data are perfect is immediately challenged to produce a listing of the data or the actual data used (if on punched cards, for example). Many problems have been caused by the letter 'O' being used instead of zero, or the input data being typed one column out.

All results produced by a program should be checked thoroughly. The attitude that the results look 'quite reasonable' often leads to the programmer overlooking some small but significant error in the program. Another tendency is to see a glaringly obvious error in the results, and correct it, while failing to see some other less obvious error. This smaller error may be helpful in diagnosing the obvious problem or, even if unconnected with that problem, could also be corrected at the same time.

The most powerful tools in debugging are thought and the attitude of mind that takes nothing for granted. All too often students are unable to find bugs because they have assumed that "that bit can't possibly be wrong". Another common failing is the combination of "it worked last time" and "well, yes I did make a small change to the program".

Having made these general observations about debugging, what techniques are available to the programmer? The most obvious technique is hand execution of the program - try to follow through part of the program, line by line, using the data read by the program and writing down all the intermediate results. This process can be started either from the beginning of the program or from a known point of success, for example, the point at which the last record was successfully printed.

A variation on this technique is reverse execution from the point of failure - starting with the erroneous results work backwards through the lines of the program which created them. Again, try to predict the values of intermediate results and see how these could have arisen.

A problem which may arise with hand execution and particularly reverse execution is establishing the exact point of failure. Many computer systems use a buffering system for output which means that the last record printed, or written to a file, may be the last but one produced by the program. Experience with a particular system and the advice of others who have used it will establish whether this is a trap to be avoided.

If these techniques fail then a very powerful additional tool is to try to convince somebody else that ones program should work. This technique is often referred to as a walkthrough and may also be undertaken by a group of programmers to test a program design. All that is required is another person who is required to act as a 'devil's advocate' and ask "why?" every time one claims that something should happen. In the author's experience, this has proved to be a very useful technique and in some cases problems have been solved even though the programming language is unfamiliar.

Some bugs will still prove intractable even after working through the program carefully and discussing it with others. In these cases the solution is to try to obtain more information about the way the program is working. The programmer needs to ascertain whether the expected values of data-items are correct and whether the program is following the correct sequence of paragraphs. Most COBOL systems include facilities to dump the values of data-items, while the program is running, and trace the flow of control through a program. Detailed discussion of these facilities is beyond the scope of this book and they tend to vary from system to system, anyway. However, in general dump and trace facilities tend to produce large amounts of output, most of which is irrelevant. They should always be used in a carefully planned manner and not as a desperation measure.

A limited form of dumping and tracing can be provided by the programmer printing the values of data-items and paragraph-names during the execution of a program. The main disadvantage of this is that by introducing additional statements to print these values the structure of the program is being changed.

Display Statements

The simplest way to print the values of data-items and paragraph-names is to use the DISPLAY statement of COBOL. This allows a mixture of nonnumeric literals and values of data-items to be printed on the "default device defined by the implementor". Where the output appears will vary from system to system but it will usually be included in some form of monitoring file associated with the execution of the program, separate from the output file.

To obtain maximum benefit from display statements their position in the program and the values to be displayed should be carefully thought out. All displayed output should be clearly identified, preferably by the paragraph-name in which the display is inserted and the names of any data-items being displayed. For example:

```
PRICE-CALCULATION.
    DISPLAY "PRICE-CALCULATION"
    DISPLAY "SALE-PRICE ", SALE-PRICE,
        " SALE-QUANTITY ", SALE-QUANTITY
    COMPUTE BASIC-PRICE = SALE-PRICE * SALE-QUANTITY
    DISPLAY "BASIC-PRICE ", BASIC-PRICE
    . . .
```

Each time PRICE-CALCULATION is performed a series of messages of the following form will appear:

```
PRICE-CALCULATION
SALE-PRICE 0765 SALE-QUANTITY 00100
BASIC-PRICE 76500
```

This shows that PRICE-CALCULATION has been entered and gives the current values of the data-items SALE-PRICE and SALE-QUANTITY. After BASIC-PRICE has been computed its new value is displayed.

Note that DISPLAY gives unmodified output so that although BASIC-PRICE may have been described as:

```
05  BASIC-PRICE     PIC 999V99.
```

only the raw digits will be displayed and the implied decimal point ignored. There is no automatic spacing between items in DISPLAY and therefore any spaces required must be included in the nonnumeric literals as shown above. For example:

```
DISPLAY "SALE-PRICE", SALE-PRICE,
    "SALE-QUANTITY", SALE-QUANTITY
```

would have resulted in output of the form:

```
SALE-PRICE0765SALE-QUANTITY00100
```

The commas between the elements in the list are optional and are included only for readability.

As shown above, DISPLAY can be used to give the equivalent of a trace, by printing paragraph-names on entry to paragraphs, and a dump, by displaying the names and contents of data-items. If the program behaves differently after the inclusion of one or more display statements then obviously the logic of the program has been changed by the insertions. This is not necessarily a problem, studying the position and effect of each inserted statement should help to pinpoint the original error.

A problem which commonly affects beginning programmers is the so-called 'infinite loop'. The program uses up its allocation of computer resources and either produces little or no output, or the same output line repeated many times. This is caused by the program executing a sequence of statements repeatedly (looping) without ever finding a condition to change the sequence.

In COBOL, this problem is usually caused by incorrect positioning of full stops. For example:

```
     . . . . .
     PERFORM GET-NEXT-CUST-AC
     PERFORM PROCESS-CUST-AC UNTIL END-OF-CUST-AC
     . . . . .
 PROCESS-CUST-AC.
     PERFORM CHECK-CUST-AC
     IF CUST-AC-OK
         PERFORM PRICE-AND-DISCOUNT-AC
     PERFORM PRINT-AC-DETAILS
     PERFORM GET-NEXT-CUST-AC.
     . . . . .
```

The paragraph CHECK-CUST-AC is a validation routine which, among other things, sets the value of CUST-AC-OK to <u>true</u> for a valid record and <u>false</u> otherwise. The first time the program gets an invalid record the program will go into an infinite loop because GET-NEXT-CUST-AC is part of the IF structure for CUST-AC-OK = <u>true</u>. Note the position of the first full stop following the IF.

Infinite loops can usually be identified by working through the program carefully checking the position of the full stops. However, if this fails then again the next step is to try to obtain more information about the behaviour of the program. The COBOL system being used may include an <u>execution flow summary</u> (or profile) option which will indicate how many times each statement in the program has been executed, this will pinpoint the position of the infinite loop. Similarly a trace facility will give the names of the paragraphs which form the infinite loop. If no debugging tools are available then the programmer will need to use the display statement to investigate which parts of the program are being executed repeatedly.

7.3 Testing

Testing is the destructive process of trying to show the presence of errors in a program and is obviously closely related to debugging. It is impossible to prove that a program does not contain errors by testing it - a test can only detect the presence of errors, never their absence. Therefore, it follows that, contrary to popular belief, a "successful" test is one which finds one or more errors in a program.

A program is the creation of a programmer and therefore he is the worst person to try to destroy it. The best person to test a program is somebody who knows what the program should do but had no part in writing it. A good exercise is to exchange a supposedly working program with another student's corresponding effort and see who can find the most errors. In practice, this approach of independent testing is often used for testing commercial programs.

One approach to testing, beloved of many students, is the 'random data method' - write down the first n records that come to mind, where n is a number chosen to impress the lecturer! This usually finds some errors, which can be corrected, but in all but the simplest programs misses as many errors as it finds. What is required is a systematic way of testing programs so that each record in the test data is there for a purpose and the likelihood of finding errors is maximized.

In this section an attempt will be made to lay down some simple guidelines for testing programs and show how these can be applied. There are two basic approaches to testing a program:

black-box testing which concentrates on the inputs and outputs of the program and ignores the actual construction of the program;

glass-box (or white box) testing which exercises the statements of the program.

Used together these two approaches should maximize the chances of finding errors.

An interesting observation, from practical experience, is that the effort of constructing test data systematically may assist in finding bugs before the program is ever run.

Black-box testing

There are two useful techniques which can be applied in this case, usually given the rather daunting titles of 'equivalence partitioning' and 'boundary-value analysis'. The reader should not be discouraged by these technical labels - both the ideas are straightforward to apply.

The basic principle of equivalence partitioning is to look at each input data-item in turn and identify the 'classes' of errors and valid data. The test data for the program should then include at least one value drawn from each equivalence class. Some examples of equivalence classes are given below.

Example 7.1
The data-item 'customer-account-type' must be a single letter, either 'W' or 'R'. The equivalence classes are:

class	customer-account-type	
1	W	valid
2	R	valid
3	anything else	invalid

Example 7.2
The 'price-per-item' must be not less than 10p. Taking a simplistic approach there are only two equivalence classes:

class	price-per-item	
1	less than 10p	invalid
2	not less than 10p	valid

More realistically, all numeric data-items used by a program should be assumed to have an extra equivalence class of 'not numeric' (unless the program specification explicitly excludes this). So in this case the classes would be:

class	price-per-item	
1	not numeric	invalid
2	less than 10p	invalid
3	not less than 10p	valid

Example 7.3
The 'quantity-sold' should never be less than 10 or greater than 1000.

class	quantity-sold	
1	not numeric	invalid
2	less than 10	invalid
3	between 10 and 1000 (incl.)	valid
4	greater than 1000	invalid

Example 7.4
The 'withdrawal-code' should be either 'C', for cash withdrawals, or 'D', for cheques drawn. This is obviously similar to Example 7.1 but suppose that the specification now goes on to state: the 'withdrawal-amount' should not exceed £250 for a cash withdrawal and cheques should only be drawn for amounts between £25 and £1000 (inclusive). To identify the equivalence classes it is now necessary to consider the two interrelated data-items: 'withdrawal-code' and 'withdrawal-amount'.

class	withdrawal-code	withdrawal-amount	
1	C	not numeric	invalid
2	C	not greater than £250	valid
3	C	greater than £250	invalid
4	D	not numeric	invalid
5	D	less than £25	invalid
6	D	between £25 and £1000	valid
7	D	greater than £1000	invalid
8	not C or D	-	invalid

Strictly, class 6 might be divided into two classes:

6a	D	between £25 and £250	valid
6b	D	over £250 up to £1000	valid

Although the £250 boundary has nothing to do with withdrawal-code = 'D' the logic of the program might be incorrect in such a way that this boundary is made significant for 'D'.

Having established the equivalence classes for each data-item, or group of related data-items, in the input record a set of test data should be constructed which includes values from every equivalence class identified. Each invalid class should be included in a record on its own to isolate the effects of combinations of errors. Valid classes can safely be combined within the same record.

The idea behind boundary-value analysis came from the observation that many programs fail when dealing with a value on the boundary between valid and invalid classes of data. Therefore to increase the chances of finding an error (a successful test) choose data values on these boundaries. Applying this method to Example 7.2 would suggest that the value in class 2 should be 9p, or 9.5p if dealing with half pennies, and a suitable lower boundary value from class 3 should be exactly 10p.

Applying the same method in Example 7.3 suggests the following values:

class	quantity-sold	
2	9	highest invalid value below 10
3	10	lower boundary of valid values
3	1000	upper boundary of valid values
4	1001	lowest invalid value above 1000

Boundary-value analysis can also be applied to output records. For each data-item in an output record the appropriate input should be included to cover the full range of output values.

Looking back to Example 7.2 again, there is apparently no need to test the upper limit of price-per-item. But if this value is to be printed then the maximum value should be included to ensure that it is correctly represented in the output data-item.

Characters are often lost because of the incorrect use of editing. For example:

```
05  CAR-BASIC-PRICE     PIC 9(5)V99.
. . . . .
05  BILL-BASIC-PRICE    PIC ££,££9.99.
. . . . .
MOVE CAR-BASIC-PRICE TO BILL-BASIC-PRICE
```

Any value of CAR-BASIC-PRICE greater than £9999.99 will be truncated because the data-item BILL-BASIC-PRICE is too short. This may be beneficial to purchasers of expensive cars but is not good programming practice.

It is also wise to test for maximum sizes of character data-items used to hold names and addresses, etc, even if they are not manipulated in the program. This should identify any problems in the layout of the output record.

It is particularly important to test for maximum values of constructed data-items. For example:

```
COMPUTE PRICE-CHARGED = SALE-PRICE * SALE-QUANTITY
```

where PRICE-CHARGED is either a temporary or output data-item constructed by multiplying two data-items from an input record. The use of PRICE-CHARGED should be tested by using the maximum permitted values of the input data-items SALE-PRICE and SALE-QUANTITY.

Totals are another area where problems often arise - it is rather embarrassing when a program which has been working perfectly well for some time suddenly starts producing rubbish when a cumulative total passes some critical value. Therefore, it is important to try to devise a set of test data to push data-items holding totals up towards their maximum values.

Although the emphasis so far has been on maximum values it should also be remembered that minimum values can cause problems. This is particularly true of numeric data-items where division by zero errors may occur or large negative values may cause truncation problems.

Applying the ideas of equivalence partitioning and boundary-value analysis should enable the programmer to construct a set of test data to systematically test the individual data-items of a program. However, this does not tackle an important problem which arises in practice - an error in one data-item may disguise an error in another data-item. A program may apparently deal quite successfully with all the errors in data-items independently but fail when some obscure combination of errors occurs. Discussion of a systematic method for dealing with combinations of errors (called 'cause-effect graphing') is beyond the scope of this book, so some simple ideas will have to suffice.

The most straightforward approach is to test every combination of error class and this is possible in programs with a small number of error classes but becomes impracticable if there are more than about four independent error classes. For programs with larger numbers of error classes it is necessary to abandon strict black-box testing and to try to guess from the structure of the program the most likely causes of error. For example, if two data-items occur within the same IF structure then their values may interact and therefore combinations of errors should be included in the test data. This type of analysis leads from black-box testing into glass-box testing.

In addition to testing at the data-item level a program should also be tested at the record level. So far, the programs studied in this book have only had one input file and the important cases to test are:

(a) no input data, the 'empty set' of test data,
(b) one record in the input file, the 'singular set' of test data,
(c) several records in the file.

The special cases of zero records or one record may be uncommon in practice but a program should work under <u>all</u> conditions. Programs with multiple input files (discussed in Chapter 9) will require combinations of these cases to be tested.

<u>Glass-box testing</u>

The objective of this type of testing is to construct a set of test data which will exercise all the statements in the PROCEDURE DIVISION of a program. The least stringent way of exercising the program is to ensure that all the statements of the procedure division have been executed at least once. Working through the program line by line it should be possible to systematically build up a file of input records containing values which will ensure that every statement is executed at least once. Some systems may provide an optional execution flow summary, or profile, which shows how many times each statement of the program has been executed. If available, this can be used to ensure that every statement has been executed at least once.

Merely checking that every statement has been executed is not sufficient as this may fail to pinpoint some obvious errors. The next stage is to add to the test data records to ensure that every condition has been either <u>true</u> or <u>false</u> at least once. This is not the same as ensuring that every statement has been executed at least once. Consider the following simple example:

```
IF TAXABLE-PAY > 0
    PERFORM TAX-CALCULATION.
PERFORM PRINT-DETAILS
```

To ensure that every statement has been executed at least once requires only that TAXABLE-PAY should have a value greater than zero. This test will not trap an error which arises because a value of TAXABLE-PAY less than zero means that the program fails to give a value to the data-item

TAX-PAID, within TAX-CALCULATION, and an employee not liable to tax is charged an arbitrary amount of tax.

Any program which contains compound conditions should have one further level of testing applied to it. For each compound condition, every simple condition making up the compound condition should take the values true and false at least once. For example:

```
PERFORM PROCESS-THIS-BATCH
    UNTIL END-OF-TRANS-FILE OR TRANS-TYPE = 1
```

To ensure that each condition in the program is either true or false at least once requires only two sets of test data, for example:

END-OF-TRANS-FILE = true	TRANS-TYPE = 1	condition = true
END-OF-TRANS-FILE = false	TRANS-TYPE = 2	condition = false

The more stringent condition that every simple condition making up a compound condition should be both true and false at least once requires four sets of test data, for example:

END-OF-TRANS-FILE = true	TRANS-TYPE = 1	condition = true
END-OF-TRANS-FILE = true	TRANS-TYPE = 2	condition = true
END-OF-TRANS-FILE = false	TRANS-TYPE = 1	condition = true
END-OF-TRANS-FILE = false	TRANS-TYPE = 2	condition = false

This example also illustrates another important point about testing - it is not always possible to combine all test cases in one run of a program. In the above example at least two runs of the program will be required because the condition END-OF-TRANS-FILE can only be true once in a simple program.

Looking at the previous example leads to another general observation that all loops in a program should be tested carefully. It is suggested that every until loop should be tested for zero, one and many repetitions. Errors often show up in the special cases of zero or one repetitions of a loop and therefore it is worth checking these as part of the testing strategy.

7.4 Case Study

To show how to apply the ideas on testing discussed in Section 7.3, the case study of Section 6.7 will be used. The description of the problem was as follows.

> The telephone billing system of the Rockall Telecom Corporation receives input records in the following format:
>
> | | |
> |---|---|
> | Area code | 3 characters (see below) |
> | Telephone number | 6 digits |
> | Customer name and address | 40 characters |
> | Rental charge | 4 digits (pence) |
> | Dialled units | 4 digits |
> | Operator-connected units | 3 digits |
>
> The area code consists of either two letters followed by a digit or a single letter followed by two digits.
>
> A program is required to check the validity of these data and to

process the valid records, calculating the amount to be charged for each customer. The following validity checks should be carried out on the records:

(a) the area code is in the correct format,
(b) the rental charge, dialled units and operator-connected units are all valid numbers,
(c) the rental charge is not less than the minimum of £8.50.

If any of these checks fails the details of the record should be printed together with a suitable error message or messages.

For each valid record calculate the amount to be charged by adding the following elements:

(a) the rental charge,
(b) charge for units used; dialled units at 2p each and operator-connected at 3p each,
(c) VAT at 12.5%.

The output from the program should consist of a tabular summary of the details of each record together with either the amount to be charged or any relevant error messages.

This description can be used to construct a set of data for black-box testing. For ease of reference, the data-items making up the input and output records will be referred to the names used in Section 6.7, reproduced below.

```
phone-record
   phone-area              area code
      phone-area-1
      phone-area-2
      phone-area-3
   phone-number            telephone number
   phone-customer          customer name and address
   phone-rental            rental charge (pence)
   phone-dialled           dialled units
   phone-op-units          operator-connected units

billing-line
   billing-area            area code
   billing-number          telephone number
   billing-customer        customer name and address
   billing-rental          rental charge (edited, pounds.pence)
   billing-dialled         dialled units (edited)
   billing-op-units        operator-connected units (edited)
   billing-charge          total charge with VAT added
```

The best approach is probably to take each data-item in turn and apply the ideas of equivalence partitioning and boundary-value analysis.

The first data-item is 'phone-area' which has four equivalence classes:

class	phone-area	
1	phone-area-1 not alphabetic	invalid
2	phone-area-2 not alphabetic nor numeric	invalid
3	phone-area-3 not numeric	invalid
4	phone-area-1 alphabetic and phone-area-2 alphabetic or numeric and phone-area-3 numeric	invalid

There are no apparent problems with boundaries but it may be necessary to consider combinations of error classes.

The second data-item 'phone-number' has no restrictions placed on it and therefore the only test required is to fill the data-item with characters to check that the corresponding output data-item 'billing-number' is large enough.

The third data-item 'phone-customer' again has no restrictions placed on it and the only useful test is therefore to ensure that a record containing a name and address which fills all character positions is constructed to test 'billing-customer'.

The fourth data-item 'phone-rental' is numeric and has a minimum permitted value specified, therefore the equivalence classes are:

class	phone-rental	
1	not numeric	invalid
2	less than £8.50	invalid
3	not less than £8.50	valid

Applying boundary-value analysis would suggest using the value £8.49 from class 2 (upper bound of error class) and £8.50 from class 3 (lower bound of valid class). To test the size of the output data-item 'billing-rental' a maximum value equivalent to £99.99 should also be included.

The last two data-items 'phone-dialled' and 'phone-op-units' are similar in that each has only two equivalence classes:

class	phone-dialled	
1	not numeric	invalid
2	numeric	valid

class	phone-op-units	
1	not numeric	invalid
2	numeric	valid

To test the effectiveness of the output data-items 'billing-dialled' and 'billing-op-units' maximum values of 9999 and 999, respectively, should be used.

Looking at the output record, there is one data-item not mentioned in the above discussion. The data-item 'billing-charge' is constructed from 'phone-rental', 'phone-dialled' and 'phone-op-units'. Therefore to test the upper boundary of 'billing-charge' all these data-items should be set to their maximum values simultaneously.

It is now possible to construct a file of test data incorporating all these classes of errors and boundaries, and the following data file is suggested. The character '-' is used to indicate that the value in this position could be any valid value for the data-item. The customer name and address field is used to indicate which data-items are being tested.

```
9BC------FIRST CHARACTER OF AREA CODE INVALID      -----------
A*3------SECOND CHARACTER OF AREA CODE INVALID     -----------
ABC------THIRD CHARACTER OF AREA CODE INVALID      -----------
---------RENTAL NOT NUMERIC                        ))!)-------
---------RENTAL TOO LOW                            0849-------
---------DIALLED UNITS NOT NUMERIC                 ----ABCD---
---------OPERATOR UNITS NOT NUMERIC                --------)*)
ZZ9999999MAXIMUM VALUES IN ALL DATA ITEMS--------99999999999
---------MINIMUM PERMITTED RENTAL                  0850-------
```

In the case of the last two records the expected results for 'billing-charge' should be calculated before running the program, and checked against the actual results. As a general rule, in all cases where a result is expected its value should be calculated before running the program.

The above file is a minimum set of test data to test the program, applying black-box techniques. Other records might be added to this collection, for example a record in which all data-items which are checked are invalid and possibly combinations of errors. Another good test is to set 'phone-dialled' and 'phone-op-units' to zero to check that there are no problems caused by this.

Applying the principles of glass-box testing to this example will not yield a significantly different set of test data. Working through the program the only statement which will not be properly exercised by the test data given above is:

```
IF PHONE-AREA-2 NOT ALPHABETIC
    AND PHONE-AREA-2 NOT NUMERIC
```

Looking at this condition there are three possible states:

PHONE-AREA-2 numeric	true AND false = false
PHONE-AREA-2 alphabetic	false AND true = false
PHONE-AREA-2 not numeric nor alphabetic	true AND true = true

The fourth state, PHONE-AREA-2 both numeric and alphabetic, simultaneously, is of course impossible. The test data should include values of PHONE-AREA-2 from all these classes.

It is left as an exercise for the reader to work through the program given in Section 6.7, and construct a set of test data using glass-box testing principles.

Exercises 7

7.1. Use the principles of black-box testing to devise suitable test data values for the following cases.

(a) The discount-rate should be 10, 15 or 20. Assume a two digit data-item.

(b) The minimum value of hourly-rate is £2.10 and the maximum is £7.25. Assume three digits - pence.

(c) If the tariff-code is 'B' (Business) then the first 200 units consumed are charged at 15p per unit and any additional units at 5p per unit. For tariff-code 'H' (Household) the first 100 units are charged at 10p per unit and any additional units at 8p per unit. Assume that tariff-code is a single letter and that units-consumed is a four digit data-item.

7.2. Apply the principles of glass-box testing to devise test data to exercise the following piece of program.

```
IF CUST-TYPE = "D"
    PERFORM DEALER-DISCOUNT
ELSE
    IF CUST-TYPE = "T" OR SPECIAL-TERMS
        PERFORM TRADE-DISCOUNT
    ELSE
        IF CUST-QUANTITY > 50
            PERFORM QUANTITY-DISCOUNT.
PERFORM PRODUCE-INVOICE.
```

7.3. Demonstrate how applying the techniques of glass-box testing would show that the following piece of COBOL:

```
QUANTITY-DISCOUNT.
    IF SALES-QUANTITY < BULK-DISCOUNT-LEVEL
        IF TRADE-CUSTOMER
            PERFORM DISCOUNT-5
    ELSE
        PERFORM DISCOUNT-10.
```

is not a correct translation of the design fragment:

```
quantity-discount
   if sales-quantity < bulk-discount-level
      if trade-customer then
         discount-5
      endif
   else
      discount-10
   endif
```

For revision and to make sure that the question has been fully understood: give a correct translation of the design fragment into COBOL and a design fragment corresponding to the piece of COBOL given.

7.4. Look at the case study discussed in Section 5.6 and devise a set of test data to test this program as thoroughly as possible.

7.5 Apply the techniques discussed in this chapter to systematically test one of the programs suggested in Programming Exercises 6.

8 Program Structure

The main objective of this chapter is to take the reader further into the structure of a COBOL program. So far the programs discussed, and those which it is hoped have been attempted by the reader, have been based on a standard program skeleton given in Appendix 1. This chapter will explain how this skeleton is actually constructed and prepare the way for looking at more complex program structures.

The four divisions making up a COBOL program were briefly introduced in Chapter 3 and each of these is explained in more detail in this chapter. One of the most important features of a COBOL program which has been largely hidden from the reader so far is the description and handling of files. The reasoning behind the structure for input and output used in the skeleton program is given in Section 8.4.

Having explained the basic file handling features of COBOL some more advanced techniques can be introduced. In Section 8.5 the production of better formatted lineprinter output is discussed and in the following section the use of multiple input records is introduced. Finally, the case study illustrates the use of some of the techniques discussed in this chapter.

8.1 Identification Division

This was intended by the original designers of COBOL to provide a unique identifier for a program and other documentary information about the program. The only obligatory entry in this division is the program identifier which is used by most systems to provide a link between the source program (in COBOL) and the object program (in a lower level language). The general format of the program identifier is:

```
PROGRAM-ID. program-name.
```

The program-name can, in theory, be any name constructed according to the rules for user-defined names (see Section 3.2). In practice, it is usually restricted in length, and possibly format, by the implementor of a particular COBOL system. This restriction is usually imposed because the program-name is used as the name, or part of the name, for a file containing the object program and each operating system imposes its own peculiar rules for file names.

There are a number of other entries which can appear in the IDENTIFICATION DIVISION but none of these are required - they simply provide additional documentation for the program. The following entries are possible:

```
AUTHOR. comment-entry.
INSTALLATION. comment-entry.
DATE-WRITTEN. comment-entry.
DATE-COMPILED. comment-entry.
SECURITY. comment-entry.
```

A 'comment-entry' is any sequence of characters extending over any number of lines - the end of one entry will be recognized by the reserved word which begins the next entry.

The entry put against DATE-COMPILED will be replaced by the current date when a listing is produced after an attempt is made to compile the program. The other comment-entries are simply listed as they appear in the source program.

A complete example of an IDENTIFICATION DIVISION using all of these options is given below.

```
IDENTIFICATION DIVISION.
PROGRAM-ID. EXAMPLE1.
AUTHOR. RAY WELLAND
INSTALLATION. UNIVERSITY OF STRATHCLYDE
DATE-WRITTEN. MAY 1982
DATE-COMPILED. TODAY
SECURITY. NONE
```

When the program is listed, after an attempt at compilation, TODAY will be replaced by the current date.

8.2 Environment Division

This division should contain all the details about the environment in which the program is to be run. The original designers of COBOL hoped that all the features peculiar to a particular type of computer would be contained in this division. Therefore to transport the program from one type of computer to another should only involve modifying the ENVIRONMENT DIVISION. This division is divided into two sections: CONFIGURATION, to specify the hardware of the system being used, and INPUT-OUTPUT which, as the name suggests, deals with input and output connections with external files.

Configuration Section

The minimum requirement for the CONFIGURATION SECTION is that SOURCE-COMPUTER and OBJECT-COMPUTER should be specified. The source-computer paragraph gives the name of the machine on which the program is to be <u>compiled</u>, while the object-computer paragraph specifies the name of the machine on which the resulting object program is to be <u>executed</u>. The source and object computers are usually the same machine but this allows for the possibility of a program being compiled on one machine and executed on another, which is sometimes called 'cross-compilation'. Such a facility would be useful if the machine named in the object-computer paragraph were not large enough to support a COBOL compiler, probably because of insufficient storage capacity, but could be used to run compiled programs.

What is actually specified in the source-computer and object-computer paragraphs is 'implementor-defined'. This means that anybody producing a COBOL compiler can specify what information should go into these paragraphs - there is no standard format given. To run a COBOL program it is therefore necessary to find out the correct entries for these paragraphs, relevant to the computer being used.

In addition to the source-computer and object-computer paragraphs there is also a facility for defining SPECIAL-NAMES in the CONFIGURATION SECTION. This facility is not usually required by the beginning programmer but is mentioned briefly as it may be encountered in reading other books or studying more advanced programs. The most common use of the SPECIAL-NAMES paragraph is to associate the name for a particular hardware feature, peculiar to the machine being used, with a 'mnemonic-name' to be used within the program.

For example, suppose that a particular COBOL system uses the name CONTROL-1 for the operator's control console of the computer. Then the programmer can choose a name to associate with that device, to be used throughout the program, by using the SPECIAL-NAMES paragraph. For example:

```
SPECIAL-NAMES.
    CONTROL-1 IS OPERATORS-CONSOLE.
```

To send a message to the operator it is possible to use a variation of the DISPLAY statement, introduced in Section 7.3. For example:

```
DISPLAY "PHASE 2 STARTING" UPON OPERATORS-CONSOLE
```

The message 'PHASE 2 STARTING' will be written on the operator's console when this statement is executed.

Now if the program is transferred to another system where the operators' console is called TYPEWRITER a simple change to the ENVIRONMENT DIVISION allows the program to continue working. The SPECIAL-NAMES paragraph would need to be altered to:

```
SPECIAL-NAMES.
    TYPEWRITER IS OPERATORS-CONSOLE.
```

The change to the program is therefore confined to the ENVIRONMENT DIVISION and any DISPLAY statements referring to OPERATORS-CONSOLE remain unchanged.

Input-output Section

The minimum required entry in the INPUT-OUTPUT SECTION is a FILE-CONTROL paragraph containing a SELECT statement for each input or output file used by the program. Select statements fulfil a similar role to the entries in the SPECIAL-NAMES paragraph; they associate names used in the program with actual files. Therefore, if within the program there is a file called TRANS-FILE it can be associated with an actual file called TRANS-2505 by the SELECT statement:

```
SELECT TRANS-FILE ASSIGN TO TRANS-2505.
```

TRANS-FILE is an internal (or logical) file-name and TRANS-2505 is an external (or physical) file-name. The rules for constructing external file-names vary from implementation to implementation but the rules for constructing internal file-names are standard. Again, programs are more 'portable', since only the external file-names have to be changed when transferring a program from one COBOL system to another.

An example of a complete ENVIRONMENT DIVISION for an imaginary COBOL system is given below.

```
ENVIRONMENT DIVISION.
CONFIGURATION SECTION.
SOURCE-COMPUTER. MM1.
OBJECT-COMPUTER. MM1.
SPECIAL-NAMES.
    MM-CONTROL IS OPERATORS-CONSOLE.
INPUT-OUTPUT SECTION.
FILE-CONTROL.
    SELECT TRANS-FILE ASSIGN TO MM-INPUT.
    SELECT OUTFILE ASSIGN TO MM-OUTPUT.
```

8.3 Data Division

The DATA DIVISION is divided into two main parts: the FILE SECTION, which contains descriptions of all input/output files used by the program, and the WORKING-STORAGE SECTION, describing all temporary data-items required by the program. In more advanced programs additional sections may appear for subprogram linkage and the report-writer feature but for the purposes of this book only two sections will be considered in detail.

File Section

Every file described in the FILE SECTION consists of a file description followed by one or more record descriptions. A file description starts with the letters FD followed by the internal file-name, the LABEL RECORDS clause and possibly some other clauses describing the file, the description being terminated by a full stop. The internal file-name is the name chosen for the file, to be used throughout the program, and must have appeared in a SELECT statement in the FILE-CONTROL paragraph of the INPUT-OUTPUT SECTION of the ENVIRONMENT DIVISION.

The LABEL RECORDS clause gives information about the structure of the file. Files held on magnetic disk or tape normally have special 'header' and 'trailer' records to mark the beginning and end of the file. The format of these special records varies from one computer system to another. If the file is described as:

```
LABEL RECORDS STANDARD
```

then the file has standard header and trailer labels for the system being used. The alternative is:

```
LABEL RECORDS OMITTED
```

which indicates that the file is unlabelled, which could possibly mean that the file is being directly input from punched cards or a keyboard, or output to a lineprinter.

Which of these alternatives should be used for a particular type of file varies from implementation to implementation. Therefore, the manual for the local system should be consulted or details given by the course tutor for a programming course.

Other optional clauses which may appear in the file description are concerned with two other aspects of the physical structure of the file. The BLOCK CONTAINS clause specifies the number of characters or records stored in a block for a file held on disk or tape. The RECORD CONTAINS clause allows for a file containing variable length records. Neither of these features is likely to be of use to the beginning programmer and, in any case, they are usually only included for documentary purposes.

Finally there is the DATA RECORDS clause which allows the programmer to list the names of different records belonging to a file containing several different types of record. However, since the record descriptions must follow immediately after the file description this clause is again of little value except for documentation.

An example of a complex file description using all of these options is given below.

```
FD  TRANS-FILE
    BLOCK CONTAINS 1000 TO 2000 CHARACTERS
    RECORD CONTAINS 300 TO 1500 CHARACTERS
    LABEL RECORDS STANDARD
    DATA RECORDS ARE TRANS-BATCH-HEADER TRANS-DETAIL.
```

This file description would then be followed by record descriptions for TRANS-BATCH-HEADER and TRANS-DETAIL.

Note that a file description consists of 'FD', followed by the file-name and any descriptive clauses required, terminated by a full stop. After finding this terminating full stop a COBOL compiler will expect to find a record description. A common error is to put the full stop after the file-name - this will give rise to a syntax error or errors.

To summarize, the minimum file description, which will suffice for this book, consists of 'FD' followed by an internal file-name, a LABEL RECORDS clause and a full stop. For example:

```
FD  CUSTOMER-FILE
    LABEL RECORDS OMITTED.
```

The file description should be followed by one or more record descriptions. All record descriptions up to the next file description or the end of the FILE SECTION will be assumed to belong to the current file. When a file has more than one record description associated with it there are problems - these are discussed in Section 8.6, below.

A record description is a data structure with the level-number 01. The simplest record description is a single data-item with level-number 01 and a picture. For example:

```
FD  OUTFILE
    LABEL RECORDS OMITTED.
01  OUT-LINE          PIC X(120).
```

This sets up an area of 120 characters, associated with the file OUTFILE, which can be accessed by the record-name OUT-LINE.

For input files the record description is usually structured so that individual data-items within the record can be accessed. The structure and type of data-items, within records, was discussed in Chapters 3 and 5 and there is little to add here.

An important restriction is that the VALUE clause must <u>not</u> be used to give initial values to any data-items in the FILE SECTION. This does not preclude the use of condition-names where VALUE is used in a different way.

Working-storage Section

This section of the program contains descriptions of all the data-items required for storage of values during execution of the program. These can be roughly categorized into the four classes given below.

(a) State-variables: describing the current state of the program. The only example used so far is the END-<input-file-name> flag but other examples will appear later in the book.

(b) Output records: data structures being used to build up one or more output records for eventual transmission to the output file.

(c) Temporary data-items: data-items used for storage of values which are used to hold intermediate results in calculations, keeping running totals, etc.

(d) Headings and other constants: areas of store which are assigned values at the start of the program and which will hold these values throughout the life of the program.

The rules for building up these data structures have already been discussed in Chapters 3 and 5 but at this point it is worth making a few general observations about the WORKING-STORAGE SECTION.

In the author's experience, one of the main stumbling blocks concerns the initial values of data-items. When a program commences execution the value of every data-item is undefined unless it has been given an initial value using a VALUE clause in the DATA DIVISION. A data-item which has no initial value can be explicitly given a value using the MOVE, COMPUTE or READ statements in the PROCEDURE DIVISION.

A caution about the use of the VALUE clause is worth repeating as it often causes trouble. For example, suppose that a program contains the following description for a data-item:

```
04  TOTAL-SALES     PIC 9(6) VALUE 0.
```

This means that when the program commences execution the value of TOTAL-SALES will be set to zero. If the value is changed by the program then it will never automatically revert to the value 0, it can only be specifically reset to zero, by a MOVE statement for example. The important point to remember is that the VALUE clause only gives an initial value to a data-item, unlike some other programming languages which have the concept of a fixed constant.

It is good programming practice to regard some data-items as constants which are to be fixed for the lifetime of the program. This idea has already been used in the construction of headings but can also be valuable in other circumstances, especially in larger programs. Programs dealing with invoicing will have to cope with VAT and a badly written program will have the current rate of 15% appearing in various invoicing calculations. For example:

```
COMPUTE VAT-SUBTOTAL = 0.15 * SALES-TOTAL
```

If the government changes the VAT rate to 12.5% next week this program will be difficult to alter because each separate reference to the VAT rate will have to be altered.

However, if a data-item called VAT-RATE is declared, given a value of 15, and not changed in the program it can be used as a constant. For example:

```
05  VAT-RATE        PIC 99V9  VALUE 15.
. . . . .
COMPUTE VAT-SUBTOTAL = 0.01 * VAT-RATE * SALES-TOTAL
```

A change in the VAT rate will now only require a single alteration in the program and there is much less likelihood of an error when making this amendment. Even if the VAT rate is changed to 13.75% the change is still confined to the one data-item.

Another piece of good programming style is to keep all the similar types of data-items together and in the same order in each program written. This saves time when searching through the WORKING-STORAGE SECTION. For example, the following format could be adopted.

```
       WORKING-STORAGE SECTION.
       01  STATE-VECTOR.
           05  END-ACCOUNT-FILE        PIC X.
               88  END-OF-ACCOUNT-FILE VALUE "E".
      *    Descriptions of other state variables such as error flags
      *        and Booleans can be added to STATE-VECTOR

       01  TEMPORARY-ITEMS.
           05  TOTAL-UNITS     PIC 9(5).
           05  TOTAL-CHARGE    PIC 9(6)V99.
      *    Descriptions of all temporary data-items can
      *        be gathered together in TEMPORARY-ITEMS

       01  CONSTANT-DATA.
           05  VAT-RATE        PIC 99V9  VALUE 15.
      *    Definitions of any constants used in the program
      *        can be collected in CONSTANT-DATA

      *    All the records associated with the output file can then
      *        be defined, possibly starting with the headings.

       01  PAGE-HEADING.
           05  FILLER      PIC X(20)  VALUE SPACES.
           05  FILLER      PIC X(24)  VALUE
               "OUTER HEBRIDES GAS BOARD".
           . . . . .

       01  COLUMN-HEADINGS.
           05  FILLER      PIC X(7)   VALUE "ACCOUNT".
           . . . . .

       01  BILLING-LINE.
           05  BILLING-CUST-NO PIC 9(6).
           05  FILLER          PIC XXXX.
           . . . . .
```

It doesn't matter what order these data structures appear in but it makes programming easier if a consistent style is used. With small programs this may seem unnecessary but it is better to learn good habits to start with rather than 'unlearn' bad ones later.

The COBOL standard includes a special level-number 77 for 'independent' data-items which appear at the beginning of the WORKING-STORAGE SECTION. The use of level-number 77 is not recommended because it is better practice to gather the various types of data-items and a special level-number is unnecessary - level number 01 with a picture has the same effect. However, other books and programs may include this feature.

8.4 Procedure Division

The PROCEDURE DIVISION is the executable, or algorithmic, part of a COBOL program. The execution of a program starts with the first statement of the first paragraph of the PROCEDURE DIVISION and continues sequentially until the special statement STOP RUN is executed. This is discussed in more detail in "Stopping a program", below.

The use of PERFORM and PERFORM ... UNTIL will change the 'flow of control' in a program by obeying the instructions in a paragraph elsewhere in the program. However, eventually execution continues sequentially, unless an execution error occurs or a STOP RUN is executed.

Consider the first paragraph of the standard program skeleton:

```
MAIN-PROGRAM.
    PERFORM INIT-STATE
    PERFORM <main-process>
    PERFORM CLOSE-DOWN.
```

No matter how many other PERFORM statements are contained within the paragraphs referenced these three statements must always be executed in the sequence shown.

It was claimed in Chapter 1 that all programs have three essential parts: initialization, processing and termination, and this structure is reflected by the highest level control structure shown above. To understand the construction of the paragraphs INIT-STATE and CLOSE-DOWN, together with the implementation of get-next-<input-file-name> and put-<record-name>, it is necessary to look in some detail at verbs hidden from the reader until now. In particular, the verbs concerned with the handling of files will need to be carefully investigated. This should then pave the way for developing programs with more complex data-processing requirements.

Stopping a Program

The format of the STOP statement used in the standard program skeleton is:

```
STOP RUN
```

The execution of this statement indicates that the program has finished and that the operating system being used to control the program should delete the program and continue with another task. It is possible for a program to contain several STOP RUN statements but this usually indicates poor design. It is strongly recommended that a program should only have one exit point and therefore only one STOP RUN statement.

An alternative form of the STOP statement is:

```
STOP "<message>"
```

Execution of this statement will temporarily stop the program and send the <message> to the operator's console. The program can be restarted by the computer operator, usually after taking some appropriate action. For example, a payroll program may require special stationery for salary slips to be loaded into the lineprinter. Therefore the program could include the statement:

```
STOP "LOAD SALARIES STATIONERY"
```

When the operator has completed the loading of the stationery the program can be restarted.

Opening and Closing Files

Any file which is to be used by a COBOL program must be _opened_ before its contents can be read or written. The record area associated with the file is also inaccessible to the program until the file has been opened. Any attempt to use a file, or its associated record area, before the file has been opened will cause an execution error and a program failure.

When opening a file it is necessary to specify whether it is an input file or an output file. A single OPEN statement can be used to open any number of files, some for input and some for output. The general form of this statement is:

```
OPEN INPUT <input-list> OUTPUT <output-list>
```

where <input-list> contains the names of one or more files to be opened for input and <output-list> contains the names of one or more files to be opened for output. For example:

```
(a)      OPEN INPUT CUSTOMER-FILE OUTPUT OUTFILE

(b)      OPEN INPUT TRANS-FILE OLD-MASTER-FILE
              OUTPUT NEW-MASTER-FILE ERRORS-FILE
```

When the OPEN statement is executed an attempt is made to open each file in turn. For an input file if the file does not exist or is not available to the user then an execution error will occur. If an output file already exists then the action taken will depend on the particular system being used. Normally a new, empty file is created for each output file opened. After the successful completion of an OPEN statement all the named files, and their associated record areas, will be accessible to the program.

The OPEN statement allows options other than input and output but these are not relevant to the development of simple programs.

When a program has finished using a file the file should be _closed_, which releases it from the program. Any number of files can be closed in a single CLOSE statement and it is not necessary to specify whether the files were used for input or output. For example:

(a) CLOSE CUSTOMER-FILE OUTFILE

(b) CLOSE TRANS-FILE ERRORS-FILE
OLD-MASTER-FILE NEW-MASTER-FILE

```
(a)        CLOSE CUSTOMER-FILE OUTFILE

(b)        CLOSE TRANS-FILE ERRORS-FILE
                OLD-MASTER-FILE NEW-MASTER-FILE
```

After the execution of a CLOSE statement the files, and their associated record areas, will no longer be accessible to the program and any attempt at using them will result in an execution error.

Looking at the standard program skeleton (see Appendix 1), it can be seen that an OPEN statement is included in INIT-STATE, to open the files required by the program, and a CLOSE statement is included in CLOSE-DOWN to release these files.

<u>Reading Records from a File</u>

To repeat an earlier point - before anything can be read from a file it must be opened for input. If the file has not been correctly opened then an attempt to read it will cause an execution error.

The read mechanism of COBOL is record based and uses a 'read-fail' approach to end of file conditions. The fact that reading is record based means that it is not possible to read individual characters or numbers from a file, only complete records as specified in the FILE SECTION of the DATA DIVISION.

The read-fail approach means that when a READ statement is executed it <u>either</u> copies the next record from the file into the input area associated with the file <u>or</u> executes a sequence of instructions specified to handle the end of file condition. After execution of this sequence of instructions the file is said to be in the 'at-end' condition and the input area for the file is inaccessible to the program. If a file is in the at-end condition then any further attempt at reading will cause an execution error.

The most commonly used form of the READ statement is:

```
READ <input-file-name>
    AT END <end-of-file-action>.
```

Where <end-of-file-action> is a sequence of "imperative statements" terminated by a full stop. Imperative statements are a subset of the statements available in COBOL and are defined in the appropriate manuals.

The recommended way to handle an end of file condition is shown in the skeleton program (see Appendix 1). The method is summarized below.

(a) Define an END-OF-<input-file-name> condition in the WORKING-STORAGE SECTION of the DATA DIVISION as follows:

```
05  END-<input-file-name>        PIC X.
    88  END-OF-<input-file-name>    VALUE "E".
```

The condition END-OF-<input-file-name> will be <u>true</u> if and only if the value "E" is moved to the associated data-item END-<input-file-name>.

(b) Initialize the END-OF-<input-file-name> condition to <u>false</u> at the beginning of the program, in the program skeleton this is done in

INIT-STATE. The initial value can be anything other than "E", in the program skeleton space is chosen as the initial value and so the initialization is:

```
MOVE SPACE TO END-<input-file-name>
```

(c) Whenever a READ statement is executed ensure that the END-OF-<input-file-name> condition is changed to <u>true</u> by the AT END part of the READ. Therefore the program skeleton contains:

```
GET-NEXT-<input-file-name>.
    READ <input-file-name>
        AT END MOVE "E" TO END-<input-file-name>.
```

(d) Ensure that every READ statement can only be executed if END-OF-<input-file-name> is <u>false</u>.

The commonly used program design:

```
get-next-<input-file-name>
until end-of-<input-file-name> do
    . . . . .
   get-next-<input-file-name>
enduntil
```

is constructed so that it is always safe to read the file. If there are no records in the input file then the get-next-<input-file-name> before the <u>until</u> will set end-of-<input-file-name> to <u>true</u> and the loop will not be executed. Otherwise the loop continues until the get-next-<input-file-name> at the end of the loop changes end-of-<input-file-name> to <u>true</u> and the loop terminates.

There is an alternative form of the READ statement:

```
READ <input-file-name> INTO <record-store>
    AT END <end-of-file-action>.
```

If a record is successfully read from the file then it will be copied from the input area to the area defined by <record-store>, which must be in the WORKING-STORAGE SECTION. An example of the use of this alternative form is given in Section 9.4.

<u>Writing to a File</u>

Before any records can be written to a file it must be open for <u>output</u> and any attempt to write to an unopened file will cause an execution error.

The simplest form of the WRITE statement is:

```
WRITE <output-record-name>
```

where <output-record-name> must be the name of a record associated with a file. This means that the FILE SECTION of the DATA DIVISION should include a description of the following form:

```
        FD  <output-file-name>
            LABEL RECORDS OMITTED.
        01  <output-record-name>
            . . . . .
```

The effect of this WRITE statement is to transfer the data stored in the output-area, referenced by <output-record-name>, to the file with which it is associated, <output-file-name>.

Note that a WRITE statement uses the name of a record while read refers to the name of a file.

If there are several records described for a particular file then a different WRITE statement is required for each of them. However, these records are not independent - there is only one output-area for the file shared by all the records. It is similar to describing one record and then regarding all subsequent records as redefining this original record.

The recommended style for writing records, used in the skeleton program, is to define a single record associated with the output file and use an alternative form of the WRITE statement:

```
WRITE <output-record-name> FROM <record-name>
```

where <output-record-name> is the name of a record associated with a file and <record-name> is a data structure described in the WORKING-STORAGE SECTION of the program.

The program still requires a WRITE statement for each different record described but the records are now independent and can, if necessary, be built up in parallel. This approach also avoids another problem, often encountered in beginners' programs, when the record output to the file contains a mixture of two or more records built up in the program.

The different records described in the WORKING-STORAGE SECTION do not have to be the same length because the effect of WRITE . . . FROM is the same as:

```
MOVE <record-name> TO <output-record-name>
WRITE <output-record-name>
```

The MOVE statement will follow the rules for a group move, explained in Section 4.2. This means that if WRITE . . . FROM is used properly the output-area will be padded with blanks for records which are shorter than the length specified in the description of <output-record-name>.

The special operation PUT-BLANK-LINE makes use of this blank padding. The record BLANK-LINE is defined as follows:

```
01  BLANK-LINE      PIC X  VALUE SPACE.
```

and the associated operation is defined as:

```
PUT-BLANK-LINE.
    WRITE OUT-LINE FROM BLANK-LINE.
```

The effect of this is to move a single blank to OUT-LINE and then fill the remainder of OUT-LINE with blanks, giving a blank line of the appropriate length to be output.

When a program commences execution the values of all data-items are undefined unless they have been given values using a VALUE clause. Therefore a record structure consisting of only variable data and FILLER data-items without values could contain any characters when the program starts executing. To ensure that the record starts with a 'clean slate' the initialization procedure, INIT-STATE, should include:

```
MOVE SPACES TO <record-name>
```

This will ensure that all the FILLER data-items in <record-name> will be correctly initialized to blanks. If there is more than one record containing only variable data and FILLER data-items then each of them should be initialized in INIT-STATE. This can be done using a special form of the MOVE statement:

```
MOVE SPACES TO <record-name-1> <record-name-2>
          . . . . . <record-name-n>
```

Having ensured that all records are correctly initialized it is also necessary to ensure that each new output record being built starts from a properly initialized state. The simplest way to do this is to re-initialize the area defined by <record-name> each time a record is written. Therefore the recommended definition of the put operation is:

```
PUT-<record-name>.
    WRITE OUT-LINE FROM <record-name>
    MOVE SPACES TO <record-name>.
```

This should ensure that each record is built up independently of the previous record output.

Record structures, such as headings, containing VALUE clauses to initialize all or part of the record must not be re-initialized otherwise all the values will disappear. Therefore they are not referenced in INIT-STATE and the put operation for these records will be of the form:

```
PUT-<constant-record>.
    WRITE OUT-LINE FROM <constant-record>.
```

8.5 Lines and Pages

The discussion in Section 8.4 about writing to a file applies to any serial output file. In general, the execution of a WRITE statement causes a record to be written to the output file immediately following the last record written. Therefore to output blank lines to the lineprinter the method has been to write complete blank records into the output file.

The WRITE statement allows a series of options specifically for the control of the vertical spacing on a lineprinter. The use of these options makes the output process more efficient and also provides pagination which is difficult writing one line at a time.

There are two forms of vertical control possible with the WRITE statement: the paper can be moved <u>after</u> a line has been printed or <u>before</u> it is printed.

The general form of the first of these WRITE statements is:

```
WRITE <output-record-name> FROM <record-name>
     AFTER ADVANCING <number> LINES
```

where <number> can be either an integer constant or the name of a data-item containing an integer value. The number of lines specified must be positive or zero. It should only be necessary to use zero lines in exceptional circumstances and it is strongly recommended that the beginner avoids this option.

The effect of this statement is to advance the paper by the specified number of lines and then print the current contents of <record-name>. The statement:

```
WRITE <output-record-name> FROM <record-name>
     AFTER ADVANCING 1 LINES
```

will have the same effect as a WRITE statement without the line-control option - the record will be printed on the line immediately below the last one. A single blank line between the current record and the preceding one can be achieved by:

```
WRITE <output-record-name> FROM <record-name>
     AFTER ADVANCING 2 LINES
```

The words ADVANCING and LINES are optional and can be omitted if desired.

The alternative is to print a record before moving the paper and so there is the general form:

```
WRITE <output-record-name> FROM <record-name>
     BEFORE ADVANCING <number> LINES
```

Apart from the timing of the paper movement, the rules are similar to the AFTER option. If <number> has the value one then again this is equivalent to the default action of the current line immediately following the last.

To ensure that a blank line follows the current record being printed the WRITE statement should be of the form:

```
WRITE <output-record-name> FROM <record-name>
     BEFORE ADVANCING 2 LINES
```

To start printing at the top of a new page the reserved word PAGE can be used instead of specifying the number of lines. There are two options:

(a)

```
WRITE <output-record-name> FROM <record-name>
     AFTER ADVANCING PAGE
```

(b)

```
WRITE <output-record-name> FROM <record-name>
     BEFORE ADVANCING PAGE
```

With format (a) the contents of <record-name> are printed at the top of a new page, while format (b) prints the contents of <record-name> and then throws a page.

It is safest to choose either the before or after option and use the option chosen consistently throughout the program. This will avoid some of the disasters which frequently occur when mixing the two options. Some implementations of COBOL force the user to choose by specifying that only one of the options may be used within a given output file. The convention used in this book will be to use the after advancing format where appropriate.

Suppose that a program is required to start its output at the top of a new page and write a main heading, described in MAIN-HEADING, followed by two blank lines and two lines of subheadings, called SUB-HEADING-1 and SUB-HEADING-2. A blank line should precede the first detail line in the report.

The following structure should achieve what is required:

```
PRINT-PAGE-HEADINGS.
    PERFORM PUT-MAIN-HEADING
    PERFORM PUT-SUB-HEADINGS
    PERFORM PUT-BLANK-LINE.

PUT-MAIN-HEADING.
    WRITE OUT-LINE FROM MAIN-HEADING
        AFTER ADVANCING PAGE.

PUT-SUB-HEADINGS.
    WRITE OUT-LINE FROM SUB-HEADING-1
        AFTER ADVANCING 3 LINES
    WRITE OUT-LINE FROM SUB-HEADING-2
        AFTER ADVANCING 1 LINES.

PUT-BLANK-LINE.
    WRITE OUT-LINE FROM BLANK-LINE
        AFTER ADVANCING 1 LINES.
```

Although AFTER ADVANCING 1 LINES is not strictly necessary it is wise to use AFTER ADVANCING in all WRITE statements for a file if it is used in any of them.

There is a temptation to replace the WRITE statement for SUB-HEADING-2 with a WRITE . . . BEFORE but this will lead to the two subheadings appearing on the same line.

Having discussed how to throw a new page, the next stage is to consider how to break a long output report into pages, each with its own heading. Suppose that a program is producing a report consisting of a lot of detail lines, each line being produced by a standard put operation as follows:

```
PUT-DETAIL-RECORD.
    WRITE OUT-LINE FROM DETAIL-RECORD
        AFTER ADVANCING 1 LINES
    MOVE SPACES TO DETAIL-RECORD.
```

The preceding example showed how to output the headings at the top of a new page at the beginning of the output. Now suppose that the number of lines per page is restricted to 50 and that after 50 lines have been printed a new page should be started with a complete set of headings.

The first thing that is required is a counter to record the number of lines currently printed. This could be called LINES-PRINTED and its description should be added to STATE-VECTOR since it reflects the state of the program. For example:

```
01  STATE-VECTOR.
    . . . . .
    05  LINES-PRINTED        PIC 99.
```

Since the maximum number of lines to be printed is 50 two digits will be sufficient for the counter. Every time a new page is started LINES-PRINTED will need to be re-initialized. Therefore PRINT-PAGE-HEADINGS could be modified as follows:

```
PRINT-PAGE-HEADINGS.
    PERFORM PUT-MAIN-HEADING
    PERFORM PUT-SUB-HEADINGS
    PERFORM PUT-BLANK-LINE
    MOVE 6 TO LINES-PRINTED.
```

The counter LINES-PRINTED could be incremented by each separate put operation but as a short cut it can simply be reset to the number of lines printed in the headings. This is possible because, in this case, the headings are always printed as a group. The initial value of LINES-PRINTED should be set to zero in INIT-STATE.

It is now necessary to modify PUT-DETAIL-RECORD to print headings for a new page when necessary and to increment the counter LINES-PRINTED by one for each line printed. The modified form of the put operation might be:

```
PUT-DETAIL-RECORD.
    IF LINES-PRINTED = 50
        PERFORM PRINT-PAGE-HEADINGS.
    WRITE OUT-LINE FROM DETAIL-RECORD
        AFTER ADVANCING 1 LINES
    MOVE SPACES TO DETAIL-RECORD
    COMPUTE LINES-PRINTED = LINES-PRINTED + 1.
```

This operation could obviously also be coded so that the output record is printed and the count incremented before the test for a new page is made. The coding shown above is better because it only prints a new page heading if it is required; that is when there is an output record to print. The alternative method can give headings with no detail lines on the final page - this causes people to wonder whether something is missing or an error has occurred.

There is a special module in COBOL called the Report-Writer which, as the name suggests, provides facilities for laying out reports. It is quite a complex feature and discussion of it is not possible within the scope of this book. In the ANS '74 standard the Report-Writer module is optional and may not be implemented on smaller systems.

8.6 Input Records of Differing Types

It is possible to have a file containing different types of input records. For example, an order file might contain an order heading record, containing customer details, followed by a number of detail records, each containing the details of an order for one type of item.

A major problem when reading a file containing two or more types of record is that it is only possible to decide the type of the next record in the file by reading it. This means that any program which depends on a particular ordering or association of the record types will be difficult to design.

The description of a file containing two or more types of records was mentioned briefly in 8.3, above. As an example, consider a finance company's file containing pairs of records, the first record containing the customer's personal details and the second record containing confidential financial data. This could be implemented as a file called CUSTOMER-FILE which contains two types of records called CUSTOMER-PERSONAL and CUSTOMER-FINANCE. Then the file description would be of the form:

```
FD  CUSTOMER-FILE
    LABEL RECORDS OMITTED.
01  CUSTOMER-PERSONAL
    . . . . .
01  CUSTOMER-FINANCE
    . . . . .
```

There is only one input-area associated with the file and so the record descriptions co-exist as if CUSTOMER-FINANCE redefines the area occupied by CUSTOMER-PERSONAL. Therefore when a record is read from the file its contents are put into the input-area and a means of distinguishing the two record types is required.

The standard 'trick' is to allocate one data-item, which identifies the record-type, in the same fixed position in each record. By testing the value of this data-item it can be decided which type of record has been read. The simplest thing is to allocate the first data-item to define the record type. Therefore in the example of the CUSTOMER-FILE, the records could be defined as follows:

```
01  CUSTOMER-PERSONAL.
    05  CUSTOMER-REC-TYPE       PIC 9.
    . . . . .
01  CUSTOMER-FINANCE.
    05  FILLER                  PIC 9.
    . . . . .
```

The second and subsequent record types do not need a named data-item in the common position because the records are all sharing the same input-area. A reference to CUSTOMER-REC-TYPE refers to the same position in every record, no matter how many different records are defined.

In many cases this technique of using a shared data-item is extended to include a second common data-item to identify the contents of associated records. In the example above it could be very embarrassing if a finance record for one customer was appended to the personal details of another. Therefore each record might also contain a customer number in a common position. For example:

```
01  CUSTOMER-PERSONAL.
    05  CUSTOMER-REC-TYPE          PIC 9.
    05  CUSTOMER-NUMBER            PIC 9(6).
    . . . . .
01  CUSTOMER-FINANCE.
    05  FILLER                     PIC 9.
    05  FILLER                     PIC 9(6).
    . . . . .
```

Having ascertained which record type has been read the program must then use the appropriate descriptions to access the non-common data-items within the records. For example:

```
01  CUSTOMER-PERSONAL.
    05  CUSTOMER-REC-TYPE          PIC 9.
    05  CUSTOMER-NUMBER            PIC 9(6).
    05  CUSTOMER-P-NAME            PIC X(30).
    . . . . .
01  CUSTOMER-FINANCE.
    05  FILLER                     PIC 9.
    05  FILLER                     PIC 9(6).
    05  CUSTOMER-F-SALARY          PIC 9(5)V99.
    05  CUSTOMER-F-LOAN            PIC 9(4).
    . . . . .
```

Suppose that CUSTOMER-PERSONAL is identified by type one and CUSTOMER-FINANCE by type two. If CUSTOMER-REC-TYPE equals one then all subsequent references should be to data-items defined in CUSTOMER-PERSONAL, for example CUSTOMER-P-NAME. Alternatively, if CUSTOMER-REC-TYPE equals two then references should be to data-items which are common to both record types or within CUSTOMER-FINANCE, for example CUSTOMER-F-SALARY and CUSTOMER-F-LOAN.

Note that attempting to treat a type one record as a type two record, or vice-versa, will result in disaster because the types of the data-items are completely dissimilar.

The different records belonging to a file may not be all of the same length. The size of the input area for the file will be chosen to accommodate the largest record defined for the file. How the data are actually represented in a file, when record lengths vary, will depend upon the implementation of COBOL. In most systems the simplest way of presenting the data is to 'pad' all records out to the same length.

The use of different types of input records within one input file will affect the program structure. So far the examples and exercises have dealt with a single record type and have been based on the design structure:

```
get-next-<input-file-name>
until end-of-<input-file-name> do
   <process-record>
   get-next-<input-file-name>
enduntil
```

Continuing with the example outlined above, suppose that a program is required to process the record types in pairs, mixing data from them to produce some unspecified output. A first approximation to the program design might be:

```
get-next-customer-file
until end-of-customer-file do
   if customer-rec-type = 1 then
      process-personal
   else
      process-finance
   endif
   get-next-customer-file
enduntil
```

In the refinement 'process-personal' the appropriate processing for a type one record (CUSTOMER-PERSONAL) would be defined. This would probably include storing some of the data from this record to be combined with data from the matching type two record (CUSTOMER-FINANCE). In the refinement 'process-finance' the processing for a type two record would then be developed.

There are a number of problems with this structure:

(a) if the data-item 'customer-rec-type' contains an invalid value then the record will be treated as a type two record,
(b) the program does not check that a type two record has been preceded by a type one record,
(c) the program should ensure that a type two record belongs to the preceding type one record, if any.

The solution to problem (a) is quite straightforward - instead of assuming that a record which is not type one must be of type two the program should include an explicit test for type two. So the program structure becomes:

```
get-next-customer-file
until end-of-customer-file do
   if customer-rec-type = 1 then
      process-personal
   else
      if customer-rec-type = 2 then
         process-finance
      else
         record-type-error
      endif
   endif
   get-next-customer-file
enduntil
```

The refinement 'record-type-error' should specify the action to be taken when an invalid type occurs in the input. This might be printing the contents of the record and an appropriate error message.

The solution to problem (b) is to record the current state of the input. The essential piece of information is whether a type one record is being held, awaiting a type two record, or not. Therefore, a Boolean data-item 'type-1-held' can be defined, which is true if a type one record has been found and not yet matched with a type two record, and false otherwise. This data-item will need to be initialized to false at the beginning of the program, set to true whenever a type one record is found and reset to false whenever a type two record is successfully processed. There are two special cases when a type two record is missing: if a type one record is read and 'type-1-held' is already true, or at the end of the program if 'type-1-held' is true.

The incorporation of this Boolean data-item leads to the following program structure:

```
transfer false to type-1-held
get-next-customer-file
until end-of-customer-file do
   if customer-rec-type = 1 then
      process-personal
   else
      if customer-rec-type = 2 then
         process-finance
      else
         record-type-error
      endif
   endif
   get-next-customer-file
enduntil
if type-1-held then
   error-no-type-2
endif

process-personal
   if type-1-held then
      error-no-type-2
   endif
   transfer true to type-1-held
    .....

process-finance
   transfer false to type-1-held
    .....
```

This still leaves problem (c) outstanding - how can the program ensure that it only processes the type two record which belongs to the type one record being held? The solution is that whenever a type one record is 'held' the value of the associated 'customer-number' must also be stored. (This may be done as part of 'process-personal' anyway.) Whenever a type two record is encountered its customer-number must be checked to see that it matches the customer-number of the type one record being held. If the customer-numbers match then processing can proceed; otherwise there is an error, and the type two record should be rejected. The modified refinements for 'process-personal' and 'process-finance' are shown below.

```
process-personal
   if type-1-held then
      error-no-type-2
   endif
   transfer true to type-1-held
   transfer customer-number to customer-number-held
    .....
```

```
process-finance
   if customer-number = customer-number-held then
      transfer false to type-1-held
      deal-with-type-2
   else
      error-no-type-1
   endif
```

The refinement 'deal-with-type-2' is where the processing of a properly matched type two record will be defined. The refinement 'error-no-type-1' should specify the action to be taken when a type two record follows a type one record but the customer-numbers do not match.

Note that this design is 'driven' by the type one records - a type one record has to be found followed by the corresponding type two record. No attempt is made to hold a type two record in the hope that a corresponding type one will appear.

This example will not be developed any further, but the reader might continue the development as an exercise. The example was included mainly to give the reader some insight into the difficulties of designing programs to use input files with different types of records. It also demonstrates how much thought needs to go into the solution of an apparently simple problem.

The above example also shows that perhaps an alternative basic program structure might be better for this type of problem. A more generally useful model for this type of program follows in the case study in the next section.

8.7 Case Study

This case study explores a problem concerned with the processing of a file containing different types of input records. The general structure of the input file is that data consists of groups of records, or 'batches', each batch relating to one customer. This grouping of records appears quite frequently in commercial data processing applications. The specification of the problem is given below.

> The input to a program which produces monthly statements for customers of XYZ Booksellers consists of three types of records:

Account record	
record type	1
account number	2 letters and 4 digits
customer name	25 characters
balance brought forward	5 digits, pence, signed

Sales record	
record type	2
account number	as above
date of transaction	8 characters (DD/MM/YY)
invoice reference number	1 letter and 4 digits
price charged	4 digits, pence

Payment record	
record type	3
account number	as above
date of payment	as Sales record above
receipt code	1 letter and 3 digits
amount received	5 digits, pence

A 'batch' of input for a particular account consists of an account record followed by a mixture of sales and payment records. If there were no transactions in the last month then a type one record will appear without any associated records of type two or three.

The records are input in batches with the type one records preceding the type two or type three records, if any. The type two and type three records for an account are entered in the order in which they occurred so that they can appear in date order on the statement. The data has already been processed by a simple data validation program which has checked that the data-items all have valid values. The data validation program does not guarantee that there are no type two or three records without corresponding type one records.

An example of a batch of input might be:

```
1 AA0012 JOE BLOGGS                00695
3 AA0012 03/07/82 C016 00695
2 AA0012 08/07/82 G0003 1525
2 AA0012 17/07/82 T0010 2695
3 AA0012 25/07/82 C345 01525
```

Note that the data-items have been separated by spaces to make the data more readable. The values would normally appear contiguously in the actual input record unless blank areas were defined in the specification.

The program that is required should produce a statement for each account. Each statement should appear on a separate page with suitable headings followed by: the balance brought forward, details of the transactions and the balance carried forward. The program should reject any type two or type three records which do not belong to the current batch. It is not necessary to check that the records are actually in date order. The output corresponding to the sample batch of data given above might be:

XYZ BOOKSELLERS

ACCOUNT: AA0012 NAME: JOE BLOGGS

DATE	REFERENCE NO.	CREDIT	DEBIT	BALANCE
	BALANCE FWD			£6.95
03/07/82	C016	£6.95		£0.00
08/07/82	G0003		£15.25	£15.25
17/07/82	T0010		£26.95	£42.20
25/07/82	C345	£15.25		£26.95
	AMOUNT DUE			£26.95

This problem has been deliberately simplified to exclude updating the balance in the account record. The general problem of sequential file updating will be considered in the next chapter.

To start solving this problem it is probably best to allocate names to all the input data-items to avoid any confusion that might arise from using common data-items and different records. A suggested naming scheme is:

account-record

account-rec-type	type of record, common to all records
account-number	customer's account number, common
account-a-name	customer's name
account-a-balance	account balance brought forward

sales-record

account-s-date	date of sale transaction
account-s-inv-num	invoice number for sale
account-s-price	amount of sales invoice

payment-record

account-p-date	date of payment
account-p-rec-code	receipt code for payment
account-p-amount	amount paid

The naming convention used is that common data-items are prefixed solely by the file-name while the data-items specific to a record type are prefixed by the file-name and a letter to indicate the record type. In the description of the second and third records there will need to be fillers for spacing but these do not affect the program design.

It would be possible to have only two record types, combining the sales and payment records using redefinition within a common record. However, these records are defined separately to emphasize their differences and improve the clarity of the program.

This problem no longer fits the pattern of earlier problems explored in this book. The records are no longer independent of one another and so a different structure for the program is required. The main unit of data which drives the program is a batch of records relating to one account. The top level of the program design could be:

```
print-statements
    find-type-1
    until end-of-account-file do
        process-batch
    enduntil
```

The program needs to ignore any records preceding the first type one (account) record as these are obviously erroneous. Once the first type one record is found, the program should process the data batch by batch. Note that there are no headings printed at the beginning of the program - the headings are associated with each batch of input.

The simplest refinement of 'find-type-1' is:

```
find-type-1
    get-next-account-file
    until account-rec-type = 1 do
        error-type-1-expected
        get-next-account-file
        enduntil
```

If the program is to work for all sets of input data then this refinement is not good enough. The design given above will not work if there are no type one records in the input. The until account-rec-type = 1 loop will never terminate and the program will run off the end of the file. To guard against this remote possibility the following structure is suggested:

```
find-type-1
    transfer false to searchover
    until searchover do
        get-next-account-file
        if end-of-account-file then
            transfer true to searchover
        else
            if account-rec-type = 1 then
                transfer true to searchover
            else
                error-type-1-expected
            endif
        endif
    enduntil
```

The exit from the loop should occur either when a type one record is found or the end of file is encountered. The loop:

```
until end-of-account-file or account-rec-type = 1 do
```

might be considered but the second condition is not testable if the first is true (see Section 6.5). Therefore a Boolean data-item, 'searchover', is used which is initialized to false and becomes true when either of the terminating conditions occurs.

To complete this part of the program the refinement of 'error-type-1-expected' can be specified at this point. To avoid mixing up messages about input errors with the printing of statements it is desirable to output these error messages to a different file, or output device, from the statements. The use of an alternative output file is discussed in Chapter 9. For the purposes of this case study the display statement, introduced in Section 7.2, can be used to identify error records. Therefore the refinement could be:

```
error-type-1-expected
   display "type 1 record expected - found ",
      account-rec-type, "  ", account-number
```

The display statement is intended only for "low-volume" output and in this case since the data has been partially validated the number of errors should be low.

The refinement of 'process-batch' also requires a loop with two terminating conditions. The end of a batch of input is normally marked by the occurrence of a new type one record but the last batch is terminated by the end of file. Again a Boolean data-item should be used to control the loop and a possible refinement is:

```
process-batch
   print-headings
   store-account-details
   get-next-account-file
   set-batch-complete
   until batch-complete do
      process-detail-record
      get-next-account-file
      set-batch-complete
   enduntil
   print-amount-due
```

At the beginning of each batch it is necessary to write the headings for the batch. It is also necessary to store any details required from the type one record because the input area will be overwritten by the next record read from the file. The processing of the current batch continues until the Boolean 'batch-complete' becomes <u>true</u>. At the end of the batch the final line of the statement is printed by 'print-amount-due'.

The refinement 'set-batch-complete' has to give a value to the Boolean batch-complete according to the current status of the input file. The refinement could be:

```
set-batch-complete
   if end-of-account-file then
      transfer true to batch-complete
   else
      if account-rec-type = 1 then
         transfer true to batch-complete
      else
         transfer false to batch-complete
      endif
```

An alternative approach, which leads to a rather neater program structure, is simply to assume that the batch is incomplete on entry to the <u>until</u> loop. The loop then starts by attempting to get the next record and deals with the current situation either by setting 'batch-complete' to <u>true</u> or processing a detail record. The refinement of 'process-batch' is then:

```
process-batch
    print-headings
    store-account-details
    transfer false to batch-complete
    until batch-complete do
        get-next-account-file
        deal-with-current-record
    enduntil
    print-amount-due
```

The first action to be refined is 'print-headings' and this could be:

```
print-headings
    put-page-heading (after page throw)
    print-account-heading
    put-column-headings (after one blank line)
    print-balance forward
```

The comments in brackets are not necessary for the program design but will remind one what is required when translating the design into COBOL.

Continuing the development of this part of the program, it is necessary to define data-items to hold the account number and customer's name in the account heading. For example:

```
account-heading
    acc-head-number          account number
    acc-head-name            customer's name
```

The refinement of 'print-account-heading' could then be:

```
print-account-heading
    transfer account-number to acc-head-number
    transfer account-a-name to acc-head-name
    put-account-heading (after two blank lines)
```

Similarly 'print-balance-forward' can be refined after defining a suitable output record. Looking ahead a little it can be seen that the lines for the balance brought forward and the amount due are similar in content and use and therefore a common output record could be defined:

```
balance-line
    balance-l-text           appropriate text for line
    balance-l-amount         balance to be printed
```

The refinement then becomes:

```
print-balance-forward
    transfer "balance fwd" to balance-l-text
    transfer account-a-balance to balance-l-amount
    put-balance-line (after one blank-line)
```

Going back to 'process-batch' the next refinement required is 'store-account-details' which needs to copy to temporary data-items any data from the type one record which is needed during the processing of the batch. There are two such data-items 'account-number' and 'account-a-balance' and these should be copied to corresponding temporary data-items, for example:

```
temporary-items
   current-account-number  account number for batch
   current-balance         balance to be updated

store-account-details
   transfer account-number to current-account-number
   transfer account-a-balance to current-balance
```

The next refinement required is 'deal-with-current-record' which is really the heart of the program. This refinement needs to establish whether the batch is complete and if not process a detail record for the batch. The next level of refinement could be:

```
deal-with-current-record
   if end-of-account-file then
      transfer true to batch-complete
   else
      if account-rec-type = 1 then
         transfer true to batch-complete
      else
         process-detail-record
      endif
   endif
```

To process a detail record the program needs to check that the record belongs to the current batch and if so then either process a sale or a payment. Therefore the refinement could be:

```
process-detail-record
   if account-number not = current-account-number then
      error-invalid-account-number
   else
      if account-rec-type = 2 then
         process-sale
      else
         process-receipt
      endif
   endif
```

The data validation program should have ensured that only records of type one, two or three reach this program and so an explicit test for type three should not be required. The invalid account numbers can be dealt with by using display statements in a similar way to the earlier error routine:

```
error-invalid-account-number
   display "invalid account number"
   display "found: ", account-number, " in batch for: ",
      current-account-number
```

To refine 'process-sale' it is necessary to decide on the names for the output data items in the detail line printed for each transaction.

Separate records could be defined for sales and payments but the two lines are sufficiently similar that a common output record can be used. For example:

```
transaction-line
   trans-date                  date of transaction
   trans-inv-num == trans-rec-code
   trans-credit                amount of credit, if any
   trans-debit                 amount of debit, if any
   trans-balance               updated balance

where:
   trans-inv-num               invoice number for sale
   trans-rec-code              receipt code for payment
```

The format of the invoice numbers and receipt codes differ only slightly and therefore these data-items can share one area using redefinition.

The refinements of 'process-sale' and 'process-receipt' are now quite straightforward:

```
process-sale
   calculate current-balance = current-balance + account-s-price
   transfer account-s-date to trans-date
   transfer account-s-inv-num to trans-inv-num
   transfer account-s-price to trans-debit
   transfer current-balance to trans-balance
   put-transaction-line

process-receipt
   calculate current-balance = current-balance - account-p-amount
   transfer account-p-date to trans-date
   transfer account-p-rec-code to trans-rec-code
   transfer account-p-amount to trans-credit
   transfer current-balance to trans-balance
   put-transaction-line
```

The final refinement required to complete the program design is 'print-amount-due' which produces the line at the bottom of the statement. The output record for this was defined when considering the headings and so the refinement is:

```
print-amount-due
   transfer "amount-due" to balance-l-text
   transfer current-balance to balance-l-amount
   put-balance-line (after one blank line)
```

The complete program design can now be put together and the whole design, including the record structures is reproduced below.

The input records are:

```
account-record
   account-rec-type            type of record, common to all records
   account-number              customer's account number, common
   account-a-name              customer's name
   account-a-balance           account balance brought forward
```

```
sales-record
   account-s-date          date of sale transaction
   account-s-inv-num       invoice number for sale
   account-s-price         amount of sales invoice

payment-record
   account-p-date          date of payment
   account-p-rec-code      receipt code for payment
   account-p-amount        amount paid
```

The output records are:

```
account-heading
   acc-head-number         account number
   acc-head-name           customer's name

balance-line
   balance-l-text          appropriate text for line
   balance-l-amount        balance to be printed

transaction-line
   trans-date              date of transaction
   trans-inv-num == trans-rec-code
   trans-credit            amount of credit, if any
   trans-debit             amount of debit, if any
   trans-balance           updated balance

where:
   trans-inv-num           invoice number for sale
   trans-rec-code          receipt code for payment
```

In addition descriptions will be required for the constant lines: 'page-heading' and 'column-headings'.

The temporary data-items required by the program are:

```
temporary-items
   current-account-number  account number for batch
   current-balance         balance to be updated
```

In addition to these, two Boolean data-items 'searchover' and 'batch-complete' were used, these should be added to the state-vector.

The complete program design is then:

```
print-statements
   find-type-1
   until end-of-account-file do
      process-batch
   enduntil
```

```
find-type-1
   transfer false to searchover
   until searchover do
      get-next-account-file
      if end-of-account-file then
         transfer true to searchover
      else
         if account-rec-type = 1 then
            transfer true to searchover
         else
            error-type-1-expected
         endif
      endif
   enduntil

error-type-1-expected
   display "type 1 record expected - found ",
      account-rec-type, "  ", account-number

process-batch
   print-headings
   store-account-details
   transfer false to batch-complete
   until batch-complete do
      get-next-account-file
      deal-with-current-record
   enduntil
   print-amount-due

print-headings
   put-page-heading (after page throw)
   print-account-heading
   put-column-headings (after one blank line)
   print-balance forward

print-account-heading
   transfer account-number to acc-head-number
   transfer account-a-name to acc-head-name
   put-account-heading (after two blank lines)

print-balance-forward
   transfer "balance fwd" to balance-l-text
   transfer account-a-balance to balance-l-amount
   put-balance-line (after one blank-line)

store-account-details
   transfer account-number to current-account-number
   transfer account-a-balance to current-balance
```

```
deal-with-current-record
   if end-of-account-file then
      transfer true to batch-complete
   else
      if account-rec-type = 1 then
         transfer true to batch-complete
      else
         process-detail-record
      endif
   endif

process-detail-record
   if account-number not = current-account-number then
      error-invalid-account-number
   else
      if account-rec-type = 2 then
         process-sale
      else
         process-receipt
      endif
   endif

error-invalid-account-number
   display "invalid account number"
   display "found: ", account-number, " in batch for: ",
      current-account-number

process-sale
   calculate current-balance = current-balance + account-s-price
   transfer account-s-date to trans-date
   transfer account-s-inv-num to trans-inv-num
   transfer account-s-price to trans-debit
   transfer current-balance to trans-balance
   put-transaction-line

process-receipt
   calculate current-balance = current-balance - account-p-amount
   transfer account-p-date to trans-date
   transfer account-p-rec-code to trans-rec-code
   transfer account-p-amount to trans-credit
   transfer current-balance to trans-balance
   put-transaction-line

print-amount-due
   transfer "amount-due" to balance-l-text
   transfer current-balance to balance-l-amount
   put-balance-line (after one blank line)
```

The complete COBOL program corresponding to this design is given below.

```
IDENTIFICATION DIVISION.
PROGRAM-ID. BOOKSTAT.
```

```
 ENVIRONMENT DIVISION.
 CONFIGURATION SECTION.
 SOURCE-COMPUTER. <computer-name>.
 OBJECT-COMPUTER. <computer-name>.
*    <computer-name> should be replaced by the name
*    of the computer being used to run programs.

 INPUT-OUTPUT SECTION.
 FILE-CONTROL.
     SELECT ACCOUNT-FILE ASSIGN TO <system-input>.
     SELECT OUTFILE ASSIGN TO <system-output>.
*        <system-input> and <system-output> must conform
*        to the rules for the system being used.

 DATA DIVISION.
 FILE SECTION.
 FD  ACCOUNT-FILE
     LABEL RECORDS OMITTED.
 01  ACCOUNT-RECORD.
     05  ACCOUNT-REC-TYPE           PIC 9.
     05  ACCOUNT-NUMBER.
         10  ACCOUNT-NUM-1          PIC AA.
         10  ACCOUNT-NUM-2          PIC 9999.
     05  ACCOUNT-A-NAME             PIC X(25).
     05  ACCOUNT-A-BALANCE          PIC S999V99.

 01  SALES-RECORD.
     05  FILLER                     PIC 9.
     05  FILLER                     PIC X(6).
     05  ACCOUNT-S-DATE             PIC X(8).
     05  ACCOUNT-S-INV-NUM.
         10  ACCOUNT-S-INV-1        PIC A.
         10  ACCOUNT-S-INV-2        PIC 9999.
     05  ACCOUNT-S-PRICE            PIC 99V99.

 01  PAYMENT-RECORD.
     05  FILLER                     PIC 9.
     05  FILLER                     PIC X(6).
     05  ACCOUNT-P-DATE             PIC X(8).
     05  ACCOUNT-P-REC-CODE.
         10  ACCOUNT-P-REC-1        PIC A.
         10  ACCOUNT-P-REC-2        PIC 999.
     05  ACCOUNT-P-AMOUNT           PIC 999V99.
 FD  OUTFILE
     LABEL RECORDS OMITTED.
 01  OUT-LINE            PIC X(120).

 WORKING-STORAGE SECTION.
 01  STATE-VECTOR.
     05  END-ACCOUNT-FILE           PIC X.
         88  END-OF-ACCOUNT-FILE VALUE "E".
     05  SEARCH-STATE               PIC X.
         88  SEARCHOVER             VALUE "T".
     05  BATCH-STATE                PIC X.
         88  BATCH-COMPLETE         VALUE "T".
```

```
01  TEMPORARY-ITEMS.
    05  CURRENT-ACCOUNT-NUMBER  PIC X(6).
    05  CURRENT-BALANCE         PIC S999V99.

01  PAGE-HEADING.
    05  FILLER        PIC X(19)  VALUE SPACES.
    05  FILLER        PIC X(15)  VALUE
        "XYZ BOOKSELLERS".

01  ACCOUNT-HEADING.
    05  FILLER             PIC X(9)  VALUE "ACCOUNT: ".
    05  ACC-HEAD-NUMBER PIC X(6).
    05  FILLER             PIC X(7)  VALUE SPACES.
    05  FILLER             PIC X(6)  VALUE "NAME: ".
    05  ACC-HEAD-NAME      PIC X(25).

01  COLUMN-HEADINGS.
    05  FILLER        PIC X(8)  VALUE "  DATE  ".
    05  FILLER        PIC X(3)  VALUE SPACES.
    05  FILLER        PIC X(13) VALUE "REFERENCE NO.".
    05  FILLER        PIC X(3)  VALUE SPACES.
    05  FILLER        PIC X(7)  VALUE " CREDIT".
    05  FILLER        PIC X(3)  VALUE SPACES.
    05  FILLER        PIC X(6)  VALUE " DEBIT".
    05  FILLER        PIC X(3)  VALUE SPACES.
    05  FILLER        PIC X(7)  VALUE "BALANCE".

01  TRANSACTION-LINE.
    05  TRANS-DATE              PIC X(8).
    05  FILLER                  PIC X(7).
    05  TRANS-INV-NUM           PIC X(5).
    05  TRANS-REC-ITEM REDEFINES TRANS-INV-NUM.
        10  TRANS-REC-CODE      PIC X(4).
        10  FILLER              PIC X.
    05  FILLER                  PIC X(7).
    05  TRANS-CREDIT            PIC £££9.99.
    05  FILLER                  PIC XXX.
    05  TRANS-DEBIT             PIC ££9.99.
    05  FILLER                  PIC XXX.
    05  TRANS-BALANCE           PIC £££9.99CR.

01  BALANCE-LINE.
    05  FILLER                  PIC X(12).
    05  BALANCE-L-TEXT          PIC X(11).
    05  FILLER                  PIC X(23).
    05  BALANCE-L-AMOUNT        PIC £££9.99CR.
```

```
PROCEDURE DIVISION.
MAIN-PROGRAM.
    PERFORM INIT-STATE
    PERFORM PRINT-STATEMENTS
    PERFORM CLOSE-DOWN.
INIT-STATE.
    MOVE SPACE TO END-ACCOUNT-FILE
    OPEN INPUT ACCOUNT-FILE OUTPUT OUTFILE
    MOVE SPACES TO BALANCE-LINE TRANSACTION-LINE.
CLOSE-DOWN.
    CLOSE ACCOUNT-FILE OUTFILE
    STOP RUN.
GET-NEXT-ACCOUNT-FILE.
    READ ACCOUNT-FILE
        AT END MOVE "E" TO END-ACCOUNT-FILE.
PUT-PAGE-HEADING.
    WRITE OUT-LINE FROM PAGE-HEADING
        AFTER ADVANCING PAGE.
PUT-ACCOUNT-HEADING.
    WRITE OUT-LINE FROM ACCOUNT-HEADING
        AFTER ADVANCING 3 LINES.
PUT-COLUMN-HEADINGS.
    WRITE OUT-LINE FROM COLUMN-HEADINGS
        AFTER ADVANCING 2 LINES.
PUT-BALANCE-LINE.
    WRITE OUT-LINE FROM BALANCE-LINE
        AFTER ADVANCING 2 LINES.
    MOVE SPACES TO BALANCE-LINE.
PUT-TRANSACTION-LINE.
    WRITE OUT-LINE FROM TRANSACTION-LINE
        AFTER ADVANCING 2 LINES.
    MOVE SPACES TO TRANSACTION-LINE.
PRINT-STATEMENTS.
    PERFORM FIND-TYPE-1
    PERFORM PROCESS-BATCH UNTIL END-OF-ACCOUNT-FILE.
FIND-TYPE-1.
    MOVE "F" TO SEARCH-STATE
    PERFORM SEARCH-FOR-1 UNTIL SEARCHOVER.
SEARCH-FOR-1.
    PERFORM GET-NEXT-ACCOUNT-FILE
    IF END-OF-ACCOUNT-FILE
        MOVE "T" TO SEARCH-STATE
    ELSE
        IF ACCOUNT-REC-TYPE = 1
            MOVE "T" TO SEARCH-STATE
        ELSE
            PERFORM ERROR-TYPE-1-EXPECTED.
ERROR-TYPE-1-EXPECTED.
    DISPLAY "TYPE 1 RECORD EXPECTED - FOUND ",
        ACCOUNT-REC-TYPE, " ", ACCOUNT-NUMBER.
PROCESS-BATCH.
    PERFORM PRINT-HEADINGS
    PERFORM STORE-ACCOUNT-DETAILS
    MOVE "F" TO BATCH-STATE
    PERFORM DETAIL-LOOP UNTIL BATCH-COMPLETE
    PERFORM PRINT-AMOUNT-DUE.
```

```
DETAIL-LOOP.
    PERFORM GET-NEXT-ACCOUNT-FILE
    PERFORM DEAL-WITH-CURRENT-RECORD.
PRINT-HEADINGS.
    PERFORM PUT-PAGE-HEADING
    PERFORM PRINT-ACCOUNT-HEADING
    PERFORM PUT-COLUMN-HEADINGS
    PERFORM PRINT-BALANCE-FORWARD.
PRINT-ACCOUNT-HEADING.
    MOVE ACCOUNT-NUMBER TO ACC-HEAD-NUMBER
    MOVE ACCOUNT-A-NAME TO ACC-HEAD-NAME
    PERFORM PUT-ACCOUNT-HEADING.
PRINT-BALANCE-FORWARD.
    MOVE "BALANCE FWD" TO BALANCE-L-TEXT
    MOVE ACCOUNT-A-BALANCE TO BALANCE-L-AMOUNT
    PERFORM PUT-BALANCE-LINE.
STORE-ACCOUNT-DETAILS.
    MOVE ACCOUNT-NUMBER TO CURRENT-ACCOUNT-NUMBER
    MOVE ACCOUNT-A-BALANCE TO CURRENT-BALANCE.
DEAL-WITH-CURRENT-RECORD.
    IF END-OF-ACCOUNT-FILE
        MOVE "T" TO BATCH-STATE
    ELSE
        IF ACCOUNT-REC-TYPE = 1
            MOVE "T" TO BATCH-STATE
        ELSE
            PERFORM PROCESS-DETAIL-RECORD.
PROCESS-DETAIL-RECORD.
    IF ACCOUNT-NUMBER NOT = CURRENT-ACCOUNT-NUMBER
        PERFORM ERROR-INVALID-ACCOUNT-NUMBER
    ELSE
        IF ACCOUNT-REC-TYPE = 2
            PERFORM PROCESS-SALE
        ELSE
            PERFORM PROCESS-RECEIPT.
ERROR-INVALID-ACCOUNT-NUMBER.
    DISPLAY "INVALID ACCOUNT NUMBER"
    DISPLAY "FOUND: ", ACCOUNT-NUMBER,
        " IN BATCH FOR: ", CURRENT-ACCOUNT-NUMBER.
PROCESS-SALE.
    COMPUTE CURRENT-BALANCE
        = CURRENT-BALANCE + ACCOUNT-S-PRICE
    MOVE ACCOUNT-S-DATE TO TRANS-DATE
    MOVE ACCOUNT-S-INV-NUM TO TRANS-INV-NUM
    MOVE ACCOUNT-S-PRICE TO TRANS-DEBIT
    MOVE CURRENT-BALANCE TO TRANS-BALANCE
    PERFORM PUT-TRANSACTION-LINE.
PROCESS-RECEIPT.
    COMPUTE CURRENT-BALANCE
        = CURRENT-BALANCE - ACCOUNT-P-AMOUNT
    MOVE ACCOUNT-P-DATE TO TRANS-DATE
    MOVE ACCOUNT-P-REC-CODE TO TRANS-REC-CODE
    MOVE ACCOUNT-P-AMOUNT TO TRANS-CREDIT
    MOVE CURRENT-BALANCE TO TRANS-BALANCE
    PERFORM PUT-TRANSACTION-LINE.
```

```
PRINT-AMOUNT-DUE.
    MOVE "AMOUNT DUE" TO BALANCE-L-TEXT
    MOVE CURRENT-BALANCE TO BALANCE-L-AMOUNT
    PERFORM PUT-BALANCE-LINE.
```

An example of an input file is given below. The data-items are separated by spaces for readability but for input to the above program should be typed without spaces between items.

```
3 QB0012 23/08/82 C003 00100
1 SU0358 STRATHCLYDE UNIVERSITY    05825
2 SU0358 02/08/82 G0351 1250
2 SU0358 05/08/82 T0057 2760
3 SU0358 08/08/82 C025 05825
2 SU0358 09/08/82 M1087 4368
2 SU0388 12/08/82 T0066 2205
3 SU0358 15/08/82 C073 10583
2 SU0358 18/08/82 M1095 2870
1 RW0001 R.C.WELLAND               00295
<end-of-input>
```

The output corresponding to these batches of input should consist of two error messages and two printed statements in the form shown below.

```
TYPE 1 RECORD EXPECTED - FOUND 3 QB0012
INVALID ACCOUNT NUMBER
FOUND: SU0388 IN BATCH FOR: SU0358

- - - - - - - - - - - - - - - - - - - - - - - - - - -

                  XYZ BOOKSELLERS


ACCOUNT: SU0358        NAME: STRATHCLYDE UNIVERSITY

  DATE     REFERENCE NO.    CREDIT     DEBIT    BALANCE

            BALANCE FWD                          £58.25
02/08/82       G0351                   £12.50    £70.75
05/08/82       T0057                   £27.60    £98.35
08/08/82       C025        £58.25                £40.10
09/08/82       M1087                   £43.68    £83.78
15/08/82       C073       £105.83                £20.05CR
18/08/82       M1095                   £28.70     £8.65

            AMOUNT DUE                            £8.65
```

- -

```
                    XYZ BOOKSELLERS

ACCOUNT: RW0001        NAME: R.C.WELLAND

  DATE     REFERENCE NO.    CREDIT    DEBIT   BALANCE

             BALANCE FWD                        £2.95

             AMOUNT DUE                         £2.95
```

Exercises 8

8.1. In order to check that no statements are lost, either accidentally or deliberately, XYZ Booksellers wish to number the statement pages consecutively. Consider how the design and the COBOL program given in Section 8.7 could be modified to add a page number at: (a) the top of each statement page, or, (b) the bottom of each statement page.

8.2. The specification for the problem in the case study discussed in Section 8.7 is modified to include an extra transaction record, type four. This record is a 'trailer' record for a batch and therefore a batch should now consist of: a type one record, any number of type two or three records, and a type four record. A batch may consist of a type one record followed by a type four record if there are no sales in the current month. The type four record contains the following data-items:

```
Trailer record
   record type                    4
   account number                 2 letters and 4 digits
   balance carried forward        5 digits, pence, signed
```

The program design and the COBOL program have to be modified as follows:

(a) an error is signalled if a batch does not terminate with a type four record,
(b) an error is signalled if the final balance calculated differs from the balance carried forward given in the type four record.

In each case the amount due printed on the statement should be that calculated for the batch.

Work through the program design in Section 8.7 and consider the changes which would be required to implement this new feature.

8.3. The following extracts are taken from a program written by a beginner who has not been reading this book.

```
. . . . .
DATA DIVISION.
FILE SECTION.
FD  CUSTOMER-FILE
    LABEL RECORDS STANDARD.
01  CUSTOMER-RECORD.
    05  CUSTOMER-ID      PIC 9(6).
    . . . . .

PROCEDURE DIVISION.
START-OFF.
    OPEN INPUT CUSTOMER-FILE OUTPUT PRINT-FILE
    MOVE 0 TO CUSTOMER-ID
    PERFORM PROCESS-CUSTOMER
        UNTIL CUSTOMER-ID = 999999
    . . . . .

PROCESS-CUSTOMER.
    READ CUSTOMER-FILE
        AT END MOVE 999999 TO CUSTOMER-ID.
    IF CUSTOMER-ID NOT = 999999
        PERFORM PROCESS-CURRENT-RECORD.
SOMETHING-ELSE.
    . . . . .
```

Explain why the loop PROCESS-CUSTOMER will not terminate correctly when end of file is reached.

8.4. Look back at the case study in Section 6.7 and consider how to include lineprinter control to give better output. The billing lines should be printed double spaced and a new page, with full headings, should be started each time 25 billing lines have been printed.

Programming Exercises 8

8.5. Input to a billing program for Brickbats Builders Merchants is in batches, each batch consisting of a delivery record followed by a number of item sale records. The contents of the records are as follows.

```
Delivery record
   record type              D
   invoice number           1 letter and 4 digits
   account number           8 digits
   customer name           25 characters
   delivery address        50 characters
   discount rate            2 digits
   payment method          AC - account
                           CP - cash paid
                           CD - cash on delivery
```

Item sale	
record type	I
invoice number	as above
item number	6 digits
quantity ordered	3 digits
retail price per item	5 digits, pence

Design and implement a COBOL program to make up an account for each batch. A batch must contain a delivery record and at least one item sale record. Any item sale record whose invoice number does not match that of the current delivery record should be rejected with a suitable error message (using DISPLAY).

Each account should be produced on a separate page with a suitable heading. For example:

```
                    BRICKBATS BUILDERS MERCHANTS


    INVOICE NO: R1001                 ACCOUNT NUMBER: 00001329

    NAME: R.BRUCE                          DISCOUNT RATE: 12%

    DELIVER TO: 1314, BANNOCKBURN ROAD, STIRLING

    ITEM NO.    QUANTITY    RETAIL PRICE    DISCOUNTED PRICE

     000001        100           £1.00              £88.00
     123456         12           £0.15               £1.58
     346700          3          £12.50              £33.00
     001245          1         £225.00             £198.00
     643218          7           £0.93               £5.73

                            TOTAL SALE             £326.31
                            VAT AT 15%              £48.95

                            AMOUNT DUE             £375.26
```

Any monetary calculation that does not yield a whole number of pence should be rounded to the nearest whole number. An account for a cash on delivery sale should have the words "CASH ON DELIVERY" added underneath the amount due.

9 Multiple Files

The model of the computer introduced in Chapter 1, and used in subsequent chapters, was based on the assumption that the machine has only one input file and one output file. This assumption underlies the program structure shown in Appendix 1 which has provided a sufficient framework for a number of different types of programs.

In this chapter the structure of programs that use more than one input file or more than one output file is considered. The previous chapter described the general guidelines for using files in a program and these guidelines are applied to show how to use multiple input or output files safely.

When a program uses two or more input files, these normally need to be combined in some way, to produce the output from the program. This can cause problems in devising a safe control structure for the program. In most cases the input files will be _ordered_, and this leads to one of the standard problems of commercial data processing - the _serial file update_. Two general solutions to this problem are outlined and compared, and the case study for this chapter gives an example of an application of this technique.

9.1 Multiple Input and Output Files

The description of the "COBOL Computer" in Section 1.1 assumed that the machine consumed a single file of records and produced a single output file of records. This model has already been slightly modified by the introduction, in Section 7.2, of the DISPLAY statement which allows low volume output to be directed to a third output channel.

The extension of the abstract machine to include multiple input and output files is quite straightforward. The program skeleton, given in Appendix 1, which has been used as the basis of all programs discussed so far, can also be quite simply extended to allow multi-file input and output. Most of the problems occur in trying to construct safe programs for handling multi-file input.

Each input file to a program will have its own input area that is independent of the areas associated with other files. The state of an input file can be defined using a separate end of file condition for each input file. Similarly, each output file has its own output area that is independent of the areas associated with other files. This is true even if there are two or more output files being directed to the lineprinter. The lines being sent to the two files will not be interleaved because the operating software for the computer will ensure that the two files appear separately.

Multiple Input Files

From Sections 8.2, 8.3 and 8.4 it is possible to collect together a set of guidelines for describing and using an input file, within the program skeleton given in Appendix 1. These guidelines for setting up an input file are summarized below.

(a) ENVIRONMENT DIVISION - each input file to be processed must be specified in a select clause of the form:

```
            SELECT <input-file-name>
                ASSIGN TO <external-file-name>.
```

The <input-file-name> is the internal name of the file which will be used to reference this file throughout the program and is constructed according to the rules for user-defined names (see 3.2). The <external-file-name> specifies the name of an actual file and the format of this name depends on the system being used.

(b) DATA DIVISION - each file must have a file description and one or more associated record descriptions in the FILE SECTION. It should also have an end of file flag defined in the WORKING-STORAGE SECTION. The general form of the file description is:

```
        FD  <input-file-name>
            LABEL RECORDS OMITTED/STANDARD.
        01  <input-record-1>.
            . . . . .
        01  <input-record-2>.
            . . . . .
```

If a file has more than one associated record description then all records share the same input area.

The end of file flag should be defined as part of STATE-VECTOR and takes the general form:

```
        01  STATE-VECTOR.
            05  END-<input-file-name>       PIC X.
                88  END-OF-<input-file-name>  VALUE "E".
```

(c) PROCEDURE DIVISION - each file must be opened for input before it can be read, the at-end condition must be handled properly and the file closed after processing is complete. A file, and its end of file flag, should be initialized in INIT-STATE and the file terminated in CLOSE-DOWN, and an appropriate get-next procedure should be defined. The general form of the initialization is:

```
        INIT-STATE.
            MOVE SPACE TO END-<input-file-name>
            OPEN INPUT <input-file-name>
            . . . . .
```

When the processing of the file is complete it should be released from the program, the general form of the termination procedure is:

```
        CLOSE-DOWN.
            CLOSE <input-file-name> . . . . .
            STOP RUN.
```

The standard form of the get-next procedure is:

```
GET-NEXT-<input-file-name>.
    READ <input-file-name>
        AT END MOVE "E" TO END-<input-file-name>.
```

In a program which uses two or more input files it is necessary to follow this set of guidelines for each of the files.

For example, suppose that a program processes two input files: ACCOUNT-FILE, a file on backing store, and CHANGES-FILE, a file created by typing data at a keyboard. Then following the guidelines given above the following parts of the program will be affected.

```
ENVIRONMENT DIVISION.
. . . . .
INPUT-OUTPUT SECTION.
FILE-CONTROL.
    SELECT ACCOUNT-FILE ASSIGN TO <external-file-in-1>.
    SELECT CHANGES-FILE ASSIGN TO <external-file-in-2>.
    . . . . .
DATA DIVISION.
FILE SECTION.
FD  ACCOUNT-FILE
    LABEL RECORDS STANDARD.
01  ACCOUNT-RECORD.
    . . . . .
FD  CHANGES-FILE
    LABEL RECORDS OMITTED.
01  CHANGES-EXIST-RECORD.
    . . . . .
01  CHANGES-ADD-RECORD.
    . . . . .
01  CHANGES-DELETE-RECORD.
    . . . . .
WORKING-STORAGE SECTION.
01  STATE-VECTOR.
    05  END-ACCOUNT-FILE            PIC X.
        END-OF-ACCOUNT-FILE  VALUE "E".
    05  END-CHANGES-FILE            PIC X.
        END-OF-CHANGES-FILE  VALUE "E".
. . . . .
PROCEDURE DIVISION.
. . . . .
INIT-STATE.
    MOVE SPACE TO END-ACCOUNT-FILE
    MOVE SPACE TO END-CHANGES-FILE
    OPEN INPUT ACCOUNT-FILE CHANGES-FILE
    . . . . .
CLOSE-DOWN.
    CLOSE ACCOUNT-FILE CHANGES-FILE . . . . .
    STOP RUN.
. . . . .
GET-NEXT-ACCOUNT-FILE.
    READ ACCOUNT-FILE
        AT END MOVE "E" TO END-ACCOUNT-FILE.
```

```
GET-NEXT-CHANGES-FILE.
    READ CHANGES-FILE
        AT END MOVE "E" TO END-CHANGES-FILE.
. . . . .
```

Multiple Output Files

A summary of the guidelines for setting up an output file, using the program skeleton of Appendix 1, is given below.

(a) ENVIRONMENT DIVISION - a select clause is required for each file. The general form is:

```
SELECT <output-file-name>
    ASSIGN TO <external-file-name>.
```

The <output-file-name> is the name used for the file within the program. The <external-file-name> has to conform to the rules for the COBOL system being used.

(b) DATA DIVISION - each file must have a file description and an associated record description in the FILE SECTION. It should have also have one or more record descriptions in the WORKING-STORAGE SECTION. The general form of the file description is:

```
FD  <output-file-name>
    LABEL RECORDS OMITTED/STANDARD.
01  <output-file-record>        PIC . . .
```

Each record description is a data structure starting with the level number 01. For example:

```
01  <output-record-1>.
    . . . . .
01  <output-record-2>.
    . . . . .
```

(c) PROCEDURE DIVISION - each file must be opened for output before it can be written and the file must be closed after output has been completed. A file should be initialized in INIT-STATE and terminated in CLOSE-DOWN, and appropriate put procedures should be defined, one for each record description in the WORKING-STORAGE SECTION. The general form of initialization is:

```
INIT-STATE.
    . . . . .
    OPEN INPUT . . . . .
        OUTPUT <output-file-name>
    MOVE SPACES TO <output-record-1>.
```

Only records containing <u>no</u> constant data should be initialized to spaces. At the end of the program the termination procedure is:

```
CLOSE-DOWN.
    CLOSE . . . . . <output-file-name>
    STOP RUN.
```

The put procedures are then based on one of the standard forms:

```
PUT-<output-record-1>.
    WRITE <output-file-record> FROM <output-record-1>
    MOVE SPACES TO <output-record-1>.

PUT-<output-record-2>.
    WRITE <output-file-record> FROM <output-record-2>.
```

The first form is used for records containing only variable data while the second is appropriate for records containing constants defined by value clauses. These procedures may of course be made more complicated by the inclusion of paper movements, or pagination, for lineprinter files.

In a program that uses several output files it is necessary to ensure that the above guidelines are adhered to for each output file.

For example, suppose that a program is required to output two files: CUSTOMER-FILE, to the backing store, and SUMMARY-FILE to the lineprinter. The first file, CUSTOMER-FILE, has an associated record CUSTOMER-DETAIL, consisting entirely of variable data. The second file, SUMMARY-FILE, has three associated records: SUMMARY-HEADING, containing only constant data, SUMMARY-DETAIL, consisting entirely of variable data, and SUMMARY-TOTAL, containing a mixture of constant and variable data. Then following the rules given above the following parts of the program would be affected.

```
ENVIRONMENT DIVISION.
. . . . .
INPUT-OUTPUT SECTION.
FILE-CONTROL.
    SELECT CUSTOMER-FILE ASSIGN TO <external-file-out-1>.
    SELECT SUMMARY-FILE  ASSIGN TO <external-file-out-2>.
    . . . . .
DATA DIVISION.
FILE SECTION.
FD  CUSTOMER-FILE
    LABEL RECORDS STANDARD.
01  CUSTOMER-RECORD          PIC . . .
FD  SUMMARY-FILE
    LABEL RECORDS OMITTED.
01  SUMMARY-LINE           PIC X(120).
. . . . .
WORKING-STORAGE SECTION.
. . . . .
01  CUSTOMER-DETAIL.
    . . . . .
01  SUMMARY-HEADING.
    . . . . .
01  SUMMARY-DETAIL.
    . . . . .
01  SUMMARY-TOTAL.
    . . . . .
. . . . .
```

```
PROCEDURE DIVISION.
. . . . .
INIT-STATE.
    . . . . .
    OPEN INPUT . . . . .
         OUTPUT CUSTOMER-FILE SUMMARY-FILE
    MOVE SPACES TO CUSTOMER-DETAIL SUMMARY-DETAIL.
CLOSE-DOWN.
    CLOSE . . . . . CUSTOMER-FILE SUMMARY-FILE
    STOP RUN.
. . . . .
PUT-CUSTOMER-DETAIL.
    WRITE CUSTOMER-RECORD FROM CUSTOMER-DETAIL
    MOVE SPACES TO CUSTOMER-DETAIL.
PUT-SUMMARY-HEADING.
    WRITE SUMMARY-LINE FROM SUMMARY-HEADING
        AFTER ADVANCING PAGE.
PUT-SUMMARY-DETAIL.
    WRITE SUMMARY-LINE FROM SUMMARY-DETAIL
        AFTER ADVANCING 2 LINES
    MOVE SPACES TO SUMMARY-DETAIL.
PUT-SUMMARY-TOTAL.
    WRITE SUMMARY-LINE FROM SUMMARY-TOTAL
        AFTER ADVANCING 3 LINES.
. . . . .
```

The procedures: PUT-SUMMARY-HEADING, PUT-SUMMARY-DETAIL and PUT-SUMMARY-TOTAL shown above will print a heading at the top of a new page, print the detail lines double spaced and leave two blank lines before the total line. They might be made more complicated by the addition of a line counter and pagination as described in Section 8.5.

9.2 Serial File Update

An important assumption which has been inherent in the type of problems that have been tackled so far is that data is input to a program, consumed and used to produce output on the lineprinter or similar human readable device. One of the great strengths of computers is that large amounts of data can be stored in machine-readable form and updated by programs. The case study of Section 8.7 was unrealistic because there is no point in typing in the account details, such as customer name, every time the program is run. The account details should have been stored in a machine-readable file and updated using the data from individual transactions.

The underlying file structure for all the files which have been used in examples so far has been the serial file organization. This means that to access an arbitrary record in the file all its predecessors have to be accessed. It is not possible to access the thirty-third record directly or to access the record for 'Joe Bloggs' without going through the file from the beginning until the required record is found.

When the records in a serial file are sorted into some predetermined order, for example by account number, then the file is an ordered serial file. This means that the systematic updating of the file is possible by using the same order for the 'master file' and the updates, usually called the 'transactions file'. However, the master file must still be processed record by record from the beginning - individual records cannot be accessed at random.

When a file is ordered, the data-item or collection of data-items that defines the ordering is said to be the key of the file. This key may be of any type which has a defined ordering, typically the key will be numeric, alphabetic or a mixture of letters and digits but other special characters may be included. The key of a file is often some specially constructed unique identifier associated with a 'thing', for example an account number, an invoice number or a part number. Accounts, for example, could be identified by customer name but although these names can be ordered there is the problem of uniqueness of names.

The ordering of records in a file may be specified in terms of a composite key, that is a combination of two or more data-items. These data-items do not necessarily need to be contiguous but the order in which they are specified is significant. Suppose that a file contains records relating to a number of different accounts, each identified by an account number, and that there may be several different records for a particular account each containing a date. Then the file could be sorted into ascending order of account number and within each account number into date order. An extract from the sorted file might appear as:

Account No.	Date
. . . . .	
00013576	050982
00013576	070982
00013576	070982
00013576	140982
00014621	030982
00014621	110982
. . . . .	

In this case the account number is called the major key and date the minor key. Alternatively this ordering can be called date order within account number. A completely different ordering would result from using date as the major key and account number as the minor key.

It is possible to specify more complex orderings, for example where the major key is in ascending order and the minor key in descending order. For simplicity, it will be assumed in this book that where a composite key is used all the elements are sorted into the same order, either ascending or descending.

The use of ordered serial files implies that it is necessary to have a means of sorting records within a file into some specified order by key. Most larger computer systems have a sort utility which will sort a file given the position, type and size of each of the data-items forming the key.

There is also a facility for sorting records from within a COBOL program but this is beyond the scope of this book for two reasons:

(a) the interface to the operating system is often quite complex and varies from system to system,
(b) the sort module is an optional part of ANS '74 COBOL and may not be implemented in COBOL systems for smaller computers.

Therefore it will be assumed that facilities exist for sorting files into a specified order and the problem of updating such files will be considered.

To update an ordered serial file, it is necessary to make a copy of the original file incorporating the updates and changes required. Therefore at least three files have to be considered: the 'old master', the 'new master' and the 'transactions'. The old master file is the file which is to be updated, using the transactions, to produce the new master file. If the old master file and transactions are both ordered on the same key then the new master file will be produced with the same ordering. In practice, there will probably be a fourth file for the output of error messages and perhaps summaries of changes, etc.

Systematic updating of a serial file is only feasible if the file is ordered. Therefore, in the remainder of this book, the term 'serial file update' will be assumed to mean the updating of an ordered serial file using a similarly ordered transactions file. The standard diagram summarizing an serial file update is given in Figure 9.1.

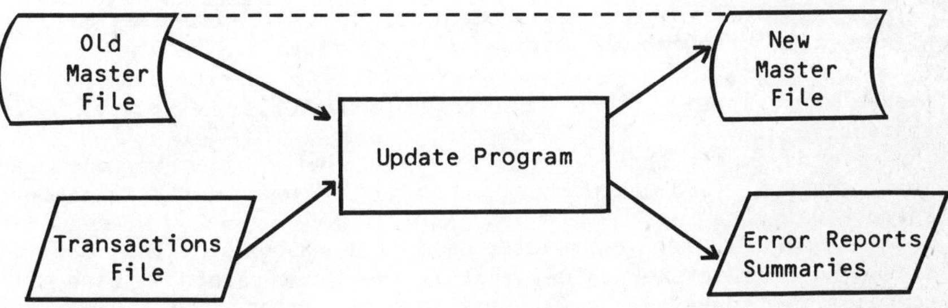

Figure 9.1

A serial file update is often associated with a processing 'cycle' where the new master file from one update becomes the old master for the next update and so on. The traditional data processing system does a master file update possibly once per day using the transactions collected during the day. Therefore a processing pattern emerges. If there are three master files identified by A, B and C then these are used as follows:

	Old Master	New Master
Monday	A	B
Tuesday	B	C
Wednesday	C	A
Thursday	A	B
etc.		

During Wednesday's processing for example the new master file will be overwriting (and destroying) the old master file from Monday. However, if a catastrophe occurs during processing, causing loss of data from the current old master file (C), it can be recreated from Tuesday's master file (B) and Tuesday's transactions file. This three file cycle is called the 'grandfather-father-son' system but can be extended to any number of generations depending on the security requirements of the system being developed. In the early days of data processing each of the files A, B and C would have been on magnetic tape. However, the same procedure can be applied to files on magnetic disk.

There are alternative ways of organizing and updating master files and some of these are discussed in Chapter 11.

In the next two sections the objective is to develop the skeletons of program designs which will perform a serial file update. Two different algorithms are outlined, one based on the techniques used so far in this book and the other to demonstrate that by introducing two simple new ideas a better algorithm can be developed. Two algorithms are also included to emphasize that for any complex problem there are many solutions and it is often difficult to find the 'best' one.

The general form of the inputs to the program will be discussed in this section and then the two algorithms developed in Sections 9.3 and 9.4.

There are two ordered streams of input coming into the update program and these have to be combined to produce a single ordered output stream - this in computing terminology is a <u>merge</u> of two files.

For the purposes of the development of these program designs, or algorithms, the following assumptions will be made.

(a) There are three files called old-master, new-master and transactions.
(b) The records in all three files contain a similar identifying data-item called old-master-key, new-master-key and trans-key, respectively.
(c) The records in the old-master and transactions files are in <u>ascending</u> order of key value, that is the first record in each file contains the lowest key value and the last record the highest key value.
(d) There may be more than one transaction associated with a particular key value. In this case, the group of transactions is assumed to appear, in the transactions file, in the order in which the transactions arose.
(e) There is a data-item in transactions called trans-type which specifies the transaction type:
    - <add>, create a new record,
    - <delete>, destroy an existing record,
    - <change>, update an existing record.

    The identifying data-items might be numeric, alphabetic or a mixture of the two, provided they are in the same format in each file and can be compared. The transaction type can be identified by a number, a letter or letters, or even a keyword; how the type is identified is an implementation detail.

    To ensure that transactions appear in the correct order, each one should be 'timestamped' with the date and time of origin. Each transaction record should include a data-item, containing this timestamp, which allows it to be distinguished, timewise, from any other transaction with the same key value. The timestamp can then be used as a minor key when sorting the transaction records. If transactions are being directly input from a computer terminal then timestamping may be provided automatically by the operating system.

    The order in which the transactions are processed is significant. Suppose that no old-master record exists with key value 2864 then the sequence of transactions:

<delete> 2864 <change> 2864 <add> 2864

is illegal because an attempt is being made to delete and then update a non-existent record. The <delete> and <change> transactions will be rejected and then a new record will be created. The same three transactions in a different order:

<add> 2864 <change> 2864 <delete> 2864

form a legal sequence of transactions.

The restriction of the algorithms to deal only with files in ascending order is necessary so that comparisons of keys can be specified. Ascending order is chosen because it is the most commonly used in practice. Changing the algorithms to operate on files in descending order is quite straightforward.

The algorithms developed will not assume that the transaction file contains perfect data. The program must be able to deal with illegal transaction types and mistyped key values leading to illegal attempts to update records, etc.

The algorithms deal with the most general case of the serial file update problem. Therefore, it is assumed that master records may be updated by any number of transactions, including the case where a new record is created by one transaction and then updated by succeeding transactions. This most general problem also includes the possibility of deleting a record with a given key value and then creating a new record with that key value.

In a particular application, rules regarding the interaction of transactions with the same key value may be specified. For example, it may not be permitted for a new record to be created with the same key as an existing record which has just been deleted. It is also possible that restrictions may be placed on the deletion of records. In some applications records may only be deleted if they have not been changed in the current update run or, alternatively, if they have not been changed for a given time period.

The algorithms given in Sections 9.3 and 9.4 are designed to deal with the most general problem and restrictions can the be added if required. It should be emphasized that these algorithms are only two out of an infinite variety of possibilities.

An alternative technique which is widely used is to have a separate data validation program which rejects illegal transactions and checks other data-items, in the transaction records, as far as possible. The validated transactions are then sorted using trans-key as the major key and transaction type as the minor key. The transactions within a particular key value are sorted into the order: <add>, <change>, <delete>. Although this restricts the sequences of transactions which are allowed it permits those of the greatest practical value.

9.3 A First Attempt at an Update Algorithm

The general problem of serial file update was discussed in Section 9.2, above. In this section the objective is to develop an algorithm for a serial file update based on the design style used so far in this book.

The merge process starts by getting one record from each of the input files, old-master and transactions. If the key of the current transaction record and the key of the current old-master record are compared then there are three possibilities, discussed below.

(a) Trans-key greater than old-master-key, which means that the current old-master record is not to be updated and can be copied unchanged to the new-master file.
(b) Trans-key less than old-master-key, which means that the transaction should be of type <add>, a request to create a new record, otherwise it is illegal.
(c) The keys are equal, which means that the current old-master record is to be updated by the current transaction and possibly succeeding transactions.

Whichever of these possibilities arises, the appropriate action should be taken, including moving on the relevant file or files ready for the next comparison. The loop must terminate as soon as one of the files has been completely used.

When the main control loop terminates it is likely that one of the input files will still have some records left unprocessed. If the old-master file is not completely processed, the remaining records should be copied to the new-master file, which is effectively possibility (a) above. Alternatively, if the transactions file is not completely processed then the only legal transactions will be concerned with setting up, and possibly updating, a new record which is effectively possibility (b) above.

The top level of the program design could therefore be:

```
merge-files
   get-next-old-master
   get-next-transactions
   until end-of-old-master or end-of-transactions do
      if trans-key > old-master-key then
         copy-old-to-new
      else
         if trans-key < old-master-key then
            should-be-new-record
         else
            update-existing-record
         endif
      endif
   enduntil

   until end-of-old-master do
      copy-old-to-new
   enduntil

   until end-of-transactions do
      should-be-new-record
   enduntil
```

It is now necessary to consider the three refinements to deal with the three possible cases. The first of these 'copy-old-to-new' is quite straightforward: the old-master record should be copied to the new-master record, the new-master record written to the new-master file and the old-master file moved on one record. Therefore the refinement could be:

```
copy-old-to-new
    transfer old-master-record to new-master-record
    put-new-master-record
    get-next-old-master
```

Since the old-master and new-master records will be in exactly the same format a group move can be used for the transfer.

The next refinement 'should-be-new-record' must have a transaction to set up a new record otherwise an error has occurred. Therefore this refinement is of the form:

```
should-be-new-record
    if trans-type = <add> then
        setup-new-record
        look-for-updates
    else
        error-new-trans-expected
        get-next-transactions
    endif
```

If a transaction of type <add> is found then the new record needs to be constructed, in new-master-record, using the details from the transaction record. There then needs to be a loop, in 'look-for-updates', to merge any subsequent transactions involving this new record into the new-master-record. If the transaction is not of type <add> then an error needs to be reported and the transaction file moved on.

The last of the second level refinements is 'update-existing-record'. There are two legal transaction types <delete> and <change> which can be applied to an existing record. If the transaction type is <delete> then both input files need to be moved on and nothing is written to the new-master file. If the transaction type is <change> then the current old-master record can be copied to the new-master record. This can be updated as many times as required by succeeding transactions, the new-master-record written to the new-master file and the old-master file needs to be moved on ready for the next comparison. The suggested refinement is therefore:

```
update-existing-record
    if trans-type = <delete> then
        get-next-old-master
        get-next-transactions
    else
        if trans-type = <change> then
            transfer old-master-record to new-master-record
            merge-trans-into-record
            put-new-master-record
            get-next-old-master
        else
            error-illegal-trans-type
            get-next-transactions
        endif
```

The refinements which deal with errors are not going to be specified at this point; they can either be implemented using a separate output file or by using display statements.

The two further refinements which have to be considered are 'look-for-updates' and 'merge-trans-into-record'. These have similar jobs to do but they are starting from different conditions. The refinement 'look-for-updates' has to establish first whether there are any updates for the new record and if there are than apply them. The refinement 'merge-trans-into-record' is given a transaction of type <change> and has to apply this and any subsequent updates. If 'look-for-updates' is coded so that it finds the first update, if any, for the new record then it can use 'merge-trans-into-record'. The suggested refinement is therefore:

```
look-for-updates
   get-next-transactions
   if not end-of-transactions then
      if trans-key = new-master-key then
         merge-trans-into-record
      endif
   endif
   put-new-master-record
```

There is an update only if there is another transaction and its key matches the new-master-key. If either of these conditions fails then the newly created record is written to the new-master file and control returns to the main control loop.

Refining 'merge-trans-into-record' has a similar problem to the above - updating normally finishes when the trans-key no longer matches the new-master-key but it may also terminate with the end of the transactions file. This double condition suggests the use of a Boolean data-item to control the loop, which could be called 'update-finished'. The suggested refinement is:

```
merge-trans-into-record
   transfer false to update-finished
   until update-finished do
      update-record
      get-next-transactions
      if end-of-transaction then
         transfer true to update-finished
      else
         if trans-key not = new-master-key then
            transfer true to update-finished
         endif
      endif
   enduntil
```

Finally, to complete the outline description of a serial file update the refinement 'update-record' needs to be considered. Here there is a difficulty with the problem specification. Normally an update will be a transaction of type <change>. A transaction of type <add> is obviously illegal but what about a transaction of type <delete>? Accepting as legal a transaction of type <delete> at this point implies that a new record can be created, or an existing record updated, and then destroyed by a subsequent transaction. If this is not allowed the refinement is quite simple:

```
update-record
   if trans-type = <change> then
      modify-new-record
   else
      error-illegal-trans-type
      get-next-transactions
   endif
```

The refinement 'modify-new-record' simply uses the data from the <change> type record to update the data in the new-master-record area. All other transaction types are treated as illegal, appropriate action is specified in 'error-illegal-trans-type' and the transaction file moved on to the next record.

An attempt to solve the more general problem, including deletions, leads to the refinement given below:

```
update-record
   if trans-type = <change> then
      modify-new-record
   else
      if trans-type = <delete> then
         destroy-new-record
         get-next-transactions
      else
         error-illegal-trans-type
         get-next-transactions
      endif
   endif
```

The refinements 'modify-new-record' and 'error-illegal-trans-type' have the same functions as those described above. The refinement 'destroy-new-master-record' should re-initialize the new-master-record area to force an exit from the update loop and leave the area in a safe state for the next operation. After deleting the record, the transactions file is moved on to the next record.

With a design of this complexity it is very rare to get everything right first time through the development process. It is often necessary to modify the design after thorough desk checking. If the above design for the more general problem is desk checked carefully a problem with deletion of records comes to light. The special cases where an existing record is updated and then deleted, and where a new record is created and then deleted are not handled properly.

Although the refinement 'destroy-new-master-record' re-initializes the new-master-record area this empty record will still be written to the new-master file in the refinements 'update-existing-record' and 'look-for-updates'. These blank records will create havoc when an attempt is made to update the new-master file subsequently. A solution to this problem is to use a Boolean data-item to indicate whether a new-master-record is to be written to the file.

A Boolean data-item 'write-new-master' can be defined which is true if a record is to be written to the new-master file and false otherwise. In 'update-existing-record' this Boolean is set to true before merging transactions into the current record, in 'merge-trans-into-record', and if it is still true after the updating the record should be written to the new-master file. Therefore the revised refinement is:

```
update-existing-record
   if trans-type = <delete> then
      get-next-old-master
      get-next-transactions
   else
      if trans-type = <change> then
         transfer old-master-record to new-master-record
         transfer true to write-new-master
         merge-trans-into-record
         if write-new-master then
            put-new-master-record
         endif
         get-next-old-master
      else
         error-illegal-trans-type
         get-next-transactions
      endif
```

The modification of 'look-for-updates' follows a similar pattern. It is assumed that the current new-master-record is to be written to the new-master file unless it is deleted by a succeeding transaction in 'merge-trans-into-record'. The revised refinement is:

```
look-for-updates
   transfer true to write-new-master
   get-next-transactions
   if not end-of-transactions then
      if trans-key = new-master-key then
         merge-trans-into-record
      endif
   endif
   if write-new-master then
      put-new-master-record
   endif
```

The only circumstances under which the new-master-record is not to be written to the new-master file is when the new-master-record is destroyed by a transaction of type <delete>. Therefore the refinement 'destroy-new-master-record' must include an operation to set the Boolean write-new-master to false. The outline of this refinement would then be:

```
destroy-new-master-record
   transfer spaces to new-master-record
   transfer false to write-new-master
```

Spaces are transferred to the new-master-record to ensure that this area is correctly initialized if the next transaction is of type <add>. It is possible that this refinement would also include printing a message indicating the record has been deleted and giving its key.

The complete program design, for the general problem including all deletions, is given below and should be followed through carefully using different combinations of transactions and old-master records.

```
merge-files
   get-next-old-master
   get-next-transactions
   until end-of-old-master or end-of-transactions do
      if trans-key > old-master-key then
         copy-old-to-new
      else
         if trans-key < old-master-key then
            should-be-new-record
         else
            update-existing-record
         endif
      endif
   enduntil

   until end-of-old-master do
      copy-old-to-new
   enduntil

   until end-of-transactions do
      should-be-new-record
   enduntil

copy-old-to-new
   transfer old-master-record to new-master-record
   put-new-master-record
   get-next-old-master

should-be-new-record
   if trans-type = <add> then
      setup-new-record
      look-for-updates
   else
      error-new-trans-expected
      get-next-transactions
   endif

update-existing-record
   if trans-type = <delete> then
      get-next-old-master
      get-next-transactions
   else
      if trans-type = <change> then
         transfer old-master-record to new-master-record
         transfer true to write-new-master
         merge-trans-into-record
         if write-new-master then
            put-new-master-record
         endif
         get-next-old-master
      else
         error-illegal-trans-type
         get-next-transactions
      endif
```

```
look-for-updates
   transfer true to write-new-master
   get-next-transactions
   if not end-of-transactions then
      if trans-key = new-master-key then
         merge-trans-into-record
      endif
   endif
   if write-new-master then
      put-new-master-record
   endif

merge-trans-into-record
   transfer false to update-finished
   until update-finished do
      update-record
      get-next-transactions
      if end-of-transaction then
         transfer true to update-finished
      else
         if trans-key not = new-master-key then
            transfer true to update-finished
         endif
      endif
   enduntil

update-record
   if trans-type = <change> then
      modify-new-record
   else
      if trans-type = <delete> then
         destroy-new-record
         get-next-transactions
      else
         error-illegal-trans-type
         get-next-transactions
      endif
   endif

destroy-new-master-record
   transfer spaces to new-master-record
   transfer false to write-new-master
```

In practice, a complete serial file update program will probably include a facility for printing a summary of changes - possibly printing the details of each record created, modified or deleted by the program.

Critical Review of this Algorithm

There are many possible solutions to any complex programming problem. Which solution is 'best' depends on the criteria which are being used to judge a particular solution. A very important criterion for judging program designs is the clarity of the algorithm - is it obvious how it works? Clarity of program design leads to another important consideration - how easy is it to change the program? In commercial data processing, programs are expected to have a long life and be frequently changed because of changing circumstances in business. This means that programs are often 'maintained' by programmers who were not responsible for the original design and implementation of those programs.

Clarity and ease of maintenance are more important than the efficiency of a program. A highly efficient program full of clever programming 'tricks' is useless if nobody but the original programmer understands it, especially if he is no longer available for consultation. Incidentally, programs written to gain maximum efficiency are also usually difficult to transport to another type of computer because they tend to use techniques peculiar to a particular COBOL system.

There are a number of criticisms of the above algorithm which indicate that there ought to be a better solution to this problem. The top level of the program description is reproduced below.

```
merge-files
    get-next-old-master
    get-next-transactions
    until end-of-old-master or end-of-transactions do
        if trans-key > old-master-key then
            copy-old-to-new
        else
            if trans-key < old-master-key then
                should-be-new-record
            else
                update-existing-record
            endif
        endif
    enduntil

    until end-of-old-master do
        copy-old-to-new
    enduntil

    until end-of-transactions do
        should-be-new-record
    enduntil
```

Looking at this, there are two major criticisms which one could make. Firstly, it is not immediately apparent why there are three loops in the program, nor is it obvious that at most two of them are actually effective in a given execution of the program.

Secondly, and probably more importantly, it is not obvious what the main control loop of the program actually does. One execution of the loop does not process one old-master record because sometimes the current old-master record is ignored. On the other hand, one execution of the loop does not always process one transaction, in some cases no transactions are relevant, while under other circumstances several transactions may be consumed by the loop.

One may therefore be tempted to think that the main control loop deals with all the records associated with a given key. This is not so because an old-master record may be deleted by a transaction in one loop execution and a new record with the same key created in the next execution of the loop.

Looking more deeply into the program design, a major problem area is the deletion of records. If some special action is required each time a record is deleted then there are two places in the program which have to be considered: 'update-existing-record' and 'update-record'. This indicates that perhaps the design could be improved - as a general rule, each function of the program should have a clearly defined point at which it is implemented.

Another measure of the complexity of this algorithm is to count the number of different points at which files are accessed. There are four uses of 'get-next-old-master', to obtain another old-master record, eight uses of 'get-next-transactions', to move on the transactions file, and three uses of 'put-new-master-record', to write a record to the new-master file. As a general rule, the fewer different points at which files are accessed the clearer the algorithm will be.

Finally, another criticism which can be made is the fact that 'merge-trans-into-record' is used by both 'update-existing-record' and 'look-for-updates' (after creating a new record). Any procedure which is used from two, or more, different points in the program is potentially dangerous. A change may be made to 'merge-trans-into-record' because of some change required in 'update-existing-record' and this could inadvertently affect the action of 'look-for-updates'.

9.4 The "Balanced Line" Algorithm

The serial file update problem has been studied by many people and a wide variety of solutions have been advocated. The solution in 9.3 was developed using the techniques explained so far in this book and based on the loop to end of file. By extending the techniques available and looking at the problem in a slightly different way it is possible to find a better, clearer solution. The method used, the balanced-line algorithm, was first described by Dijkstra in *A Discipline of Programming*.

As has already been indicated, one difficulty with the solution given in 9.3 is that the main control loop is driven by the status of the files whereas what is really at the heart of the problem is the record *keys*. The input data is naturally grouped where a group of records consists of all those records with the same key. A group can contain at most one old-master record but it may include any number of transaction records. The main control loop of the program should process one group of records and keep going until there are no more groups. The key of a group can be established by comparing the keys of the current transaction and old-master records and assigning the lowest value to a data-item, say 'current-key'. One process should then deal with all the records containing the value current-key.

To drive the program by key value an alternative technique for dealing with end of file can be used. Suppose a new operation called

```
getin-next-<input-file-name>
```

is defined which will attempt to read another record from <input-file-name> and if no record is available will set the record key to an impossibly high value. For example, getin-next-transactions would attempt to read a record from transactions and if no record is available set trans-key to <high-value>.

The algorithm uses a Boolean data-item 'master-present' to record the current state of the new-master-record area. If master-present is true then there is valid data in new-master-record area otherwise new-master-record is empty.

Based on the above observations and techniques, the top level of the design for the serial file update is:

```
balanced-line
   getin-next-transactions
   getin-next-old-master
   find-current-key
   until current-key = <high-value> do
      process-group-of-current-key
      find-current-key
   enduntil
```

The algorithm starts by attempting to read one record from each of the input files and establishes a value for current key. The program then loops until both files are exhausted indicated by current-key taking the high-value associated with the getin-next operations. Within the loop the group associated with the current-key is processed and then a new value of current-key is established.

The first refinement is quite straightforward:

```
find-current-key
   if trans-key < old-master-key then
      transfer trans-key to current-key
   else
      transfer old-master-key to current-key
   endif
```

The other refinement at this level, 'process-group-of-current-key', needs to specify the starting conditions for the group, process all the transactions matching current-key and then terminate the group. This refinement is given below.

```
process-group-of-current-key
   start-group
   until trans-key not = current-key do
      process-current-trans
      getin-next-transactions
   enduntil
   finish-group
```

The first refinement, from this procedure, is 'start-group', to define the starting conditions for a group of records. If the current group contains an old-master record then this record is copied to new-master-record, master-present is set to true to indicate that there is valid data in new-master-record and the old-master file is moved on. If there is no old-master record in the current group then master-present is set to false because there is no valid data in new-master-record. The refinement can be developed as:

```
start-group
   if old-master-key = current-key then
      transfer old-master-record to new-master-record
      transfer true to master-present
      getin-next-old-master
   else
      transfer false to master-present
   endif
```

The refinement of 'process-current-trans' is simply a four-way selection:

```
process-current-trans
   if trans-type = <add> then
      create-record
   else
      if trans-type = <delete> then
         destroy-record
      else
         if trans-type = <change> then
            update-record
         else
            error-illegal-transaction
         endif
      endif
   endif
```

Finally, at this level of refinement the group is completed by writing a record to new-master file, if there is valid data in new-master-record:

```
finish-group
   if master-present then
      put-new-master-record
   endif
```

The three important refinements coming from 'process-current-trans' should all be quite clear now. If the transaction is of type <add>, to create a record, then if master-present is true there is an error. Otherwise, a new record should be set up by copying data from the transaction to new-master-record and master-present set to true to indicate the presence of this new data. Therefore, the refinement is:

```
create-record
   if master-present then
      error-illegal-create
   else
      setup-new-record
      transfer true to master-present
   endif
```

A transaction of type <delete> is only legal if master-present is true, indicating that there is a record to delete. If this is so then new-master-record is re-initialized and master-present is set to false, otherwise an error occurs:

```
destroy-record
   if master-present then
      transfer spaces to new-master-record
      transfer false to master-present
   else
      error-illegal-delete
   endif
```

Similarly, a transaction of type <change> is only valid if master-present is true:

```
update-record
   if master-present then
      modify-record
   else
      error-illegal-update
   endif
```

Some refinements are still left to be developed - these are the ones which are problem dependent and do not affect the overall structure of the design. There are six refinements unspecified:

(a) error-illegal-transaction, to deal with a transaction of invalid type;
(b) error-illegal-create, an attempt to create a new record where one already exists with the same key;
(c) setup-new-record, copy the details from a transaction of type <add> to new-master-record;
(d) error-illegal-delete; an attempt to delete a non-existent record;
(e) modify-record, carry out amendments to an existing record specified in a transaction of type <change>;
(f) error-illegal-update, an attempt to change a non-existent record.

A complete example of the implementation of this algorithm is given in the case study in Section 9.5.

The top level of the program design for the balanced line algorithm, described in this section, is much clearer than that of the earlier algorithm, described in Section 9.3. There are no extra loops for dealing with the 'tail' of the old master or transactions file but a single loop dealing with the current group of records. The structure of the program, in the balanced line algorithm, is a better reflection of the structure of the data.

Another reason for the balanced line algorithm being clearer is the technique of driving the program by the key values and treating the end of file conditions as special key values. This avoids the double conditions, which were unavoidable in the first algorithm, where before comparing keys it was necessary to check for end-of-transactions.

In the first attempt at the algorithm the deletion of records is rather untidy as a record can be deleted at two places in the program design. This problem disappears in the balanced line algorithm where each transaction type has a clearly defined point in the design at which it takes effect. If, for example, any special action is to be associated with deletion it obviously belongs in 'destroy-record'.

The number of points at which files are accessed is much smaller in the balanced-line algorithm. There are only two uses of 'getin-next-old-master' and 'getin-next-transactions', in each case once for initialization and once inside a loop. and there is only one use of 'put-new-master-record'.

Implementation in COBOL

To be able to implement the above algorithm the techniques available have to be extended to cope with the idea of <high-value> and the implementation of getin-next-<input-file-name>.

The first is apparently quite simple as COBOL provides a special figurative constant called HIGH-VALUES which represents any number of occurrences of the highest value which can be represented in the COBOL system being used. The use of this constant is similar to SPACES. For example:

```
MOVE HIGH-VALUES TO TRANS-KEY
```

will fill TRANS-KEY with the appropriate number of high-value characters. This technique can be used as long as a key containing all high-values cannot occur in the data. This will be true for most applications.

However, there is a trap in the definition of HIGH VALUES which will cause difficulties in many COBOL systems. In the above example, one might assume that if TRANS-KEY is of numeric type then HIGH-VALUES will be the largest numeric value which will fit into TRANS-KEY. In many systems this is not the case and the value associated with HIGH-VALUES will be fixed as the highest character code in the 'collating sequence' which is unlikely to be a numeric character. Therefore, in the above example, if TRANS-KEY is of numeric type undesirable results may occur because this MOVE statement involves an alphanumeric to numeric data transfer.

If this problem arises then one solution is to describe all key data-items as <u>alphanumeric</u>, even if they normally contain only numeric data. This is quite straightforward unless there is a requirement to carry out arithmetic on key values or to edit them for output. An alternative solution is to use a numeric value of all 9's as the <high-value> provided that this cannot occur as a legal key value. This technique is used in the case study in Section 9.5.

There is an analogous figurative constant called LOW-VALUES which represents any number of occurrences of the lowest value which can be represented in the COBOL system being used. This can be useful as an artificial starting value for a sequence of values or when files are in descending order of key value. The discussion above about the type of the figurative constant HIGH-VALUES also applies to LOW-VALUES.

The implementation of getin-next-<input-file-name> needs to use an alternative form of the read statement:

```
READ <input-file-name> INTO <store-record-name>
    AT END . . . . .
```

This statement will attempt to read a record from <input-file-name>. If the read is successful the input-area will be copied to <store-record-name>, which must be a data structure, with level-number 01, in the WORKING-STORAGE SECTION. If the read is unsuccessful, because there are no more records to be processed, then the statement(s) following AT END will be executed. This could be considered as equivalent to:

```
READ <input-file-name>
    AT END . . . . .
IF <read-successful>
    MOVE <input-area> TO <store-record-name>.
```

It might seem that the implementation of getin-next-<input-file-name> could be based on:

```
READ <input-file-name>
    AT END MOVE <high-value> TO <input-record-key>.
```

where <input-record-key> is specified in the input-area for <input-file-name>. However, as soon as the at-end condition occurs the input-area for the file is no longer accessible, therefore it cannot have a value moved into it nor can data-items within the input-area be used in comparisons.

The implementation suggested for getin-next-<input-file-name> is:

```
GETIN-NEXT-<input-file-name>.
    READ <input-file-name> INTO <store-record-name>
        AT END MOVE <high-value> TO <store-record-key>.
```

There is one slight disadvantage of read-into and that is that redefinition must be used to define alternative types of records. In the outline program design above the transactions file has three types of records and these could be defined as follows:

```
01  TRANS-STORE.
    05  TRANS-TYPE   . . . . .
    05  TRANS-KEY    . . . . .
    05  TRANS-TYPE-NEW.
        . . . . . .
    05  TRANS-TYPE-DELETE REDEFINES TRANS-TYPE-NEW.
        . . . . . .
    05  TRANS-TYPE-CHANGE REDEFINES TRANS-TYPE-NEW.
        . . . . . .
```

Each of the data structures TRANS-TYPE-NEW, TRANS-TYPE-DELETE and TRANS-TYPE-CHANGE must be of the same length.

The definition of the getin-next operation for the file would then be:

```
GETIN-NEXT-TRANSACTIONS.
    READ TRANSACTIONS INTO TRANS-STORE
        AT END MOVE <high-value> TO TRANS-KEY.
```

The file description for TRANSACTIONS need contain only a single record description defining enough characters to contain the largest record in the file. For example:

```
FD  TRANSACTIONS
    LABEL RECORDS OMITTED.
01  TRANS-RECORD         PIC X(<length>).
```

where <length> is chosen as the size of the largest possible transaction record.

9.5 Case Study

This case study is an illustration of the use of the balanced-line algorithm for serial file update discussed in Section 9.4. The problem specification is:

> The Bank of Ruritania maintains a master file of account records containing the following data:
>
> | | |
> |---|---|
> | Account number | 8 digits |
> | Account name | 30 characters |
> | Current balance | 8 digits (signed, pence) |
> | Date of last update | 6 digits (DDMMYY) |
>
> These records are stored in ascending order of account number and there is no account with number 99999999.
>
> Transactions relating to these accounts are recorded using three types of transaction:
>
> <u>Add customer</u>
>
> | | |
> |---|---|
> | Record type | A |
> | Account number | 8 digits |
> | Date of addition | 6 digits (DDMMYY) |
> | Account name | 30 characters |
> | Opening balance | 8 digits (pence) |
>
> <u>Delete customer</u>
>
> | | |
> |---|---|
> | Record type | D |
> | Account number | 8 digits |
> | Date of deletion | 6 digits (DDMMYY) |
> | Authorization code | 3 letters followed by 2 digits |
>
> <u>Change balance</u>
>
> | | |
> |---|---|
> | Record type | C |
> | Account number | 8 digits |
> | Date of change | 6 digits (DDMMYY) |
> | Type of change | 1 = cash withdrawal |
> | | 2 = cheque |
> | | 3 = standing order |
> | | 4 = cash/cheques paid in |
> | | 5 = credit transfer |
> | Amount | 6 digits (pence) |
> | Reference number | 5 digits |
>
> A program is required which will update the master file using an ordered file of transactions. The transactions are sorted into ascending order of account number but within each account number appear in the order in which they arose. The transactions have been validated by a previous program to ensure that all relevant data-items contain numeric values and that the type of change is a digit in the range one to five.
>
> The program should produce a new master file of update records together with two printed reports: a summary of all amendments made to the file and a report of all errors encountered in the transaction data. The amendment summary should include a line for:

(a) each record which is deleted, showing the authorization code and closing balance,
(b) each new record created, showing the account name and opening balance,
(c) the final amended balance of any record which has been updated during the program run.

Before starting on the program design, names can be assigned to the data-items within the records associated with the master and transaction files. The old-master file contains four data-items:

```
old-master-record
   oldm-acc-number          account number
   oldm-acc-name            account name
   oldm-balance             current balance
   oldm-last-date           date of last update
```

The new-master file has a corresponding structure:

```
new-master-record
   newm-acc-number          account number
   newm-acc-name            account name
   newm-balance             amended balance
   newm-last-date           date of last update
```

The transactions file has three record types which will need to be defined in one record structure as follows:

```
trans-record
   trans-type                  A,C or D
   trans-acc-number            account number
   trans-date                  date of transaction
   trans-add
      trans-a-acc-name         account name
      trans-a-balance          opening balance
   trans-delete == trans-add
      trans-d-auth-code        authorization code for deletion
   trans-change == trans-add
      trans-c-type             type of change, 1-5
      trans-c-amount           amount withdrawn / paid in
      trans-c-refno            reference number for change
```

The basic structure of the program design will follow that described in Section 9.4 with the addition of extra coding for the printing of the amendment file. The outline design from Section 9.4 is given below, modified to include the appropriate names and values for the problem under consideration. As there is no account with number 99999999 this value can be used as the <high-value> to terminate the main control loop.

```
update-accounts
   getin-next-transactions
   getin-next-old-master
   find-current-acc-number
   until current-acc-number = 99999999 do
      process-current-acc-number
      find-current-acc-number
   enduntil

find-current-acc-number
   if trans-acc-number < oldm-acc-number then
      transfer trans-acc-number to current-acc-number
   else
      transfer oldm-acc-number to current-acc-number
   endif

process-current-acc-number
   start-group
   until trans-acc-number not = current-acc-number do
      process-current-trans
      getin-next-transactions
   enduntil
   finish-group

start-group
   if oldm-acc-number = current-acc-number then
      transfer old-master-record to new-master-record
      transfer true to master-present
      getin-next-old-master
   else
      transfer false to master-present
   endif

process-current-trans
   if trans-type = "A" then
      create-record
   else
      if trans-type = "D" then
         destroy-record
      else
         if trans-type = "C" then
            update-record
         else
            error-illegal-transaction
         endif
      endif
   endif

finish-group
   if master-present then
      put-new-master-record
   endif
```

```
create-record
   if master-present then
      error-illegal-create
   else
      setup-new-record
      transfer true to master-present
   endif

destroy-record
   if master-present then
      transfer spaces to new-master-record
      transfer false to master-present
   else
      error-illegal-delete
   endif

update-record
   if master-present then
      modify-record
   else
      error-illegal-update
   endif
```

Looking at the additional coding required for the printing of the amendment summary, there are three records to be written to the amendment summary file for deletions, additions and amended balances. Taking the fist of these, deletion, the only point in the program where a record is deleted is in 'destroy-record' therefore this can be modified to include the necessary printing. The revised refinement is:

```
destroy-record
   if master-present then
      print-deletion-summary
      transfer spaces to new-master-record
      transfer false to master-present
   else
      error-illegal-delete
   endif
```

Similarly, the second type of amendment, addition, can be dealt with quite straightforwardly because all new records are added in 'create-record'. Therefore this can be revised as follows:

```
create-record
   if master-present then
      error-illegal-create
   else
      setup-new-record
      transfer true to master-present
      print-addition-summary
   endif
```

The third type of summary record, for amended balances, requires more thought. Records are updated in 'update-record' but a summary record is not required for each change to a master record, only the final amended balance is to be printed. Therefore in 'update-record' it is necessary to note that the balance has been amended but nothing should be printed at that point. If a record is noted as having been amended then the printing should be included in 'finish-group'.

Suppose a Boolean data-item called 'record-changed' is defined which is to be set to true if an amendment is made to a record. Then at the beginning of each group it will need to be set to false. Therefore 'start-group' should be modified to:

```
start-group
    transfer false to record-changed
    if oldm-acc-number = current-acc-number then
        transfer old-master-record to new-master-record
        transfer true to master-present
        getin-next-old-master
    else
        transfer false to master-present
    endif
```

Whenever a record is updated it will be necessary to set record-changed to true, this requires a modification to 'update-record' as follows:

```
update-record
    if master-present then
        modify-record
        transfer true to record-changed
    else
        error-illegal-update
    endif
```

At the end of each group it will be necessary to check whether an amendment has been made and if so print a summary record. There is no point in checking for an amendment if there is no data in new-master-record, therefore the modified form of 'finish-group' could be:

```
finish-group
    if master-present then
        if record-changed then
            print-change-summary
        endif
        put-new-master-record
    endif
```

It would now be wise to desk check the overall design before getting down to the detailed coding of the various lower level refinements. If the above design is checked through with various combinations of transactions a minor problem with the design of the summary output becomes apparent.

Suppose that the following group occurs:

```
oldm-acc-number  = 00001234
trans-acc-number = 00001234     trans-type = C  (Change)
trans-acc-number = 00001234     trans-type = D  (Delete)
trans-acc-number = 00001234     trans-type = A  (Add)
```

The summary printed would be of the form:

```
deletion        with closing balance
addition        with opening balance
amendment       with same balance as addition, above
```

The last line is unnecessary and will perhaps cause confusion. The problem is caused by the creation of a new record without the resetting of record-changed back to false. Therefore 'create-record' needs to be further modified to:

```
create-record
   if master-present then
      error-illegal-create
   else
      setup-new-record
      transfer true to master-present
      print-addition-summary
      transfer false to record-changed
   endif
```

Now if the design is desk checked again it should work correctly even for unlikely combinations involving amendment, addition and deletion. It now remains to develop the various lower-level refinements which were left.

The first refinement which will be considered is 'setup-new-record' which is quite straightforward:

```
setup-new-record
   transfer trans-acc-number to newm-acc-number
   transfer trans-date to newm-last-date
   transfer trans-a-acc-name to newm-acc-name
   transfer trans-a-balance to newm-balance
```

There is then the refinement 'modify-record' to update the existing new-master-record. This again is quite straightforward:

```
modify-record
   transfer trans-date to newm-last-date
   if trans-c-type < 4 then
      calculate newm-balance = newm-balance - trans-c-amount
   else
      calculate newm-balance = newm-balance + trans-c-amount
   endif
```

There are now two groups of refinements remaining - those concerned with printing the summary records and those dealing with errors. In each case it is necessary to decide on the contents of the output records and then develop the refinements.

For the summary records the data-items which might be required are the account number, the account name, the current balance and a message indicating the type of summary record. Therefore the record could be defined as:

```
summary-record
   summary-acc-number                account number
   summary-acc-name                  account name
   summary-balance                   current balance
   summary-auth-code                 authorization code, deletions only
   summary-type                      type of summary record
```

Then the three refinements: 'print-deletion-summary', 'print-addition-summary' and 'print-change-summary' are all straightforward. All these refinements will need to fill the summary-record from the new-master-record and add the appropriate message. Therefore they can all use a common procedure. The refinements could be:

```
print-deletion-summary
   transfer trans-d-auth-code to summary-auth-code
   transfer "record deleted" to summary-type
   print-summary-record

print-addition-summary
   transfer "new account added" to summary-type
   print-summary-record

print-change-summary
   transfer "balance amended" to summary-type
   print-summary-record

print-summary-record
   transfer newm-acc-number to summary-acc-number
   transfer newm-acc-name to summary-acc-name
   transfer newm-balance to summary-balance
   put-summary-record
```

The error-record will need to contain data-items to hold the transaction type, account number, date of transaction, account name, amount and a message for the type of error. Therefore the record could be defined as:

```
error-record
   error-trans-type       transaction type
   error-acc-number       account-number
   error-trans-date       date of transaction
   error-acc-name         account name, if any
   error-amount           amount involved, if any
   error-type             type of error
```

A similar strategy to that for the summary records could be adopted, extracting the common elements of the error-record construction. The refinements could then be:

```
error-illegal-transaction
   transfer "illegal transaction type" to error-type
   print-error-record
```

```
error-illegal-create
   transfer trans-a-acc-name to error-acc-name
   transfer trans-a-balance to error-amount
   transfer "create: existing account" to error-type
   print-error-record

error-illegal-delete
   transfer "delete: no master record" to error-type
   print-error-record

error-illegal-update
   transfer trans-c-amount to error-amount
   transfer "update: no master record" to error-type
   print-error-record

print-error-record
   transfer trans-type to error-trans-type
   transfer trans-acc-number to error-acc-number
   transfer trans-date to error-trans-date
   put-error-record
```

Finally, it will be necessary to produce headings for the two reports and these will need to be printed at the beginning of the program. Therefore the top level of the program design will need to include this. The complete program design, incorporating this change, is given below.

```
update-accounts
   print-headings
   getin-next-transactions
   getin-next-old-master
   find-current-acc-number
   until current-acc-number = 99999999 do
      process-current-acc-number
      find-current-acc-number
   enduntil

print-headings
   put-summary-page-heading (after new page)
   put-summary-col-headings (after two blank lines)
   put-error-page-heading (after new page)
   put-error-col-headings (after two blank lines)

find-current-acc-number
   if trans-acc-number < oldm-acc-number then
      transfer trans-acc-number to current-acc-number
   else
      transfer oldm-acc-number to current-acc-number
   endif
```

```
process-current-acc-number
   start-group
   until trans-acc-number not = current-acc-number do
      process-current-trans
      getin-next-transactions
   enduntil
   finish-group

start-group
   transfer false to record-changed
   if oldm-acc-number = current-acc-number then
      transfer old-master-record to new-master-record
      transfer true to master-present
      getin-next-old-master
   else
      transfer false to master-present
   endif

process-current-trans
   if trans-type = "A" then
      create-record
   else
      if trans-type = "D" then
         destroy-record
      else
         if trans-type = "C" then
            update-record
         else
            error-illegal-transaction
         endif
      endif
   endif

finish-group
   if master-present then
      if record-changed then
         print-change-summary
      endif
      put-new-master-record
   endif

create-record
   if master-present then
      error-illegal-create
   else
      setup-new-record
      transfer true to master-present
      print-addition-summary
      transfer false to record-changed
   endif
```

```
destroy-record
   if master-present then
      print-deletion-summary
      transfer spaces to new-master-record
      transfer false to master-present
   else
      error-illegal-delete
   endif

update-record
   if master-present then
      modify-record
      transfer true to record-changed
   else
      error-illegal-update
   endif

setup-new-record
   transfer trans-acc-number to newm-acc-number
   transfer trans-date to newm-last-date
   transfer trans-a-acc-name to newm-acc-name
   transfer trans-a-balance to newm-balance

modify-record
   transfer trans-date to newm-last-date
   if trans-c-type < 4 then
      calculate newm-balance = newm-balance - trans-c-amount
   else
      calculate newm-balance = newm-balance + trans-c-amount
   endif

print-deletion-summary
   transfer trans-d-auth-code to summary-auth-code
   transfer "record deleted" to summary-type
   print-summary-record

print-addition-summary
   transfer "new account added" to summary-type
   print-summary-record

print-change-summary
   transfer "balance amended" to summary-type
   print-summary-record

print-summary-record
   transfer newm-acc-number to summary-acc-number
   transfer newm-acc-name to summary-acc-name
   transfer newm-balance to summary-balance
   put-summary-record

error-illegal-transaction
   transfer "illegal transaction type" to error-type
   print-error-record
```

```
error-illegal-create
    transfer trans-a-acc-name to error-acc-name
    transfer trans-a-balance to error-amount
    transfer "create: existing account" to error-type
    print-error-record

error-illegal-delete
    transfer "delete: no master record" to error-type
    print-error-record

error-illegal-update
    transfer trans-c-amount to error-amount
    transfer "update: no master record" to error-type
    print-error-record

print-error-record
    transfer trans-type to error-trans-type
    transfer trans-acc-number to error-acc-number
    transfer trans-date to error-trans-date
    put-error-record
```

After desk checking this design thoroughly the corresponding COBOL program can be developed.

```
       IDENTIFICATION DIVISION.
       PROGRAM-ID. UPDATE01.

       ENVIRONMENT DIVISION.
       CONFIGURATION SECTION.
       SOURCE-COMPUTER. <computer-name>.
       OBJECT-COMPUTER. <computer-name>.
      *    <computer-name> should be replaced by the name
      *    of the computer being used to run programs.

       INPUT-OUTPUT SECTION.
       FILE-CONTROL.
           SELECT TRANSACTIONS ASSIGN TO <input-file-1>.
           SELECT OLD-MASTER   ASSIGN TO <input-file-2>.
           SELECT NEW-MASTER   ASSIGN TO <output-file-1>.
           SELECT SUMMARY-FILE ASSIGN TO <output-file-2>.
           SELECT ERROR-FILE   ASSIGN TO <output-file-3>.
      *        <input-file-name-n> and <output-file-name-n>
      *        must conform to the rules for the COBOL system.

       DATA DIVISION.
       FILE SECTION.
       FD  TRANSACTIONS
           LABEL RECORDS OMITTED.
       01  TRANSACTION-INPUT-AREA       PIC X(53).
       FD  OLD-MASTER
           LABEL RECORDS STANDARD.
       01  OLD-MASTER-INPUT-AREA        PIC X(52).
       FD  NEW-MASTER
           LABEL RECORDS STANDARD.
       01  NEW-MASTER-OUTPUT-AREA       PIC X(52).
       FD  SUMMARY-FILE
```

```
    LABEL RECORDS OMITTED.
01  SUMMARY-LINE                  PIC X(81).
FD  ERROR-FILE
    LABEL RECORDS OMITTED.
01  ERROR-LINE                    PIC X(93).

WORKING-STORAGE SECTION.
01  STATE-VECTOR.
    05  RECORD-STATUS             PIC X.
        88  RECORD-CHANGED  VALUE "T".
    05  MASTER-STATUS             PIC X.
        88  MASTER-PRESENT  VALUE "T".
    05  CURRENT-ACC-NUMBER        PIC 9(8).

01  TRANS-RECORD.
    05  TRANS-TYPE                PIC A.
    05  TRANS-ACC-NUMBER          PIC 9(8).
    05  TRANS-DATE                PIC 9(6).
    05  TRANS-ADD.
        10  TRANS-A-ACC-NAME      PIC X(30).
        10  TRANS-A-BALANCE       PIC 9(6)V99.
    05  TRANS-DELETE REDEFINES TRANS-ADD.
        10  TRANS-D-AUTH-CODE     PIC X(5).
        10  FILLER                PIC X(33).
    05  TRANS-CHANGE REDEFINES TRANS-ADD.
        10  TRANS-C-TYPE          PIC 9.
        10  TRANS-C-AMOUNT        PIC 9999V99.
        10  TRANS-C-REFNO         PIC 9(5).
        10  FILLER                PIC X(26).

01  OLD-MASTER-RECORD.
    05  OLDM-ACC-NUMBER     PIC 9(8).
    05  OLDM-ACC-NAME       PIC X(30).
    05  OLDM-BALANCE        PIC S9(6)V99.
    05  OLDM-LAST-DATE      PIC 9(6).

01  NEW-MASTER-RECORD.
    05  NEWM-ACC-NUMBER     PIC 9(8).
    05  NEWM-ACC-NAME       PIC X(30).
    05  NEWM-BALANCE        PIC S9(6)V99.
    05  NEWM-LAST-DATE      PIC 9(6).

01  SUMMARY-PAGE-HEADING.
    05  FILLER          PIC X(24) VALUE SPACES.
    05  FILLER          PIC X(33) VALUE
        "SUMMARY OF MASTER FILE AMENDMENTS".

01  SUMMARY-COL-HEADINGS.
    05  FILLER      PIC X(7)  VALUE " NUMBER".
    05  FILLER      PIC X(12) VALUE SPACES.
    05  FILLER      PIC X(12) VALUE "ACCOUNT NAME".
    05  FILLER      PIC X(13) VALUE SPACES.
    05  FILLER      PIC X(7)  VALUE "BALANCE".
    05  FILLER      PIC X(6)  VALUE SPACES.
    05  FILLER      PIC X(5)  VALUE "AUTH.".
    05  FILLER      PIC X(3)  VALUE SPACES.
```

```
    05  FILLER        PIC X(14) VALUE "TYPE OF UPDATE".

01  SUMMARY-RECORD.
    05  SUMMARY-ACC-NUMBER        PIC 9(8).
    05  FILLER                    PIC XX.
    05  SUMMARY-ACC-NAME          PIC X(30).
    05  FILLER                    PIC XX.
    05  SUMMARY-BALANCE           PIC ££££,££9.99DB.
    05  FILLER                    PIC XX.
    05  SUMMARY-AUTH-CODE         PIC X(5).
    05  FILLER                    PIC XX.
    05  SUMMARY-TYPE              PIC X(17).

01  ERROR-PAGE-HEADING.
    05  FILLER        PIC X(34) VALUE SPACES.
    05  FILLER        PIC X(24) VALUE
        "TRANSACTION ERROR REPORT".

01  ERROR-COL-HEADINGS.
    05  FILLER        PIC XXXX  VALUE "TYPE".
    05  FILLER        PIC XXX   VALUE SPACES.
    05  FILLER        PIC X(6)  VALUE "NUMBER".
    05  FILLER        PIC XXXX  VALUE SPACES.
    05  FILLER        PIC XXXX  VALUE "DATE".
    05  FILLER        PIC X(12) VALUE SPACES.
    05  FILLER        PIC X(12) VALUE "ACCOUNT NAME".
    05  FILLER        PIC X(14) VALUE SPACES.
    05  FILLER        PIC X(6)  VALUE "AMOUNT".
    05  FILLER        PIC X(9)  VALUE SPACES.
    05  FILLER        PIC X(13) VALUE "TYPE OF ERROR".

01  ERROR-RECORD.
    05  FILLER                    PIC X.
    05  ERROR-TRANS-TYPE          PIC X.
    05  FILLER                    PIC X(4).
    05  ERROR-ACC-NUMBER          PIC 9(8).
    05  FILLER                    PIC XX.
    05  ERROR-TRANS-DATE          PIC 9(6).
    05  FILLER                    PIC XX.
    05  ERROR-ACC-NAME            PIC X(30).
    05  FILLER                    PIC XX.
    05  ERROR-AMOUNT              PIC ££££,££9.99.
    05  FILLER                    PIC XX.
    05  ERROR-TYPE                PIC X(24).

PROCEDURE DIVISION.
MAIN-PROGRAM.
    PERFORM INIT-STATE
    PERFORM UPDATE-ACCOUNTS
    PERFORM CLOSE-DOWN.
INIT-STATE.
    OPEN INPUT TRANSACTIONS OLD-MASTER
         OUTPUT NEW-MASTER SUMMARY-FILE ERROR-FILE
    MOVE SPACES TO NEW-MASTER-RECORD
        SUMMARY-RECORD ERROR-RECORD.
```

```
CLOSE-DOWN.
    CLOSE TRANSACTIONS OLD-MASTER NEW-MASTER
        SUMMARY-FILE ERROR-FILE
    STOP RUN.
GETIN-NEXT-TRANSACTIONS.
    READ TRANSACTIONS INTO TRANS-RECORD
        AT END MOVE 99999999 TO TRANS-ACC-NUMBER.
GETIN-NEXT-OLD-MASTER.
    READ OLD-MASTER INTO OLD-MASTER-RECORD
        AT END MOVE 99999999 TO OLDM-ACC-NUMBER.
PUT-NEW-MASTER-RECORD.
    WRITE NEW-MASTER-OUTPUT-AREA FROM NEW-MASTER-RECORD
    MOVE SPACES TO NEW-MASTER-RECORD.
PUT-SUMMARY-PAGE-HEADING.
    WRITE SUMMARY-LINE FROM SUMMARY-PAGE-HEADING
        AFTER ADVANCING PAGE.
PUT-SUMMARY-COL-HEADINGS.
    WRITE SUMMARY-LINE FROM SUMMARY-COL-HEADINGS
        AFTER ADVANCING 2 LINES.
PUT-SUMMARY-RECORD.
    WRITE SUMMARY-LINE FROM SUMMARY-RECORD
        AFTER ADVANCING 1 LINES
    MOVE SPACES TO SUMMARY-RECORD.
PUT-ERROR-PAGE-HEADING.
    WRITE ERROR-LINE FROM ERROR-PAGE-HEADING
        AFTER ADVANCING PAGE.
PUT-ERROR-COL-HEADINGS.
    WRITE ERROR-LINE FROM ERROR-COL-HEADINGS
        AFTER ADVANCING 2 LINES.
PUT-ERROR-RECORD.
    WRITE ERROR-LINE FROM ERROR-RECORD
        AFTER ADVANCING 1 LINES
    MOVE SPACES TO ERROR-RECORD.
UPDATE-ACCOUNTS.
    PERFORM PRINT-HEADINGS
    PERFORM GETIN-NEXT-TRANSACTIONS
    PERFORM GETIN-NEXT-OLD-MASTER
    PERFORM FIND-CURRENT-ACC-NUMBER
    PERFORM LOOP-FOR-ONE-ACC-NUMBER
        UNTIL CURRENT-ACC-NUMBER = 99999999.
LOOP-FOR-ONE-ACC-NUMBER.
    PERFORM PROCESS-CURRENT-ACC-NUMBER
    PERFORM FIND-CURRENT-ACC-NUMBER.
PRINT-HEADINGS.
    PERFORM PUT-SUMMARY-PAGE-HEADING
    PERFORM PUT-SUMMARY-COL-HEADINGS
    PERFORM PUT-ERROR-PAGE-HEADING
    PERFORM PUT-ERROR-COL-HEADINGS.
FIND-CURRENT-ACC-NUMBER.
    IF TRANS-ACC-NUMBER < OLDM-ACC-NUMBER
        MOVE TRANS-ACC-NUMBER TO CURRENT-ACC-NUMBER
    ELSE
        MOVE OLDM-ACC-NUMBER TO CURRENT-ACC-NUMBER.
```

```
PROCESS-CURRENT-ACC-NUMBER.
    PERFORM START-GROUP
    PERFORM TRANS-LOOP
        UNTIL TRANS-ACC-NUMBER NOT = CURRENT-ACC-NUMBER
    PERFORM FINISH-GROUP.
TRANS-LOOP.
    PERFORM PROCESS-CURRENT-TRANS
    PERFORM GETIN-NEXT-TRANSACTIONS.
START-GROUP.
    MOVE "F" TO RECORD-STATUS
    IF OLDM-ACC-NUMBER = CURRENT-ACC-NUMBER
        MOVE OLD-MASTER-RECORD TO NEW-MASTER-RECORD
        MOVE "T" TO MASTER-STATUS
        PERFORM GETIN-NEXT-OLD-MASTER
    ELSE
        MOVE "F" TO MASTER-STATUS.
PROCESS-CURRENT-TRANS.
    IF TRANS-TYPE = "A"
        PERFORM CREATE-RECORD
    ELSE
        IF TRANS-TYPE = "D"
            PERFORM DESTROY-RECORD
        ELSE
            IF TRANS-TYPE = "C"
                PERFORM UPDATE-RECORD
            ELSE
                PERFORM ERROR-ILLEGAL-TRANSACTION.
FINISH-GROUP.
    IF MASTER-PRESENT
        PERFORM CHECK-RECORD-CHANGED
        PERFORM PUT-NEW-MASTER-RECORD.
CHECK-RECORD-CHANGED.
    IF RECORD-CHANGED
        PERFORM PRINT-CHANGE-SUMMARY.
CREATE-RECORD.
    IF MASTER-PRESENT
        PERFORM ERROR-ILLEGAL-CREATE
    ELSE
        PERFORM SETUP-NEW-RECORD
        MOVE "T" TO MASTER-STATUS
        PERFORM PRINT-ADDITION-SUMMARY
        MOVE "F" TO RECORD-STATUS.
DESTROY-RECORD.
    IF MASTER-PRESENT
        PERFORM PRINT-DELETION-SUMMARY
        MOVE SPACES TO NEW-MASTER-RECORD
        MOVE "F" TO MASTER-STATUS
    ELSE
        PERFORM ERROR-ILLEGAL-DELETE.
UPDATE-RECORD.
    IF MASTER-PRESENT
        PERFORM MODIFY-RECORD
        MOVE "T" TO RECORD-STATUS
    ELSE
        PERFORM ERROR-ILLEGAL-UPDATE.
```

```
SETUP-NEW-RECORD.
    MOVE TRANS-ACC-NUMBER TO NEWM-ACC-NUMBER
    MOVE TRANS-DATE TO NEWM-LAST-DATE
    MOVE TRANS-A-ACC-NAME TO NEWM-ACC-NAME
    MOVE TRANS-A-BALANCE TO NEWM-BALANCE.
MODIFY-RECORD.
    MOVE TRANS-DATE TO NEWM-LAST-DATE
    IF TRANS-C-TYPE < 4
        COMPUTE NEWM-BALANCE = NEWM-BALANCE - TRANS-C-AMOUNT
    ELSE
        COMPUTE NEWM-BALANCE = NEWM-BALANCE + TRANS-C-AMOUNT.
PRINT-DELETION-SUMMARY.
    MOVE TRANS-D-AUTH-CODE TO SUMMARY-AUTH-CODE
    MOVE "RECORD DELETED" TO SUMMARY-TYPE
    PERFORM PRINT-SUMMARY-RECORD.
PRINT-ADDITION-SUMMARY.
    MOVE "NEW ACCOUNT ADDED" TO SUMMARY-TYPE
    PERFORM PRINT-SUMMARY-RECORD.
PRINT-CHANGE-SUMMARY.
    MOVE "BALANCE AMENDED" TO SUMMARY-TYPE
    PERFORM PRINT-SUMMARY-RECORD.
PRINT-SUMMARY-RECORD.
    MOVE NEWM-ACC-NUMBER TO SUMMARY-ACC-NUMBER
    MOVE NEWM-ACC-NAME TO SUMMARY-ACC-NAME
    MOVE NEWM-BALANCE TO SUMMARY-BALANCE
    PERFORM PUT-SUMMARY-RECORD.
ERROR-ILLEGAL-TRANSACTION.
    MOVE "ILLEGAL TRANSACTION TYPE" TO ERROR-TYPE
    PERFORM PRINT-ERROR-RECORD.
ERROR-ILLEGAL-CREATE.
    MOVE TRANS-A-ACC-NAME TO ERROR-ACC-NAME
    MOVE TRANS-A-BALANCE TO ERROR-AMOUNT
    MOVE "CREATE: EXISTING ACCOUNT" TO ERROR-TYPE
    PERFORM PRINT-ERROR-RECORD.
ERROR-ILLEGAL-DELETE.
    MOVE "DELETE: NO MASTER RECORD" TO ERROR-TYPE
    PERFORM PRINT-ERROR-RECORD.
ERROR-ILLEGAL-UPDATE.
    MOVE TRANS-C-AMOUNT TO ERROR-AMOUNT
    MOVE "UPDATE: NO MASTER RECORD" TO ERROR-TYPE
    PERFORM PRINT-ERROR-RECORD.
PRINT-ERROR-RECORD.
    MOVE TRANS-TYPE TO ERROR-TRANS-TYPE
    MOVE TRANS-ACC-NUMBER TO ERROR-ACC-NUMBER
    MOVE TRANS-DATE TO ERROR-TRANS-DATE
    PERFORM PUT-ERROR-RECORD.
```

To illustrate the operation of this program examples of an old-master and transactions file are given below. The data-items are separated by spaces for readability and the balances in the old-master records are shown with minus signs where appropriate. This is not the way the records would be represented in the above program.

Old-master

```
01002546 C.CAMPBELL                          00000123  090982
01002681 M.CAMPBELL                          00001036- 060982
02001481 D.MCDONALD                          00100200  020982
02001732 D.MCDONALD                          00001000- 260882
02002812 F.J.MCDONALD                        00000000  090982
02002915 J.T.MCDONALD                        00221316- 030982
02003016 K.MCDONALD BLACK                    00056521  200882
02006058 W.W.MCDONALD                        00102532  030982
03001231 J.MACLEOD                           00001225- 060982
03002314 T.J.W.MACLEOD                       00256210- 010982
```

Transactions

```
D 01002681 100982 RCW01
C 01003515 100982 2 002595 01258
D 01004218 100982 RCW02
A 02001533 100982 D.MCDONALD                      00001000
F 02001732 100982 RCW03
A 02002915 100982 J.T.W.MCDONALD                  00000100
C 02003016 100982 1 005000 99999
C 02003016 100982 2 015010 00258
C 02003016 100982 3 002500 18281
C 03001231 100982 5 010432 56214
```

The resulting new-master file after running the program would be:

New-master

```
01002546 C.CAMPBELL                          00000123  090982
02001481 D.MCDONALD                          00100200  020982
02001533 D.MCDONALD                          00001000  100982
02001732 D.MCDONALD                          00001000- 260882
02002812 F.J.MCDONALD                        00000000  090982
02002915 J.T.MCDONALD                        00221316- 030982
02003016 K.MCDONALD BLACK                    00034011  100982
02006058 W.W.MCDONALD                        00102532  030982
03001231 J.MACLEOD                           00009207  100982
03002314 T.J.W.MACLEOD                       00256210- 010982
```

The summary of changes and error files, associated with this update are shown in Figures 9.2 and 9.3, respectively.

SUMMARY OF MASTER FILE AMENDMENTS

NUMBER	ACCOUNT NAME	BALANCE	AUTH.	TYPE OF UPDATE
01002681	M.CAMPBELL	£10.36DB	RCW01	RECORD DELETED
02001533	D.MCDONALD	£10.00		NEW ACCOUNT ADDED
02003016	K.MCDONALD BLACK	£340.11		BALANCE AMENDED
03001231	J.MACLEOD	£92.07		BALANCE AMENDED

Figure 9.2

TRANSACTION ERROR REPORT

TYPE	NUMBER	DATE	ACCOUNT NAME	AMOUNT	TYPE OF ERROR
C	01003515	100982		£25.95	UPDATE: NO MASTER RECORD
D	01004218	100982			DELETE: NO MASTER RECORD
F	02001732	100982			ILLEGAL TRANSACTION TYPE
A	02002915	100982	J.T.W.MCDONALD	£1.00	CREATE: EXISTING ACCOUNT

Figure 9.3

Exercises 9

9.1. The Bank of Ruritania wants to modify the summary report devised for the case study in Section 9.5. The first two digits of the account number are used to identify different categories of customers. Therefore each time there is a change in the first two digits of the account number the summary report should start on a new page. Consider how to incorporate this change into the program design and program given in Section 9.5.

Look back to the first attempt algorithm given in Section 9.3 and consider at what point in the design a similar type of test for change of category could be incorporated.

9.2. Outline a set of test data for thoroughly testing the program given in Section 9.5. [Hint: Break this task down into a number of subtasks, for example: consider the different combinations of transactions with old-master records, look at the creation and subsequent updating of records, identify the ways in which errors can arise, test the various possibilities for each transaction type.]

9.3. Study the balanced-line algorithm, given in Section 9.4, and suggest how it will need to be modified to deal with files in descending order of key value.

What changes are required to the first attempt algorithm, given in Section 9.3, to deal with files in descending order?

Programming Exercises 9

9.4. A motor factor maintains a large stock of spare parts for various types of motor vehicles. A master file of stock records has been set up with each record containing the following data-items:

part number	10 digits
brief description of part	25 characters
quantity on hand	4 digits
reorder level	4 digits
reorder quantity	4 digits
parts on order flag	R = parts on order

This file is sorted into ascending order of part number and is to be updated regularly by a transactions file containing the changes required to the file. The first type of transaction concerns a sale resulting in a withdrawal from stock, this is of the form:

Stock Withdrawal

transaction type	WI
part number	10 digits
quantity withdrawn	3 digits

If after adjusting the quantity on hand it is below the reorder level and the parts on order flag is not set to "R" then a message should be printed indicating the quantity to be ordered (reorder quantity) and the parts on order flag set to "R". If a withdrawal from stock results in the quantity on hand becoming negative then a warning message should be printed.

When stock is received a transactions record is created for each type of part received:

```
Stock Receipt
   transaction type      RE
   part number           10 digits
   quantity received      4 digits
```

The data from this record should be used to update the quantity on hand and the parts on order flag should be reset to some value other than "R".

To create a record for a new part the full details of the part should be input as follows:

```
New Part
   transaction type                NP
   part number                     10 digits
   brief description of part       25 characters
   initial quantity stocked         4 digits
   reorder level                    4 digits
   reorder quantity                 4 digits
```

The Parts Manager needs a facility for changing the reorder levels or reorder quantities of any given part. These changes are specified by transactions of the form:

```
Change Parameters
   transaction type                CP
   part number                     10 digits
   type of change required          1 = reorder level
                                    2 = reorder quantity
                                    3 = both level and quantity

   new reorder level                4 digits
   new reorder quantity             4 digits
```

Finally there has to be a facility for deleting records relating to obsolete stock. This gives rise to a transaction of the form:

```
Obsolete Stock
   transaction type                OS
   part number                     10 digits
```

An obsolete stock record should only be removed from the master file if the quantity on hand is zero.

A program is required that will accept a file of transactions, sorted into ascending order of part number, and update the master file accordingly. This program should print two reports: one on illegal transactions and the other summarizing the program's actions, such as records added, deleted and amended, and actions required, such as reorders required and negative stock balances found.

10 Tables

Information presented in tabular form appears quite frequently in everyday life. In a typical newspaper there might be tables summarizing the benefits of life insurance for a given premium and age of proposer, football league tables and tables of currency conversion rates. The characteristic of all of these things is repetition of similar information - the figures are repeated for many key values or combinations of key values.

Some of the data input to computers is repetitive, for example figures given for each month or data for a large organization presented as a set of similar figures for each branch or department. Computer programs are quite often required to produce tabular output by analyzing or summarizing input data. Therefore this chapter is concerned with the representation of tables in COBOL programs.

The approach used here is to present examples and then to try to extract more general techniques. The first section is concerned with repetitive data in the input records processed by a program. This is followed by a section dealing with tabular data built up within the program. The next two sections develop this theme further, leading to a simple algorithm for building tables summarizing input data. The description of more complex tables is dealt with briefly because a more comprehensive coverage is beyond the scope of this book. Finally, there is a case study to illustrate the development of a complete COBOL program using tables.

10.1 Repetitive Data in an Input Record

Suppose that a file of sales statistics exists for a multi-branch retail organization such as a supermarket chain. Each record in the file contains the following data:

branch identifier
sales value in January, last year
sales value in February, last year
. . . . .
sales value in December, last year

A given record summarizes the monthly value of sales, for each month of the trading year, for a particular branch.

Looking at the individual records independently, the type of analyses required might be the yearly value of sales, the average monthly sales or the best/worst monthly sales for each branch. Similar figures might be required for the whole organization, using the accumulated values of the branch results.

What is required to solve any of these problems is a way of representing repetitive data such as the monthly sales values in the above example. Using the techniques which have been discussed so far in this book the following record description might be used:

```
sales-record
    sales-branch-id          branch identifier
    sales-value-jan          sales value for January
    sales-value-feb          sales value for February
     . . . . .
    sales-value-dec          sales value for December
```

To illustrate the use of this approach, consider two simple problems involving processing the records independently to produce values for a branch. To find the total annual sales value for a given branch would involve writing an operation of the form:

```
calculate-yearly-sales
    calculate yearly-sales-value =
        sales-value-jan + sales-value-feb +
        sales-value-mar + . . . . . + sales-value-dec
```

To find the maximum monthly sales value during the year would involve a sequence of operations as follows:

```
find-maximum-sale
    transfer sales-value-jan to max-sales-value
    if sales-value-feb > max-sales-value then
        transfer sales-value-feb to max-sales-value
    endif
     . . . . .
    if sales-value-dec > max-sales-value then
        transfer sales-value-dec to max-sales-value
    endif
```

In the above design fragments the ellipses, '. . . . .', have been used to denote repetition of similar constructs. When translating into COBOL no such shorthand exists - every operation will have to be explicitly stated.

These design fragments could be translated into COBOL and incorporated into a complete working program. However, the method is extremely clumsy and the prospect of processing fifty-two weekly sales values for the last year, using a similar method, would be very daunting.

Therefore a notation is required which will allow a collection of similar data-items to be named and described while allowing the value of each individual data-item to be picked out and used. In COBOL this data structure is called a _table_ and each data-item within the table is called an _element_ of the table. To represent the data in the example described above the following structure could be used:

```
sales-record
    sales-branch-id          branch identifier
    sales-value              sales value for one month
        repeated 12 times
```

The elements have to be identified by _subscripts_. A subscript must be an integer (whole number) value and in this case must be a number between one and twelve, as there are twelve elements in the table. To identify an element the name of the table is given followed by the subscript, of the element required, in parentheses. In this example the elements are:

sales-value (1)	sales value for January
sales-value (2)	sales value for February
. . . . .	
sales-value (12)	sales value for December

The subscript need not be a constant; indeed the power of tables comes from using data-items, containing integer values, as subscripts. To go back to the problems discussed earlier: if we wanted to find the total yearly sales value for a given branch we would now need to write a sequence of operations as follows:

```
calculate-yearly-sales
   transfer 0 to yearly-sales-value
   transfer 1 to month-no
   until month-no > 12 do
      calculate yearly-sales-value =
              yearly-sales-value + sales-value (month-no)
      calculate month-no = month-no + 1
   enduntil
```

The data-item 'month-no' must be of type integer (without a decimal point) and at least two digits in order to hold values up to 12. The data-item 'yearly-sales-value' should be able to hold a value twelve times the maximum value which can be held in a single element of the table 'sales-value'.

To illustrate the action of this procedure, consider the simplified set of sales values given in Figure 10.1.

sales-value

1	2	3	4	5	6	7	8	9	10	11	12
3.5	6.7	4.9	8.1	5.3	6.7	7.4	8.2	2.4	3.8	5.4	6.3

Figure 10.1

There are two temporary data-items 'yearly-sales-value' and 'month-no' which are initialized to one and zero, respectively. Therefore before entering the until loop the state of these temporary data-items is:

yearly-sales-value	month-no
0.0	1

The condition 'month-no > 12' is false therefore the body of the loop is executed. The first operation is:

```
calculate yearly-sales-value =
        yearly-sales-value + sales-value (month-no)
```

which means add the value of the element of the table sales-value identified by month-no to the current value of yearly-sales-value and put the result in yearly-sales-value. The value of month-no is one and the value of sales-value (1) is 3.5, therefore 3.5 is added to zero giving the result 3.5 which is stored in yearly-sales-value. The state of the temporary data-items is now:

yearly-sales-value	month-no
3.5	1

The second operation is:

    calculate month-no = month + 1

which adds one to the value of month-no. At the end of the loop the state of the temporary data-items is:

yearly-sales-value	month-no
3.5	2

Following the loop through again: the condition 'month-no > 12' is still false, therefore the value of sales-value (2), which is 6.7, is added to yearly-sales-value giving the result 10.2, in yearly-sales-value. The value of month-no is increased by one and the state after executing the loop twice is:

yearly-sales-value	month-no
10.2	3

The reader can follow through successive executions of the loop until eventually the state of the temporary data-items at the end of the twelfth execution of the loop should be:

yearly-sales-value	month-no
68.7	13

which causes an exit from the loop with yearly-sales-value containing the required total.

To find the maximum sales value in the table it is again possible to construct an until loop which works through the table processing each element in turn. The following procedure could be used to find the maximum monthly sales value during the year.

```
find-maximum-sale
   transfer sales-value (1) to max-sales-value
   transfer 2 to month-no
   until month-no > 12 do
      if sales-value (month-no) > max-sales-value then
         transfer sales-value (month-no) to max-sales-value
      endif
      calculate month-no = month-no + 1
   enduntil
```

The data-item 'month-no' again needs to be a two digit integer and 'max-sales-value' needs to be a data-item of the same type as one element of the table 'sales-value'. The reader is urged to work through the above procedure using the data values given in Figure 10.1. The initial state of the temporary data-items is:

max-sales-value	month-no
3.5	2

and the final state, on exit from the until loop, should be:

max-sales-value	month-no
8.2	13

The For Loop

Looking back at the versions of the two procedures 'calculate-yearly-sales' and 'find-maximum-sale' which process the elements of the table 'sales-value', there is an obvious similarity in the loop structure. In each case the sequence is:

(a) initialize: give an initial value to month-no (and possibly other data-items),

(b) test: see whether the value of month-no is greater than the final value required; if so exit from the loop,

(c) execute the operations in the body of the loop,

(d) increment: add one to the value of month-no,

(e) loop: go back to step (b).

In this case 'month-no' is called the control-item of the loop.

This structure is so common in programs involving tables that COBOL, like many other programming languages, has a special type of loop structure incorporating the above steps. In the design language this will be called the for loop which has the following structure:

```
for <control-data-item> = <initial-value> to <final-value> do
   <procedure>
endfor
```

The action of this construct is defined as follows:

(a) set the value of the <control-data-item> equal to <initial-value>,

(b) if the value of <control-data-item> is greater than <final-value> then jump to step (f),

(c) execute <procedure>,

(d) increase the value of the <control-data-item> by one,

(e) return to step (b),

(f) continue by executing the next statement after endfor.

Note that, like until, the for loop tests the condition before executing the body of the loop. Therefore if <initial-value> is greater the <final-value> the body of the loop will not be executed at all.

The two previous examples can now be rewritten using for loops as follows:

```
calculate-yearly-sales
   transfer 0 to yearly-sales-value
   for month-no = 1 to 12 do
      calculate yearly-sales-value =
               yearly-sales-value + sales-value (month-no)
   endfor

find-maximum-sale
   transfer sales-value (1) to max-sales-value
   for month-no = 2 to 12 do
      if sales-value (month-no) > max-sales-value then
         transfer sales-value (month-no) to max-sales-value
      endif
   endfor
```

The Overall Program Structure

The above fragments of program have been developed without reference to an overall program design. These procedures can be fitted into a simple program design to process all the records in the file and print the total sales and maximum sale for each branch.

The top level of the program design will be the familiar structure to process each record in a file:

```
branch-summaries
   print-headings
   get-next-branch
   until end-of-branch do
      deal-with-branch
      get-next-branch
   enduntil
```

The refinement of 'print-headings' should print any necessary page and column headings for the output report and is left for the reader to develop.

Under 'deal-with-branch' there will be three further refinements, the two developed above, for total sales and maximum monthly sale, and a procedure to print the results. Therefore, the refinement could be:

```
deal-with-branch
   calculate-yearly-sales
   find-maximum-sale
   print-branch-results
```

The two procedures developed above fit in at this point.

```
calculate-yearly-sales
   transfer 0 to yearly-sales-value
   for month-no = 1 to 12 do
      calculate yearly-sales-value =
               yearly-sales-value + sales-value (month-no)
   endfor

find-maximum-sale
   transfer sales-value (1) to max-sales-value
   for month-no = 2 to 12 do
      if sales-value (month-no) > max-sales-value then
         transfer sales-value (month-no) to max-sales-value
      endif
   endfor
```

Finally, the procedure 'print-branch-results' should print a summary line for the branch, so this might be of the form:

```
print-branch-results
   transfer sales-branch-id to summary-branch-id
   transfer yearly-sales-value to summary-yearly-sales
   transfer max-sales-value to summary-max-sale
   put-summary-line
```

The above example demonstrates that the use of tables in the input data does not affect the overall structure of the program, simply the detailed processing of each record.

Translation into COBOL

When a table consists of a repetition of single data-items then the representation in COBOL is quite straightforward. The picture of the repeated data-item is followed by the clause:

```
OCCURS <number-of-repetitions> TIMES
```

where <number-of-repetitions> is an integer constant defining the number of times the data-item is to be repeated. The elements of the table must be referenced by subscripts taking values from one to <number-of-repetitions>.

In the example of the monthly sales values, discussed earlier in this section, the description of the sales record might be:

```
01  SALES-RECORD.
    05  SALES-BRANCH-ID      PIC AAAA.
    05  SALES-VALUE          PIC 9(6)V99  OCCURS 12 TIMES.
```

Note that the occurs-clause is part of the description of the data-item, therefore the full stop which terminates the description comes after the occurs-clause.

The translation of the <u>for</u> loop into COBOL uses the same technique as the translation of <u>until</u>. The body of the loop becomes a paragraph and another variation of the PERFORM verb is used to implement the control of the loop. The design construct:

```
for <control-data-item> = <initial-value> to <final-value> do
    <procedure>
endfor
```

is translated into COBOL as:

```
        PERFORM <paragraph-name>
            VARYING <control-data-item> FROM <initial-value>
            BY 1 UNTIL <control-data-item> > <final-value>
    . . . . .
    <paragraph-name>.
        translation of <procedure>.
```

For example, the procedure:

```
find-maximum-sale
    transfer sales-value (1) to max-sales-value
    for month-no = 2 to 12 do
        if sales-value (month-no) > max-sales-value then
            transfer sales-value (month-no) to max-sales-value
        endif
    endfor
```

could be translated into COBOL as:

```
FIND-MAXIMUM-SALE.
    MOVE SALES-VALUE (1) TO MAX-SALES-VALUE
    PERFORM COMPARE-WITH-MAX
        VARYING MONTH-NO FROM 2
        BY 1 UNTIL MONTH-NO > 12.

COMPARE-WITH-MAX.
    IF SALES-VALUE (MONTH-NO) > MAX-SALES-VALUE
        MOVE SALES-VALUE (MONTH-NO) TO MAX-SALES-VALUE.
```

In this example the data-item MONTH-NO will need to be described as:

```
01  TEMPORARY-ITEMS.
    05  MONTH-NO          PIC 99.
```

One of the commonest reasons for beginners' programs which use tables failing with execution errors is the incorrect description of subscripts. In the above example, if the data-item MONTH-NO is described as PIC 9 the program will fail with a subscript error, or some similar message, which indicates that an attempt has been made to use a non-existent element of the table. This is because the sequence of values generated for MONTH-NO will be

2, 3, 4, 5, 6, 7, 8, 9, 0

It is impossible to represent the value 10 in a single digit and therefore the value stored is truncated to zero. Since SALES-VALUE (0) does not exist, the program fails. Whenever describing a data-item to be used as a subscript - ensure that it is big enough to hold all possible subscript values.

An associated problem which arises occasionally is caused by the subscript going one value past the end of the table. If there are twenty elements in a table then after executing a <u>for</u> loop the subscript will contain the value twenty-one. Therefore a table with ninety-nine elements needs a three digit subscript.

The PERFORM . . . VARYING option may not be implemented in low-level ANS COBOL compilers; an alternative translation of the <u>for</u> loop is given in Appendix 5.5.

10.2 Tables in Working-Storage

There is a group of problems which can be classified as frequency counting problems. An example of this type of problem, used in many programming textbooks, is the accumulation of election results. Suppose that there are, say, 10 candidates in an election, numbered from one to ten. A file contains one record for each vote cast giving the number of the candidate voted for. The records will be in the order in which the votes were cast and one possible approach is to work through the file tallying the votes for each of the candidates.

One can visualize this process being done with a pile of voting slips and a pencil and paper. The process starts by writing down the numbers of the ten candidates on the sheet of paper. Taking each voting slip in turn, the candidate number is read and one is added to the total for the appropriate candidate. After processing all the voting slips the final totals for each candidate are given on the paper and the winner can be selected.

Within a program the piece of paper used to accumulate the totals becomes a table in temporary storage. This table will have ten elements, one for each candidate. As each voting record is processed the appropriate element of the table will be increased by one to show another vote cast for a particular candidate. At the end of the program the contents of the table can be printed to summarize the votes cast for each candidate. The winning candidate can be identified by finding the largest value in the table.

The program will be complicated by the fact that the data has to be checked to ensure that no invalid candidate numbers are entered. A person using the equivalent pencil and paper method will recognize an invalid candidate number and ignore it. If a candidate number is read by the program which is not in the range one to ten and there is no check then the program will fail with an execution error.

This is a comparatively simple problem, as the candidates are identified by a contiguous set of numbers. If the candidates were identified by name, the problem becomes more difficult to solve by using a program, although the person using the pencil and paper doesn't need to change his method. This is because people are much better at pattern recognition than computers.

Many similar problems exist in data processing. One particular example will be studied in some detail to introduce the idea of a temporary storage table and to show the variety of techniques for using the table.

Every time an item, or quantity of similar items, is sold by a shop a record is written to a cumulative file. Each record contains:

Date of sale
Till number
Item number
Quantity sold
Price per item

This data could be collected automatically from some of the 'point-of-sale' checkouts currently used in large stores. This cumulative file is mainly used by the shop's auditors and is called the transaction _log_. One of the auditor's main tasks is to analyse the sales of specific items, or groups of items, to cross-check these with the stock control figures. The file is so large that sorting all the records into item number order and picking out those required is not feasible. Therefore, one possible solution is to write a program which will search through the file and accumulate totals for the specified items.

At its simplest, when the specified item numbers form a contiguous group, this problem is similar to vote counting in an election. It becomes more difficult when there are ranges of item numbers involved and much more complex when a random set of item numbers is specified. The problem might also be extended in other directions, for example, to accumulate the value of sales as well as the quantity sold for each specified item, assuming the price per item is not necessarily constant for a particular item.

The simplest problem is to write a program which will produce a summary of the quantity sold for each of the items numbered, say, one to twenty-five. There will need to be a table, called say 'total-quantity', containing twenty-five elements to accumulate the quantities. As each record from the log file is processed it will need to be checked to see if it belongs to the required group. If the item number is in the range one to twenty-five then the quantity sold can be added to the appropriate element of the table. After processing all the records in the log file the contents of the table can be printed out.

Each element of a table used for the accumulation of data has to be initialized to zero in the same way as a simple data-item used for accumulating a running total.

The basic structure of the required program is:

```
accumulate-totals
   initialize-table
   get-next-log-file
   until end-of-log-file do
      update-table
      get-next-log-file
   enduntil
   print-table
```

The structure of this program is similar to that for a program which accumulates some simple totals from a file (see Example 2.5, page 16). The only difference is that a table of data-items is being used for accumulation rather than a simple data-item or several simple data-items.

The first refinement is 'initialize-table' which should set the value of each element of the table to zero. This can be done using a for loop of the form:

```
initialize-table
   for tq-subscript = 1 to 25 do
      transfer 0 to total-quantity (tq-subscript)
   endfor
```

The temporary data-item 'tq-subscript' is associated with the table 'total-quantity' and must be described so that it is large enough to hold any legal subscript value for that table. The name 'tq-subscript' was chosen to show the use of this data-item as a subscript and its association with 'total-quantity'.

Before refining 'update-table', it is necessary to allocate names to the data-items in the input record. A possible set of names is:

```
log-record
   log-sale-date          date of sale
   log-till-no            till number of sale
   log-item-no            item number
   log-quantity-sold      quantity of item sold
   log-item-price         price per item
```

To update the element of the table corresponding to the current item number the operation is:

```
calculate total-quantity (log-item-no) =
   total-quantity (log-item-no) + log-quantity-sold
```

However, it is only quantities sold for item numbers in the range one to twenty-five, inclusive, which are to be accumulated in the table. Therefore the refinement should be:

```
update-table
   if log-item-no > 0 and log-item-no < 26 then
      calculate total-quantity (log-item-no) =
         total-quantity (log-item-no) + log-quantity-sold
   endif
```

After processing all the records in the log file the program needs to print the contents of the table. Suppose that the output record is:

```
summary-line
   summary-item-no
   summary-total-quantity
```

Then, to produce a listing of the contents of the table requires a simple for loop of the form:

```
print-table
   for tq-subscript = 1 to 25 do
      transfer tq-subscript to summary-item-no
      transfer total-quantity (tq-subscript)
         to summary-total-quantity
      put-summary-line
   endfor
```

There are two main points to note about this refinement. Firstly, the item numbers for the summary-line are being generated by the for loop as they correspond to the subscripts of the table, they are not actually stored in the table. Secondly, the 'put-summary-line' must be inside the for loop as one line is required for each element of the table.

If the reader is in any doubt about the operation of this program then it is suggested that the program should be executed by hand.

The size of the table is not important; therefore, to make the hand execution less tedious, substitute 5 for 25 (and 6 for 26) in the above design. Draw a table with five elements, as shown in Figure 10.2.

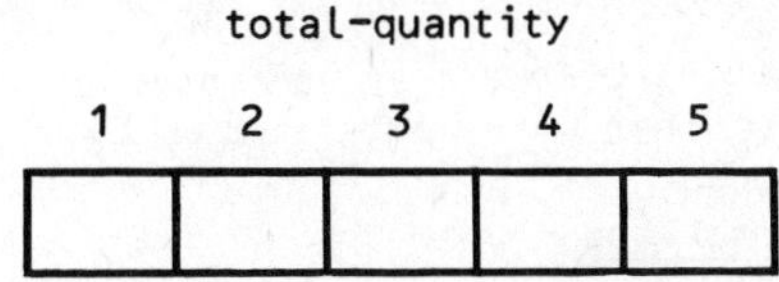

Figure 10.2

Now work through the program design obeying the instructions, using the following input data:

log-item-no	log-quantity-sold
2	3
36	16
3	12
2	4
0	5
4	26
1	2
3	24

The output from the program should be:

1	2
2	7
3	36
4	26
5	0

Implementation in COBOL

The only difference between the implementation of this program and the one given in 9.1 is that 'total-quantity' needs to be described in the WORKING-STORAGE SECTION of the program.

Therefore, the following would appear in the corresponding COBOL program:

```
WORKING-STORAGE SECTION.
01  STATE-VECTOR.
    05  END-LOG-FILE          PIC X.
        88  END-OF-LOG-FILE   VALUE "E".
01  TOTAL-QUANTITY-TABLE.
    05  TOTAL-QUANTITY        PIC 9(6)   OCCURS 25 TIMES.
    05  TQ-SUBSCRIPT          PIC 99.
```

The name of the data-item for the subscript is just another data-name but it should be chosen so as to emphasize the use of the data-item. If the data-item for the subscript is described immediately following the elements of the table, in the same data structure, then this should assist somebody reading the program to associate the subscript with the table.

There is a rule in COBOL that an occurs clause must not be associated with a data-item with level-number 01.

More Complex Transformations

Suppose that, instead of item numbers in the range one to twenty-five, the auditors wanted to accumulate quantities for each of the numbers in the range 1016 to 1040. This is apparently a different problem to the one solved above but note that there are still twenty-five different item numbers required. What is required is to accumulate the quantities for item number 1016 in the first table element, 1017 in the second element and so on, with item number 1040 being associated with the twenty-fifth table element. This means that the item numbers have to be 'mapped' from their present range onto the range one to twenty-five. This mapping is quite simple - subtract 1015 from the item number to give the corresponding subscript of the table.

The general structure of the program is the same as the one developed earlier in this section. There are only two refinements that are affected by this change in problem specification: 'update-table' and 'print-table'. The first of these needs to be modified to pick out the correct range of values and to map these item numbers onto the subscripts of the table. The revised version could be:

```
update-table
   if log-item-no > 1015 and log-item-no < 1041 then
      calculate tq-subscript = log-item-no - 1015
      calculate total-quantity (tq-subscript) =
         total-quantity (tq-subscript) + log-quantity-sold
   endif
```

In order to print a meaningful output summary the subscripts of the table must be mapped back to the corresponding item numbers. This can be done quite simply by adding 1015 to the subscript. The revised refinement of 'print-table' might be:

```
print-table
   for tq-subscript = 1 to 25 do
      calculate summary-item-no = tq-subscript + 1015
      transfer total-quantity (tq-subscript)
         to summary-total-quantity
      put-summary-line
   endfor
```

There are, then, only three changes required in the program design: the range checking, the mapping from item number to subscript and the mapping back from subscript to item number.

The basic design can be used to solve any problem where it is possible to define a mapping from item numbers to table subscripts. Suppose that the stock numbering system in the example is designed so that similar items are grouped together. The auditors are interested in checking on quantities sold within each group rather than for individual items. As an example, consider the problem of accumulating the quantities sold for each of the following groups of item numbers: 2000-2009, 2010-2019, 2020-2029, ... 2190-2199. There are twenty groups of item numbers; so a table of twenty elements is required and the mapping needed is:

log-item-no	subscript
2000 - 2009	1
2010 - 2019	2
2020 - 2029	3
. . . . .	.
2190 - 2199	20

If the last digit of log-item-no is ignored, there are twenty numbers in the range 200 to 219. To map these truncated values onto a table with twenty elements simply requires the subtraction of 199.

To ignore the last digit of log-item-no, it would be possible to use a simple 'trick' in describing this data-item. The description of log-item-no could be:

```
05  LOG-ITEM-NO.
    10  LOG-ITEM-NO-1-3     PIC 999.
    10  LOG-ITEM-NO-4       PIC 9.
```

The mapping from log-item-no to subscript is then of the form:

```
calculate tq-subscript = log-item-no-1-3 - 199
```

A more generally applicable technique, which does not depend on the data structuring features of COBOL, is to divide log-item-no by ten and discard the fractional part. To do this in COBOL a temporary data-item could be described with one digit less than log-item-no. For example, assuming log-item-no has four digits:

```
01  TEMPORARY-ITEMS.
    05  TRUNC-ITEM-NO        PIC 999.
```

Then the operation:

```
calculate trunc-item-no = log-item-no / 10
```

removes the last digit of log-item-no. The complete mapping would then be:

```
calculate trunc-item-no = log-item-no / 10
calculate tq-subscript = trunc-item-no - 199
```

This mapping can then be substituted into 'update-table' to give the following revised refinement.

```
update-table
   if log-item-no > 1999 and log-item-no < 2200 then
      calculate trunc-item-no = log-item-no / 10
      calculate tq-subscript = trunc-item-no - 199
      calculate total-quantity (tq-subscript) =
         total-quantity (tq-subscript) + log-quantity-sold
   endif
```

To produce meaningful output a reverse mapping from subscript to item number has to be defined. Since the program is now dealing with ranges of values it would seem sensible to redefine summary-line as follows:

```
summary-line
   summary-low-item-no              lowest item number in range
   summary-high-item-no             highest item number in range
   summary-total-quantity           total quantity sold for range
```

To transform the subscript to the lowest value in the range the operation could be:

```
calculate summary-low-item-no = (tq-subscript + 199) * 10
```

and for the highest value in the range:

```
calculate summary-high-item-no = (tq-subscript + 199) * 10 + 9
```

The revised refinement for printing the table is then:

```
print-table
   for tq-subscript = 1 to 25 do
      calculate summary-low-item-no =
         (tq-subscript + 199) * 10
      calculate summary-high-item-no =
         (tq-subscript + 199) * 10 + 9
      transfer total-quantity (tq-subscript)
         to summary-total-quantity
      put-summary-line
   endfor
```

Although it is possible to extend this approach by using ever more complex mapping algorithms it is not really very instructive to do so. A more general solution to the problem is given in Section 10.4.

10.3 Repeated Group-items

In the examples discussed in Sections 10.1 and 10.2 it was assumed that a table consisted of a number of repetitions of an elementary-item. It is also possible to have repeated group-items as part of a data structure.

Suppose that the input to a program consists of records containing the details from an employee's time sheet for one week. Each record might contain: employee number, employee's department, six sets of daily figures for normal time and overtime working, and normal and overtime rates of pay. This record structure could be described as:

```
employee-record
   employee-number                  employee number
   employee-dept                    employee's department code
   employee-hours                   hours worked per day
         repeated 6 times
      employee-h-normal                normal hours worked
      employee-h-overtime              overtime hours worked
   employee-normal-rate             normal rate of pay
   employee-overtime-rate           overtime rate of pay
```

There are six elements of the table 'employee-hours' which can be identified using a subscript, so it is possible to refer to employee-hours (1), employee-hours (day-no), etc. However, each element of the table is subdivided into 'employee-h-normal' and 'employee-h-overtime'. If reference is made to either of these elementary-items then the name must be subscripted.

To add up the number of 'normal' hours that an employee had worked in a week would require a for loop of the form:

```
transfer 0 to total-normal-hours
for day-no = 1 to 6 do
   calculate total-normal-hours =
      total-normal-hours + employee-h-normal (day-no)
endfor
```

The structure of the record can be visualized as shown in Figure 10.3.

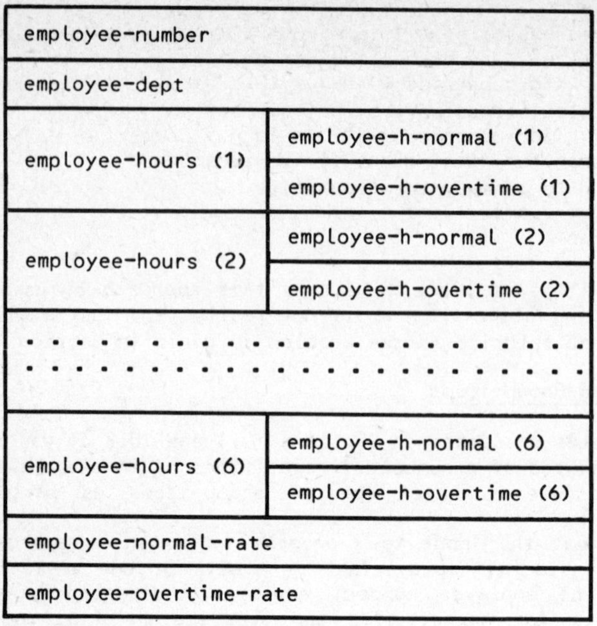

employee-number	
employee-dept	
employee-hours (1)	employee-h-normal (1)
	employee-h-overtime (1)
employee-hours (2)	employee-h-normal (2)
	employee-h-overtime (2)
. . . .	
employee-hours (6)	employee-h-normal (6)
	employee-h-overtime (6)
employee-normal-rate	
employee-overtime-rate	

Figure 10.3

The description of this record in COBOL is quite straightforward. The occurs clause, to indicate repetition, is associated with the name of the group-item; all subordinate items in the group will be repeated by implication. A possible description for the employee record is:

```
01  EMPLOYEE-RECORD.
    05  EMPLOYEE-NUMBER                PIC 9(6).
    05  EMPLOYEE-DEPT                  PIC AA.
    05  EMPLOYEE-HOURS  OCCURS 6 TIMES.
        10  EMPLOYEE-H-NORMAL          PIC 9.
        10  EMPLOYEE-H-OVERTIME        PIC 99.
    05  EMPLOYEE-NORMAL-RATE           PIC 9V99.
    05  EMPLOYEE-OVERTIME-RATE         PIC 9V99.
```

The group-item to be repeated may have more than one level of subordinate data-items. However many levels are involved in the structure ali the data-items belonging to the repeated group-item must be subscripted when referenced. For example:

```
insurance-record
   insurance-name                  name of policyholder
   insurance-policy                details for each policy
        repeated 10 times
      insurance-p-number           policy number
      insurance-p-matdate          date of maturity of policy
         insurance-p-m-month       month of maturity
         insurance-p-m-year        year of maturity
      insurance-p-amount           sum assured
   insurance-age                   age of the policyholder
```

To pick out the year in which the third policy reaches maturity will require a reference to insurance-p-m-year (3). Note that a table may only consist of a fixed number of elements. Therefore if any elements in the table 'insurance-policy' are not used they must be filled with spaces or zeros. Conversely, if a policyholder has more than ten policies, a continuation record will be required or the table size will have to be adjusted for <u>all</u> records.

It is possible to have a repeated item within a repeated group-item; this will be discussed in Section 10.6.

A repeated group-item can also be useful for accumulating data. In the main example discussed in Section 10.2, only the quantities sold were accumulated. It might be more realistic to accumulate both the quantity sold and the value of sales for each of the specified ranges of item numbers. To do this a table could be described in the WORKING-STORAGE SECTION of the form:

```
totals-for-item
      repeated <number-of-ranges> times
   total-quantity
   total-value
```

The program design developed at the end of Section 10.2 could be extended to include the accumulation of sales values. The input data is:

```
log-record
   log-sale-date           date of sale
   log-till-no             till number of sale
   log-item-no             item number
   log-quantity-sold       quantity of item sold
   log-item-price          price per item
```

To output the total value of sales an extra data-item needs to be added to the output record, 'summary-line', for example:

```
summary-line
   summary-low-item-no             lowest item number in range
   summary-high-item-no            highest item number in range
   summary-total-quantity          total quantity sold for range
   summary-total-value             total sales value for range
```

The revised program design, to include totalling values is given below. The name of the subscript for the table has been changed to 'tfi-subscript' as the subscript refers to elements of the table 'totals-for-items'.

```
accumulate-totals
   initialize-table
   get-next-log-file
   until end-of-log-file do
      update-table
      get-next-log-file
   enduntil
   print-table

initialize-table
   for tfi-subscript = 1 to 25 do
      transfer 0 to total-quantity (tfi-subscript)
      transfer 0 to total-value (tfi-subscript)
   endfor

update-table
   if log-item-no > 1999 and log-item-no < 2200 then
      calculate trunc-item-no = log-item-no / 10
      calculate tfi-subscript = trunc-item-no - 199
      calculate total-quantity (tfi-subscript) =
         total-quantity (tfi-subscript) + log-quantity-sold
      calculate total-value (tfi-subscript) =
         total-value (tfi-subscript)
         + log-quantity-sold * log-item-price
   endif

print-table
   for tfi-subscript = 1 to 25 do
      calculate summary-low-item-no =
         (tfi-subscript + 199) * 10
      calculate summary-high-item-no =
         (tfi-subscript + 199) * 10 + 9
      transfer total-quantity (tfi-subscript)
         to summary-total-quantity
      transfer total-value (tfi-subscript)
         to summary-total-value
      put-summary-line
   endfor
```

The description of the table in the corresponding COBOL program should now be:

```
WORKING-STORAGE SECTION.
01  STATE-VECTOR.
    05  END-LOG-FILE          PIC X.
        88  END-OF-LOG-FILE VALUE "E".
01  ITEM-TOTALS-TABLE.
    05  TOTALS-FOR-ITEM OCCURS 20 TIMES.
        10  TOTAL-QUANTITY   PIC 9(6).
        10  TOTAL-VALUE      PIC 9(8)V99.
    05  TFI-SUBSCRIPT        PIC 99.
```

10.4 Searching a Table

The algorithms outlined in Section 10.2 all dealt with a fixed set of item numbers which may be useful in some circumstances but in general will be too restrictive.

The more general solution is to read in the required item numbers from a separate file and store them in a table. Each element of this table should then be a group-item consisting of elementary-items to hold an item number and the associated quantity and sales value for that item. The log file is then processed and the item number in each record is compared with the item numbers in the table. If the item number in a record matches an item number in the table then the associated data-items, for quantity and sales value, are updated using values from the record.

The general structure of the program is similar to that used throughout Sections 10.2 and 10.3 and is given below.

```
table-search
   initialize-table
   get-next-log-file
   until end-of-log-file do
      update-table
      get-next-log-file
   enduntil
   print-table
```

However, the refinements of 'initialize-table' and 'update-table' are much more complex now.

The table to hold the required item numbers and their associated quantities and values could be described as:

```
search-item
      repeated <table-size> times
   search-item-no
   search-quantity
   search-value
```

The number of elements in the table, given by <table-size>, defines the maximum number of required item numbers that can be specified but the table does not need to be filled with item numbers. To subscript the table a data-item 'si-subscript' can be described and to indicate the position of the last item number in the table an additional data-item 'si-limit' can be defined. This means that at any time the only elements of 'search-item' that hold information are 'search-item (1)' to 'search-item (si-limit)' inclusive.

If the required item numbers are to be read from a file called 'req-file' in which each record contains a data-item 'req-item-no' then a first attempt at refining 'update-table' might be:

```
initialize-table
    transfer 0 to si-subscript
    get-next-req-file
    until end-of-req-file do
        calculate si-subscript = si-subscript + 1
        transfer req-item-no to search-item-no (si-subscript)
        transfer 0 to search-quantity (si-subscript)
        transfer 0 to search-value (si-subscript)
        get-next-req-file
    enduntil
    transfer si-subscript to si-limit
```

This piece of program works through 'req-file' and for each record in it initializes an element in the table 'search-item' by storing the required item number, 'req-item-no', and setting the associated data-items to zero. When the file of required item numbers is exhausted the data-item 'si-limit' is set to the current subscript value to show how many item numbers are stored in the table. The data-item 'si-limit' will then be treated as a constant for the rest of the program.

The refinement shown above will work correctly until somebody inadvertently puts more item numbers into 'req-file' than can be stored in the table. The program will then fail with a subscript error when the value of 'si-subscript' exceeds <table-size>. It would be possible to leave the user with a system error but it is better practice to trap the error inside the program, give the user an intelligible error message and take appropriate action.

In this case, there are two obvious alternative courses of action; either ignore any required item numbers which cannot be stored in the table or exit from the program, not attempting to do any accumulation. The latter course of action is probably more sensible because if a user specifies, say, fifty item numbers then presumably the first thirty, if that is all the table will hold, are not sufficient for his needs.

Therefore, if the value of 'si-subscript' exceeds <table-size>, a message should be displayed and the program stopped. One way of doing this is shown below.

```
initialize-table
    transfer 0 to si-subscript
    get-next-req-file
    until end-of-req-file do
        calculate si-subscript = si-subscript + 1
        check-table-overflow
        transfer req-item-no to search-item-no (si-subscript)
        transfer 0 to search-quantity (si-subscript)
        transfer 0 to search-value (si-subscript)
        get-next-req-file
    enduntil
    transfer si-subscript to si-limit

check-table-overflow
    if si-subscript > <table-size> then
        display "too many item numbers specified"
        display "maximum possible is <table-size>"
        close-down
    endif
```

The reference to 'close-down' causes the standard end of program procedure to be executed and the program will stop because there is a STOP RUN in close-down. If 'initialize-table' is successfully executed, the table 'search-item' should be properly initialized with item numbers stored in the first and succeeding elements up to and including the element with subscript 'si-limit'.

To update the table it is necessary to set up a search loop which compares 'log-item-no' with each 'search-item-no' in turn. If a match is found then the corresponding quantity and value should be updated. A first attempt at the refinement of 'update-table' might be:

```
update-table
   for si-subscript = 1 to si-limit do
      if log-item-no = search-item-no (si-subscript) then
         accumulate-data
      endif
   endfor

accumulate-data
   calculate search-quantity (si-subscript) =
      search-quantity (si-subscript) + log-quantity-sold
   calculate search-value (si-subscript) =
      search-value (si-subscript)
      + log-quantity-sold * log-item-price
```

This solution does not make use of the fact that if an item number has been found in the table then there is no point in continuing the search. A slightly more efficient algorithm would be:

```
update-table
   transfer false to end-of-search
   transfer 1 to si-subscript
   until end-of-search do
      if log-item-no = search-item-no (si-subscript) then
         accumulate-data
         transfer true to end-of-search
      else
         calculate si-subscript = si-subscript + 1
         if si-subscript > si-limit then
            transfer true to end-of-search
         endif
      endif
   enduntil
```

The Boolean end-of-search is used to control the search loop. Initially it is set to <u>false</u> and the search continues until either a match is found or there is no possibility of finding a match, when 'si-subscript' goes beyond 'si-limit'.

To complete the program description the final refinement 'print-table' can be added. The output record can be defined as follows:

```
summary-line
   summary-item-no               required item number
   summary-total-quantity        total quantity of item sold
   summary-total-value           total value of item sales
```

The refinement is a straightforward for loop of the form:

```
print-table
   for si-subscript = 1 to si-limit do
      transfer search-item-no (si-subscript)
         to summary-item-no
      transfer search-quantity (si-subscript)
         to summary-total-quantity
      transfer search-value (si-subscript)
         to summary-total-value
      put-summary-line
   endfor
```

Implementation in COBOL

To implement the above algorithm in COBOL what is needed is a table containing a repeated group-item, as described in Section 10.4, and two input files, one for the required item numbers and the other for the log file. The DATA DIVISION of the corresponding program could be:

```
DATA DIVISION.
FILE SECTION.
FD  REQ-FILE
    LABEL RECORDS OMITTED.
01  REQ-RECORD.
    05  REQ-ITEM-NO                 PIC 9(8).

FD  LOG-FILE
    LABEL RECORDS STANDARD.
01  LOG-RECORD.
    05  LOG-SALE-DATE               PIC 9(8).
    05  LOG-TILL-NO                 PIC 9(4).
    05  LOG-ITEM-NO                 PIC 9(8).
    05  LOG-QUANTITY-SOLD           PIC 9(4).
    05  LOG-ITEM-PRICE              PIC 999V99.

FD  OUTFILE
    LABEL RECORDS OMITTED.
01  OUT-LINE           PIC X(120).

WORKING-STORAGE SECTION.
01  STATE-VECTOR.
    05  END-LOG-FILE          PIC X.
        88  END-OF-LOG-FILE VALUE "E".
    05  END-REQ-FILE          PIC X.
        88  END-OF-REQ-FILE VALUE "E".

01  SEARCH-ITEM-TABLE.
    05  SEARCH-ITEM  OCCURS 30 TIMES.
        10  SEARCH-ITEM-NO          PIC 9(8).
        10  SEARCH-QUANTITY         PIC 9(6).
        10  SEARCH-VALUE            PIC 9(6)V99.
    05  SI-SUBSCRIPT                PIC 99.
    05  SI-LIMIT                    PIC 99.
```

```
01  SUMMARY-LINE.
    05  SUMMARY-ITEM-NO          PIC 9(8).
    05  FILLER                   PIC X(4).
    05  SUMMARY-TOTAL-QUANTITY   PIC Z(5)9.
    05  FILLER                   PIC X(4).
    05  SUMMARY-TOTAL-VALUE      PIC ££££,££9.99.
```

The size of the table must be chosen to exceed the maximum number of required item numbers expected to be specified by the user of the program. In the above example an arbitrary limit of 30 has been chosen.

A General Table Search Algorithm

The idea of searching a table has been introduced in this section using the example which was introduced in Section 10.2 and has gone through a number of variations since then. It is possible to remove the parts of the program design specific to that problem and identify a framework for an algorithm to initialize and search a table of key values.

This algorithm will work for any type of key: alphabetic, numeric or alphanumeric, unlike some of the earlier algorithms which depended on the transformation of numeric values into subscripts. The general form of the problem requires input from two files: 'req-file', the list of required key values, and 'data-file', containing the raw data to be analyzed. These two files will be assumed to contain the following record structures:

```
req-record
   req-key           required key value

data-record
   data-key          key value, in same format as req-key
   data-details      other data-items containing values
```

For output of the accumulated values it will be assumed that there is a file called 'summary-file' which contains records in the form:

```
summary-record
   summary-key             required key value
   summary-details         data-items for the output of
                                   accumulated values
```

In order to accumulate values from 'data-file' there will need to be a table in WORKING-STORAGE of the form:

```
stored-data
      repeated <table-size> times
   stored-key              key value (from req-file)
   stored-details          data-items for accumulation
```

To access the table there will need to be a data-item 'sd-subscript' and a data-item to record the number of elements in the table which are used, 'sd-limit'.

The general form of the algorithm is given below. The actual updating of the table depends on the number and type of different values which are to be accumulated. The production of output will similarly be affected by the structure of the table and is therefore left incomplete. Points which are problem specific are enclosed between '<' and '>'.

```
table-search
   initialize-table
   get-next-data-file
   until end-of-data-file do
      update-table
      get-next-data-file
   enduntil
   print-table

initialize-table
   transfer 0 to sd-subscript
   get-next-req-file
   until end-of-req-file do
      calculate sd-subscript = sd-subscript + 1
      check-table-overflow
      transfer req-key to stored-key (sd-subscript)
      <initialize stored-details>
      get-next-req-file
   enduntil
   transfer sd-subscript to sd-limit

check-table-overflow
   if sd-subscript > <table-size> then
      <write message to user>
      close-down
   endif

update-table
   transfer false to end-of-search
   transfer 1 to sd-subscript
   until end-of-search do
      if data-key = stored-key (sd-subscript) then
         <update stored details>
         transfer true to end-of-search
      else
         calculate sd-subscript = sd-subscript + 1
         if sd-subscript > sd-limit then
            transfer true to end-of-search
         endif
      endif
   enduntil

print-table
   print-headings
   for sd-subscript = 1 to sd-limit do
      transfer stored-key (sd-subscript) to summary-key
      <transfer stored-details to summary-details>
      put-summary-line
   endfor

print-headings
   <print headings for output>
```

10.5 Multi-dimensional Tables

So far the tables discussed have been "one-dimensional", that is one element, an elementary-item or group-item, repeated a number of times. It is possible to have tables with two or more dimensions, "multi-dimensional tables", by having repeated data-items within group-items which are themselves repeated and so on. In this book, the principal examples developed (and exercises given) are all based on one-dimensional tables but two-dimensional tables will be introduced briefly and the reader can experiment with them if he or she so desires.

As an example of a two-dimensional table, consider the following structure:

```
branch-table
   branch-sales                         year's sales for branch
          repeated 30 times
      branch-s-code                     branch identifier
      branch-s-month-value              sales value for one month
             repeated 12 times
```

The table element branch-sales is repeated 30 times and within each of these elements there is one occurrence of 'branch-s-code' and twelve repetitions of 'branch-s-month-value'. To identify a particular occurrence of 'branch-sales' the name must be subscripted, for example: branch-sales (25), branch-sales (bs-subscript). To access the corresponding 'branch-s-code' this must also be subscripted, for example: branch-s-code (25), branch-s-code (bs-subscript).

Within each occurrence of the repeated group-item branch-sales there are twelve occurrences of 'branch-s-month-value'. Therefore to identify one of these <u>two</u> subscripts are needed, one to identify which 'branch-sales' is required and the other to indicate which of the 'branch-s-month-value' elements within this group-item is required. These subscripts are written in the order in which the occurs-clauses appear in the data-structure. So a reference to

```
branch-s-month-value (bs-subscript, 3)
```

means the third branch-s-month-value element within the branch-sales element subscripted by bs-subscript. Alternatively: find the branch-sales element subscripted by bs-subscript and within that element find the third occurrence of 'branch-s-month-value'.

The structure of the table could be visualized as shown in Figure 10.4.

The description of this table in a COBOL program would be of the form:

```
01  BRANCH-TABLE.
    05  BRANCH-SALES  OCCURS 30 TIMES.
        10  BRANCH-S-CODE                PIC XXX.
        10  BRANCH-S-MONTH-VALUE         PIC 9(5)V99
            OCCURS 12 TIMES.
```

branch-table

<table>
<tr><td rowspan="5">branch-sales (1)</td><td>branch-s-code (1)</td></tr>
<tr><td>branch-s-month-value (1,1)</td></tr>
<tr><td>branch-s-month-value (1,2)</td></tr>
<tr><td>. . . . .</td></tr>
<tr><td>branch-s-month-value (1,12)</td></tr>
<tr><td rowspan="5">branch-sales (2)</td><td>branch-s-code (2)</td></tr>
<tr><td>branch-s-month-value (2,1)</td></tr>
<tr><td>branch-s-month-value (2,2)</td></tr>
<tr><td>. . . . .</td></tr>
<tr><td>branch-s-month-value (2,12)</td></tr>
<tr><td colspan="2">. . . . .
. . . .</td></tr>
<tr><td rowspan="5">branch-sales (30)</td><td>branch-s-code (30)</td></tr>
<tr><td>branch-s-month-value (30,1)</td></tr>
<tr><td>branch-s-month-value (30,2)</td></tr>
<tr><td>. . . . .</td></tr>
<tr><td>branch-s-month-value (30,12)</td></tr>
</table>

Figure 10.4

Figure 10.5 shows a fictitious example of the type of table, often presented by insurance companies, showing the relationship between premiums paid and the expected surrender value of the policy if bonuses continue to accrue at the present level.

	Guaranteed Life Cover of £5,000		Guaranteed Life Cover of £10,000		Guaranteed Life Cover of £20,000	
Age	Monthly Premium	Expected Return	Monthly Premium	Expected Return	Monthly Premium	Expected Return
18	2.85	8,672	4.82	18,545	9.21	39,128
19	2.96	8,593	4.97	18,427	9.43	38,974
.. ..	. . . . . .	. . . . . .	. . . . . .	. . . . . .	. . . . . .	. . . . . .
50	5.22	5,825	10.13	11,742	20.11	23,818

Figure 10.5

To represent the information contained in the body of this table within a COBOL program would require a two-dimensional table of the form:

```
plan-table
   plan-line                          line for one age
         repeated 33 times
      plan-l-age                      age of proposer
      plan-l-column                   column of premiums and returns
            repeated 3 times
         plan-l-c-premium             monthly premium
         plan-l-c-return              expected return
```

The monthly premium payable by a nineteen year old person requiring life cover of £10,000 would then be given by 'plan-l-c-premium (2,2)' and the expected return for a thirty year old requiring life cover of £20,000 would be given by 'plan-l-c-return (13,3)'.

The description of the corresponding table in COBOL would be of the form:

```
01  PLAN-TABLE.
    05  PLAN-LINE  OCCURS 33 TIMES.
        10  PLAN-L-AGE             PIC 99.
        10  PLAN-L-COLUMN  OCCURS 3 TIMES.
            15  PLAN-L-C-PREMIUM   PIC 99V99.
            15  PLAN-L-C-RETURN    PIC 9(5).
```

10.6 Case Study

This case study is intended to illustrate the use of tables, giving an example of a slightly different type of table search to that discussed in Section 10.4. The problem specification is as follows:

The computer system for a motor trader, Honest Joe (Motors) Ltd., includes a file containing the details of all vehicles sold during the last month. Among the details held in the file are the model code for the vehicle sold, the gross value of the sale and the profit on the sale.

The simplified format of the input record is:

```
Vehicle sales record
    Model code              3 characters
    Gross sale value        7 digits (pence)
    Profit on sale          6 digits (pence, signed)
```

A model code consists of a mixture of alphabetic and numeric characters, and there are less than fifty model codes in use. The vehicle sales file is held in invoice number order.

A program is required which will produce a summary of the numbers of each model sold during the last month, together with the average gross value and average profit for each model.

This problem differs from that discussed in Section 10.4 as the search keys are not being provided separately but will need to be built up from the model codes in the vehicle sales file. A table will be required in which each different model code can be stored, together with the accumulated data for that model. For each record in the vehicle sales file it will be necessary to check whether its model code is already in the table. If the model code is present in the table then the details for that model will need to be updated, otherwise the model code will need to be stored in the table together with the sales details.

The program is required to produce the numbers of a particular model sold, the average gross value and average profit for that model. Therefore the table will need to be a repeated group-item made up of four elementary-items. For example:

```
model-table
    model-counter
          repeated 50 times
        model-c-code               stored model code
        model-c-numbers            number of this model sold
        model-c-gross    gross value of sales for this model
        model-c-profit   profit on sales for this model
```

The size of the table can be fixed at fifty elements because the problem specification states that there are "less than fifty model codes in use".

Once all the data has been accumulated from the vehicle sales file the averages for the gross value and profit on each model can be calculated and printed.

The vehicle sales file will probably contain a great deal of detail about the sale of each vehicle but for the purposes of this example only the data-items directly relevant to the problem will be identified. Each record in the vehicle sales file, 'vehicle-file', will include the following data-items:

```
vehicle-record
    vehicle-code              model code for vehicle
    vehicle-gross             gross value of sale
    vehicle-profit            profit on this sale
```

The general structure of the program will follow that of the earlier examples discussed in Sections 10.2 and 10.4.

```
vehicle-summary
    initialize-table
    get-next-vehicle-file
    until end-of-vehicle-file do
        update-table
        get-next-vehicle-file
    enduntil
    print-table
```

The simplest way to initialize the table is to read the first record from 'vehicle-file' and store the details of that record in the first element of the table. Therefore the refinement 'initialize-table' might be:

```
initialize-table
    get-next-vehicle-file
    transfer vehicle-code to model-c-code (1)
    transfer 1 to model-c-numbers (1)
    transfer vehicle-gross to model-c-gross (1)
    transfer vehicle-profit to model-c-profit (1)
    transfer 1 to mc-limit
```

This refinement sets up the first element of the table and defines the current limit on the number of table elements, 'mc-limit', as one. This limit will increase as new model codes are stored in the table.

The next step is to refine 'update-table'. This requires a table search with either an update of an existing element or the addition of a new element. The general structure of this refinement is:

```
update-table
    transfer true to new-model
    for mc-subscript = 1 to mc-limit do
        if vehicle-code = model-c-code (mc-subscript) then
            transfer false to new-model
            accumulate-details
        endif
    endfor
    if new-model then
        append-model-to-table
    endif
```

This refinement starts with the pessimistic assumption that the current record will contain a new model code (one not stored in the table) by setting the Boolean new-model to true. The table is then searched to see if the current model code, 'vehicle-code', is already stored in the table. If it is then the appropriate element of the table is updated and the Boolean new-model set to false, to indicate that the current record was for a model code already stored in the table. At the end of the search loop if 'new-model' is still true then the model code and relevant details need to be appended to the table.

There are two lower level refinements to be developed from 'update-table' and these are both quite straightforward:

```
accumulate-details
    calculate model-c-numbers (mc-subscript) =
       model-c-numbers (mc-subscript) + 1
    calculate model-c-gross (mc-subscript) =
       model-c-gross (mc-subscript) + vehicle-gross
    calculate model-c-profit (mc-subscript) =
       model-c-profit (mc-subscript) + vehicle-profit

append-model-to-table
    calculate mc-limit = mc-limit + 1
    transfer vehicle-code to model-c-code (mc-limit)
    transfer 1 to model-c-numbers (mc-limit)
    transfer vehicle-gross to model-c-gross (mc-limit)
    transfer vehicle-profit to model-c-profit (mc-limit)
```

Looking back to the refinement of 'initialize-table', there is obviously a strong similarity between this and 'append-model-to-table'. This is because both refinements are effectively doing the same thing. Therefore, the refinement of 'initialize-table' could be modified to:

```
initialize-table
    get-next-vehicle-file
    transfer 0 to mc-limit
    append-model-to-table
```

After all the records in 'vehicle-file' have been processed the refinement of 'print-table' should produce the required summaries of numbers and averages. An output line can be described to hold these values:

```
summary-line
    summary-code             model code
    summary-numbers          number of this model sold
    summary-av-gross         average gross price of model
    summary-av-profit        average profit on model
```

The refinement of 'print-table' is then straightforward:

```
print-table
    print-headings
    for mc-subscript = 1 to mc-limit do
       transfer model-c-code (mc-subscript) to summary-code
       transfer model-c-numbers (mc-subscript) to summary-numbers
       calculate summary-av-gross =
          model-c-gross (mc-subscript) /
          model-c-numbers (mc-subscript)
       calculate summary-av-profit =
          model-c-profit (mc-subscript) /
          model-c-numbers (mc-subscript)
       put-summary-line
    endfor
```

The refinement of 'print-headings' might involve the printing of a company heading at the top of a page, followed by a report heading for this monthly analysis, and two lines of column headings separated from the details by a blank line. This could be expressed as:

```
    print-headings
       put-company-heading      (at top of new page)
       put-report-heading       (leaving 2 blank lines)
       put-col-heading-1        (leaving 1 blank line)
       put-col-heading-2
       put-blank-line
```

The complete program design, including the record and table descriptions, is reproduced below. The input record is:

```
    vehicle-record
       vehicle-code             model code for vehicle
       vehicle-gross            gross value of sale
       vehicle-profit           profit on this sale
```

In the WORKING-STORAGE SECTION, the table and its associated subscript and limit have to be described:

```
    model-table
       model-counter
             repeated 50 times
          model-c-code             stored model code
          model-c-numbers          number of this model sold
          model-c-gross    gross value of sales for this model
          model-c-profit   profit on sales for this model
       mc-subscript                subscript for model-counter
       mc-limit                    limit of elements used
                                      in model-counter
```

In addition to these temporary data-items, the Boolean new-model will need to be added to STATE-VECTOR.

The output record is quite simple in this case:

```
    summary-line
       summary-code             model code
       summary-numbers          number of this model sold
       summary-av-gross         average gross price of model
       summary-av-profit        average profit on model
```

The complete design, using the above data structures, is given below.

```
    vehicle-summary
       initialize-table
       get-next-vehicle-file
       until end-of-vehicle-file do
          update-table
          get-next-vehicle-file
       enduntil
       print-table
```

```
initialize-table
   get-next-vehicle-file
   transfer 0 to mc-limit
   append-model-to-table

update-table
   transfer true to new-model
   for mc-subscript = 1 to mc-limit do
      if vehicle-code = model-c-code (mc-subscript) then
         transfer false to new-model
         accumulate-details
      endif
   endfor
   if new-model then
      append-model-to-table
   endif

accumulate-details
   calculate model-c-numbers (mc-subscript) =
      model-c-numbers (mc-subscript) + 1
   calculate model-c-gross (mc-subscript) =
      model-c-gross (mc-subscript) + vehicle-gross
   calculate model-c-profit (mc-subscript) =
      model-c-profit (mc-subscript) + vehicle-profit

append-model-to-table
   calculate mc-limit = mc-limit + 1
   transfer vehicle-code to model-c-code (mc-limit)
   transfer 1 to model-c-numbers (mc-limit)
   transfer vehicle-gross to model-c-gross (mc-limit)
   transfer vehicle-profit to model-c-profit (mc-limit)

print-table
   print-headings
   for mc-subscript = 1 to mc-limit do
      transfer model-c-code (mc-subscript) to summary-code
      transfer model-c-numbers (mc-subscript) to summary-numbers
      calculate summary-av-gross =
         model-c-gross (mc-subscript) /
         model-c-numbers (mc-subscript)
      calculate summary-av-profit =
         model-c-profit (mc-subscript) /
         model-c-numbers (mc-subscript)
      put-summary-line
   endfor

print-headings
   put-company-heading     (at top of new page)
   put-report-heading      (leaving 2 blank lines)
   put-col-heading-1       (leaving 1 blank line)
   put-col-heading-2
   put-blank-line


   IDENTIFICATION DIVISION.
   PROGRAM-ID. TABLES01.
```

```
 ENVIRONMENT DIVISION.
 CONFIGURATION SECTION.
 SOURCE-COMPUTER. <computer-name>.
 OBJECT-COMPUTER. <computer-name>.
*    <computer-name> should be replaced by the name
*    of the computer being used to run programs.

 INPUT-OUTPUT SECTION.
 FILE-CONTROL.
     SELECT VEHICLE-FILE ASSIGN TO <system-input>.
     SELECT OUTFILE ASSIGN TO <system-output>.
*        <system-input> and <system-output> must conform
*        to the rules for the system being used.

 DATA DIVISION.
 FILE SECTION.
 FD  VEHICLE-FILE
     LABEL RECORDS OMITTED.
 01  VEHICLE-RECORD.
     05  VEHICLE-CODE        PIC XXX.
     05  VEHICLE-GROSS       PIC 9(5)V99.
     05  VEHICLE-PROFIT      PIC S9(4)V99.
 FD  OUTFILE
     LABEL RECORDS OMITTED.
 01  OUT-LINE        PIC X(120).

 WORKING-STORAGE SECTION.
 01  STATE-VECTOR.
     05  END-VEHICLE-FILE        PIC X.
         88  END-OF-VEHICLE-FILE VALUE "E".
     05  MODEL-FLAG          PIC X.
         88  NEW-MODEL  VALUE "T".

 01  MODEL-TABLE.
     05  MODEL-COUNTER  OCCURS 50 TIMES.
         10  MODEL-C-CODE            PIC XXX.
         10  MODEL-C-NUMBERS         PIC 99.
         10  MODEL-C-GROSS           PIC 9(7)V99.
         10  MODEL-C-PROFIT          PIC S9(6)V99.
     05  MC-SUBSCRIPT                PIC 99.
     05  MC-LIMIT                    PIC 99.

 01  COMPANY-HEADING.
     05  FILLER        PIC X(5)  VALUE SPACES.
     05  FILLER        PIC X(24) VALUE
         "HONEST JOE (MOTORS) LTD.".

 01  REPORT-HEADING.
     05  FILLER        PIC X     VALUE SPACE.
     05  FILLER        PIC X(32) VALUE
         "MONTHLY SUMMARY OF VEHICLES SOLD".
```

```
01  COL-HEADINGS-1.
    05  FILLER       PIC X(5)  VALUE "MODEL".
    05  FILLER       PIC XXX   VALUE SPACES.
    05  FILLER       PIC X(6)  VALUE "NUMBER".
    05  FILLER       PIC XXX   VALUE SPACES.
    05  FILLER       PIC X(7)  VALUE "AVERAGE".
    05  FILLER       PIC XXXX  VALUE SPACES.
    05  FILLER       PIC X(7)  VALUE "AVERAGE".

01  COL-HEADINGS-2.
    05  FILLER       PIC XXXX  VALUE "CODE".
    05  FILLER       PIC X(5)  VALUE SPACES.
    05  FILLER       PIC XXXX  VALUE "SOLD".
    05  FILLER       PIC X(5)  VALUE SPACES.
    05  FILLER       PIC X(5)  VALUE "GROSS".
    05  FILLER       PIC X(5)  VALUE SPACES.
    05  FILLER       PIC X(6)  VALUE "PROFIT".

01  BLANK-LINE.
    05  FILLER       PIC X     VALUE SPACE.

01  SUMMARY-LINE.
    05  FILLER                     PIC X.
    05  SUMMARY-CODE               PIC XXX.
    05  FILLER                     PIC X(6).
    05  SUMMARY-NUMBERS            PIC Z9.
    05  FILLER                     PIC XXX.
    05  SUMMARY-AV-GROSS           PIC £££,££9.99.
    05  FILLER                     PIC XX.
    05  SUMMARY-AV-PROFIT          PIC ££££9.99DB.

PROCEDURE DIVISION.
MAIN-PROGRAM.
    PERFORM INIT-STATE
    PERFORM VEHICLE-SUMMARY
    PERFORM CLOSE-DOWN.
INIT-STATE.
    MOVE SPACE TO END-VEHICLE-FILE
    OPEN INPUT VEHICLE-FILE OUTPUT OUTFILE
    MOVE SPACES TO SUMMARY-LINE.
CLOSE-DOWN.
    CLOSE VEHICLE-FILE OUTFILE
    STOP RUN.
GET-NEXT-VEHICLE-FILE.
    READ VEHICLE-FILE
        AT END MOVE "E" TO END-VEHICLE-FILE.
PUT-SUMMARY-LINE.
    WRITE OUT-LINE FROM SUMMARY-LINE
        AFTER ADVANCING 1 LINES.
    MOVE SPACES TO SUMMARY-LINE.
PUT-COMPANY-HEADING.
    WRITE OUT-LINE FROM COMPANY-HEADING
        AFTER ADVANCING PAGE.
PUT-REPORT-HEADING.
    WRITE OUT-LINE FROM REPORT-HEADING
        AFTER ADVANCING 3 LINES.
```

```
PUT-COL-HEADINGS-1.
    WRITE OUT-LINE FROM COL-HEADINGS-1
        AFTER ADVANCING 2 LINES.
PUT-COL-HEADINGS-2.
    WRITE OUT-LINE FROM COL-HEADINGS-2
        AFTER ADVANCING 1 LINES.
PUT-BLANK-LINE.
    WRITE OUT-LINE FROM BLANK-LINE
        AFTER ADVANCING 1 LINES.
VEHICLE-SUMMARY.
    PERFORM INITIALIZE-TABLE.
    PERFORM GET-NEXT-VEHICLE-FILE
    PERFORM PROCESS-VEHICLE-RECORD
        UNTIL END-OF-VEHICLE-FILE
    PERFORM PRINT-TABLE.
PROCESS-VEHICLE-RECORD.
    PERFORM UPDATE-TABLE
    PERFORM GET-NEXT-VEHICLE-FILE.
INITIALIZE-TABLE.
    PERFORM GET-NEXT-VEHICLE-FILE
    MOVE 0 TO MC-LIMIT
    PERFORM APPEND-MODEL-TO-TABLE.
UPDATE-TABLE.
    MOVE "T" TO MODEL-FLAG
    PERFORM SEARCH-TABLE
        VARYING MC-SUBSCRIPT FROM 1
        BY 1 UNTIL MC-SUBSCRIPT > MC-LIMIT
    IF NEW-MODEL
        PERFORM APPEND-MODEL-TO-TABLE.
SEARCH-TABLE.
    IF VEHICLE-CODE = MODEL-C-CODE (MC-SUBSCRIPT)
        MOVE "F" TO MODEL-FLAG
        PERFORM ACCUMULATE-DETAILS.
ACCUMULATE-DETAILS.
    COMPUTE MODEL-C-NUMBERS (MC-SUBSCRIPT) =
        MODEL-C-NUMBERS (MC-SUBSCRIPT) + 1
    COMPUTE MODEL-C-GROSS (MC-SUBSCRIPT) =
        MODEL-C-GROSS (MC-SUBSCRIPT) + VEHICLE-GROSS
    COMPUTE MODEL-C-PROFIT (MC-SUBSCRIPT) =
        MODEL-C-PROFIT (MC-SUBSCRIPT) + VEHICLE-PROFIT.
APPEND-MODEL-TO-TABLE.
    COMPUTE MC-LIMIT = MC-LIMIT + 1
    MOVE VEHICLE-CODE TO MODEL-C-CODE (MC-LIMIT)
    MOVE 1 TO MODEL-C-NUMBERS (MC-LIMIT)
    MOVE VEHICLE-GROSS TO MODEL-C-GROSS (MC-LIMIT)
    MOVE VEHICLE-PROFIT TO MODEL-C-PROFIT (MC-LIMIT)
PRINT-TABLE.
    PERFORM PRINT-HEADINGS.
    PERFORM PRINT-MODEL-DETAILS
        VARYING MC-SUBSCRIPT FROM 1
        BY 1 UNTIL MC-SUBSCRIPT > MC-LIMIT.
```

```
PRINT-MODEL-DETAILS.
    MOVE MODEL-C-CODE (MC-SUBSCRIPT) TO SUMMARY-CODE
    MOVE MODEL-C-NUMBERS (MC-SUBSCRIPT) TO SUMMARY-NUMBERS
    COMPUTE SUMMARY-AV-GROSS =
        MODEL-C-GROSS (MC-SUBSCRIPT) /
        MODEL-C-NUMBERS (MC-SUBSCRIPT)
    COMPUTE SUMMARY-AV-PROFIT =
        MODEL-C-PROFIT (MC-SUBSCRIPT) /
        MODEL-C-NUMBERS (MC-SUBSCRIPT)
    PERFORM PUT-SUMMARY-LINE.
PRINT-HEADINGS.
    PERFORM PUT-COMPANY-HEADING
    PERFORM PUT-REPORT-HEADING
    PERFORM PUT-COL-HEADINGS-1
    PERFORM PUT-COL-HEADINGS-2
    PERFORM PUT-BLANK-LINE.
```

An example of the output from this program is shown in Figure 10.6. Note that the averages for gross value and profit will be truncated by the division operations specified in PRINT-MODEL-DETAILS.

HONEST JOE (MOTORS) LTD.

MONTHLY SUMMARY OF VEHICLES SOLD

MODEL CODE	NUMBER SOLD	AVERAGE GROSS	AVERAGE PROFIT
XX3	2	£17,142.00	£1215.00
E11	15	£4,976.23	£416.38
65R	1	£6,450.00	£250.00DB
U10	5	£623.44	£27.98
UX3	1	£75.00	£0.00
U93	6	£987.34	£2.85DB

Figure 10.6

Exercises 10

10.1. Looking back at the case study of Section 10.6, explain what assumption is made about the maximum numbers of a given model which are expected to be sold. Identify the data-items which are dependent upon this assumption.

Honest Joe's business expands and the number of model codes in use increases to 150. Specify the changes which will be required in the program design and the corresponding program.

10.2. The following data structure appears in a COBOL program used by a bureau de change.

```
01  TEMPORARY-ITEMS.
    05  AMOUNT-REQUIRED               PIC 999V99.
01  CURRENCY-TABLE.
    05  CURRENCY-RATE  OCCURS 40 TIMES.
        10  CURRENCY-R-CODE           PIC AAA.
        10  CURRENCY-R-EXCHANGE       PIC 9(5)V99.
    05  NUMBER-OF-CURRENCIES          PIC 99.
```

Various foreign currencies are given three letter codes (CURRENCY-R-CODE) and these are stored in a table together with the exchange rate (CURRENCY-R-EXCHANGE). The exchange rate is expressed as the amount of foreign currency purchased for one pound sterling. The number of currencies currently quoted is given in NUMBER-OF-CURRENCIES. The data-item AMOUNT-REQUIRED is used to express an amount in pounds sterling.

Assuming that all relevant data-items in the above structure have been initialized correctly, write pieces of program design, and the corresponding pieces of COBOL, to carry out the following operations.

(a) Update the exchange rate for 'GDM' to 4.21.
(b) Look up the exchange rate for 'FFR' and calculate the amount of this currency which corresponds to the current value of AMOUNT-REQUIRED.
(c) Add a new currency to the table with code 'NGU' and exchange rate 3.88.

Give descriptions for any subscripts used and any other temporary data-items required.

Progamming Exercises 10

10.3. Develop the example of 10.1 into a full COBOL program which prints the average, best and worst sales for each branch. Use the following input record format for the program:

```
Sales record
   Branch identifier              2 letters and 4 digits
   Monthly sales value            6 digits (pence)
      repeated 12 times
```

The program should include a suitable page heading and column headings for the output.

When you have managed to get this comparatively simple program working, consider extending the program to include calculating the average monthly sales, the best monthly total sales and the worst monthly sales for the whole organization.
[Hint: a table will be required in WORKING-STORAGE to accumulate the monthly totals for the whole organization. After processing all the branch records this table can be analyzed to give the three values required.]

10.4. A large firm which writes software for a number of different clients has a project numbering system where the first three digits of the project number are unique to a particular client. A number of projects for a particular client may be undertaken simultaneously.

Each employee of the firm completes a weekly timesheet recording the time he or she has spent on each project in which they are involved. Clients then pay labour charges based on these time allocations. A large file exists containing the details of the weekly allocation of employees to projects. Each record contains the following data:

timesheet record

employee number	6 digits
week number	2 digits
project number	6 digits
time spent on project	2 digits (hours)
employee's hourly rate	4 digits (pence)

In order to cross-check the labour charges made to clients, a program is required that will process all the records in this file and accumulate the total time allocated and the total labour charge for each client.

Assume that all projects for the first client have project numbers starting '100', the second client starting '110', etc. There are currently twenty clients, numbered contiguously, and therefore the last one has project numbers starting '290'.

Would the method you have chosen still work if projects were numbered so that the first client was allocated project numbers in the range 100-124, the second client 125-149, etc.?

10.5. Every transaction processed by a company's credit sales section is recorded in a transaction log in the form:

transaction record

transaction reference	1 letter, 5 digits
date of transaction	6 digits (ddmmyy)
account number	2 letters, 3 digits, 1 letter
transaction value	5 digits (pence, signed)

A transaction may be a sale in which case the transaction value is negative or a payment when the transaction is positive.

A program is required which will accept a random selection of account numbers together with the opening balances for the corresponding accounts. The program should then process the transaction log and produce a summary of the number of transactions and the closing balance for each of the specified accounts. For example, the output might start:

PROJECT CODE	NUMBER OF TRANSACTIONS	CLOSING BALANCE
100	12	£234.56
110	0	£23.75DB
. .	.	. . .

The required accounts will be specified in a file in which each record is of the form:

account record

account number	2 letters, 3 digits, 1 letter
opening balance	7 digits (pence, signed)

There will never be more than 40 different account numbers specified in this file.

11 Additional Features of COBOL

This chapter is designed to give brief coverage of a number of useful COBOL features for which there is insufficient space to cover in detail.

The first feature discussed is the unconditional jump, the GO TO statement, which provides an extra mechanism for transfer of control within a program. The disciples of pure structured programming argue (and can prove) that unconditional jump statements are unnecessary in a language which provides the 'proper' control structures (sequence, selection and iteration). In the author's opinion, there are some special circumstances in which an unconditional jump is useful and these are discussed in the first section.

The technique for program development advocated in this book is stepwise refinement - breaking a problem down into subproblems and continuing this process until the subproblems are easy to solve. However, all the solutions so far have been in the form of a single program. For complex problems it may be necessary to implement the solution using a collection of interrelated _subprograms_. Inter-program communication is discussed in the second section of this chapter.

Hitherto it has been assumed that all input and output files, used by a program, are serial access, sequential files. Many problems can be solved more naturally by using files from which a given record can be extracted without reference to other records in the file; this can be achieved using _direct-access_ files. Two types of direct-access file structures are provided in COBOL: _relative_ and _indexed_; these are discussed in the next two sections of this chapter.

11.1 The GO TO Statement

The main emphasis of this book has been on methodical programming using stepwise refinement. Quite complex programs have been built up using the structured programming control primitives: _if_, _until_ and _for_, together with refinement.

In common with many other programming languages, COBOL provides an unconditional jump statement which takes the form:

```
GO TO paragraph-name
```

This has the effect of transferring control to the named paragraph, that is the next statement to be executed will be the first executable statement following paragraph-name. Unlike 'PERFORM paragraph-name', there is no return to the statement following the GO TO statement.

The general philosophy of structured programming is to avoid the use of GO TO statements as they are unnecessary and tend to obscure the meaning of the program if used indiscriminately. The use of GO TO should be restricted to circumstances where it is necessary to define a special exit from a loop or a program.

In the algorithm for searching a table, given in Section 10.4, a problem arose if the table was about to overflow; the following refinement was suggested:

```
check-table-overflow
   if si-subscript > <table-size> then
      display "too many item numbers specified"
      display "maximum possible is <table-size>"
      close-down
   endif
```

When the refinement close-down is executed the program will stop because this refinement includes a STOP RUN statement. However, the program would be clearer if the above refinement used an explicit jump to 'close-down'. For example:

```
check-table-overflow
   if si-subscript > <table-size> then
      display "too many item numbers specified"
      display "maximum possible is <table-size>"
      goto close-down
   endif
```

This emphasizes that there is a jump to the exit point of the program rather than the execution of a refinement followed by a transfer of control back to the main sequence of operations.

If <table-size> has the value thirty then the equivalent COBOL paragraph would be:

```
CHECK-TABLE-OVERFLOW.
    IF SI-SUBSCRIPT > 30
        DISPLAY "TOO MANY ITEM NUMBERS SPECIFIED"
        DISPLAY "MAXIMUM POSSIBLE IS 30"
        GO TO CLOSE-DOWN.
```

Readers using low-level ANS COBOL compilers may need to use GO TO statements to translate until or for operations; these translations are discussed in Appendix 5.3 and Appendix 5.5, respectively.

11.2 Inter-program Communication

The size of any single COBOL program is physically limited by the memory and addressing limitations of the computer system being used. With some small computer systems, it may be necessary to consider segmentation of large programs - this involves overlaying sections of the program and is beyond the scope of this book. However, in most systems, segmentation is unnecessary because the physical limit on the size of a program exceeds the size limit for an easily understood and manageable program.

When tackling complex problems it may not be sufficient to break the problem solution into refinements contained within one program. It might be necessary to subdivide the task and use either a collection of separate programs, communicating via files, or a structure of interrelated programs. This latter technique requires a facility for one program to call another program to carry out some subtask. In any interaction between programs there is a calling program and a called program. When the called progam has completed its specified task control is returned to the calling program by a similar mechanism to the PERFORM statement within a program.

Calling Programs

In the calling program a CALL statement is used to transfer control to the called program. For example:

```
CALL "ERROR-MODULE"
```

would transfer control for the current program to the program called ERROR-MODULE. No data is directly transferred between the calling and called programs, although data may be indirectly transferred via files.

An extended form of the CALL statement enables data to be passed to the called program and results to be returned from the called program to the calling program. For example:

```
CALL "DATE-CONV" USING SALE-DATE FULL-DATE
```

would call the program DATE-CONV and allow the data-items SALE-DATE and FULL-DATE to be used for data transfer between the calling program and the called program, DATE-CONV.

In this example, the called program is designed to convert an abbreviated date, in the form of a day-number from the beginning of a decade, into a full date. For example, the day-number 1106 would be converted to 10 January 1983, if day-numbers are stored using 1 January 1980 as the first day. The data-items SALE-DATE and FULL-DATE might be described, in the calling program, as follows:

```
05  SALE-DATE                PIC 9999.
. . . . .
05  FULL-DATE.
    10  FULL-DAY             PIC 99.
    10  FULL-MONTH           PIC A(9).
    10  FULL-YEAR            PIC 9999.
```

It is now necessary to look at the construction of the called program to see how these data-items may be used.

Called Programs

There are three essential features of a called program:

- the description of any data-items used for transferring data to or from the calling program,
- establishing the correspondence between these data-items and those in the CALL statement of the calling program,
- defining the exit point from the called program.

The data-items used for inter-program communication are specified in the LINKAGE-SECTION of the DATA DIVISION. This is a third section of the DATA DIVISION which is used only in called programs. Its general format is similar to that of the WORKING-STORAGE SECTION. Therefore, in the example program DATE-CONV, the LINKAGE SECTION could be defined as:

```
LINKAGE SECTION.
01  IN-DATE              PIC 9999.
01  OUT-DATE.
    05  OUT-DAY          PIC 99.
    05  OUT-MONTH        PIC A(9).
    05  OUT-YEAR         PIC 9999.
```

To establish the correspondence between these data-items and those used in the CALL statement of the calling program, the record-descriptions given in the LINKAGE SECTION are listed in a USING clause appended to the PROCEDURE DIVISION heading of the called program. For example:

```
PROCEDURE DIVISION USING IN-DATE OUT-DATE.
```

The data-items listed after USING are matched to those in the corresponding CALL statement which in this case was:

```
CALL "DATE-CONV" USING SALE-DATE FULL-DATE
```

Therefore SALE-DATE is matched with IN-DATE and FULL-DATE with OUT-DATE.

The calling program should have put a value into SALE-DATE before calling DATE-CONV; the called program can then use this value from IN-DATE and put results into OUT-DATE. On return to the calling program these results will be available in FULL-DATE. If DATE-CONV changes the value of IN-DATE then this will be reflected in the calling program (SALE-DATE will be changed).

In other programming languages IN-DATE and OUT-DATE would be called 'formal parameters' and SALE-DATE and FULL-DATE 'actual parameters'. Technically the method of parameter passing in COBOL is 'call by reference'. The called program is equivalent to a subroutine subprogram in FORTRAN or to a procedure in Pascal or Algol.

The data-items in the list following USING are matched by position, not by name, and therefore it would be possible to call DATE-CONV with different data-items, for example:

```
CALL "DATE-CONV" USING INVOICE-DATE EXPANDED-DATE
```

The data-items will now be matched so that INVOICE-DATE corresponds to IN-DATE and EXPANDED-DATE to OUT-DATE.

To return control from a called program to the calling program the last paragraph to be executed must be a paragraph containing the single statement EXIT PROGRAM. For example:

```
RETURN-TO-CALLING.
    EXIT PROGRAM.
```

In the first example of a CALL statement given above:

```
CALL "ERROR-MODULE"
```

there is no direct data transfer. Therefore the only difference between the program ERROR-MODULE and a normal program would be the use of EXIT PROGRAM rather than STOP RUN.

A called program may call other programs provided it does not directly or indirectly call the calling program, that is, recursion is not allowed in COBOL.

11.3 Source Library and Copy Directives

It is possible to maintain a library of COBOL program fragments which can be copied into a program prior to compilation. This would allow, for example, a particular installation to have a standard CONFIGURATION SECTION which could be copied from the library into all COBOL programs being written.

It would also allow a team of programmers working on interrelated programs to store file-descriptions for commonly used files and copy these into each of their programs. In this way any change in the format of a file will be automatically inserted into to all relevant programs.

The COPY verb, used to copy text from the library into a program, is called a compiler directive: that is, it affects the compilation of the program rather than the execution. A COPY directive can appear anywhere in a program; it is not restricted to a particular division or context.

The simplest form of the COPY directive is:

```
COPY library-entry-name.
```

where library-entry-name is the unique name for a piece of text stored in a COBOL source library. For example:

```
. . . . .
ENVIRONMENT DIVISION.
COPY CONFIG-SECTION.
INPUT-OUTPUT SECTION.
. . . . .
```

The directive 'COPY CONFIG-SECTION.' will be replaced by the piece of COBOL text with the name CONFIG-SECTION in the source library.

Suppose the library entry CONFIG-SECTION contains:

```
CONFIGURATION SECTION.
SOURCE-COMPUTER. MM1.
OBJECT-COMPUTER. MM1.
SPECIAL-NAMES.
    MM-CONTROL IS OPERATORS-CONSOLE.
```

Then this whole piece of text will be copied into the program before it is compiled. Therefore the expanded form of the program will be:

```
. . . . .
ENVIRONMENT DIVISION.
CONFIGURATION SECTION.
SOURCE-COMPUTER. MM1.
OBJECT-COMPUTER. MM1.
SPECIAL-NAMES.
    MM-CONTROL IS OPERATORS-CONSOLE.
INPUT-OUTPUT SECTION.
. . . . .
```

A more advanced form of the COPY directive allows text to be copied from the COBOL library systematically replacing parts of the text in the library by new pieces of text. This would allow, for example, a general algorithm to be stored in the source library and then copied into a program substituting appropriate data-names for the current program.

To illustrate the format of the COPY directive with the REPLACING option, suppose that a program is required with a modified CONFIGURATION SECTION, based on the library entry CONFIG-SECTION. It would be possible to write:

```
COPY CONFIG-SECTION
    REPLACING MM1 BY XYZ-82
              MM-CONSOLE BY XYZ-TYPEWRITER.
```

The expanded form of the program will now contain:

```
. . . . .
ENVIRONMENT DIVISION.
CONFIGURATION SECTION.
SOURCE-COMPUTER. XYZ-82.
OBJECT-COMPUTER. XYZ-82.
SPECIAL-NAMES.
    XYZ-TYPEWRITER IS OPERATORS-CONSOLE.
INPUT-OUTPUT SECTION.
. . . . .
```

A COPY directive can specify any number of replacements to be carried out when a library entry is copied into a program.

How the pieces of COBOL text are actually added to the library and the format of the library file(s) is implementor-defined and will therefore vary from system to system.

11.4 Relative Files

A relative file can be considered as an extension of the idea of a one-dimensional table where the elements of the table become records in a file. A relative file can be visualized as a sequence of data areas, each area being large enough to hold one record of the file.

An area is uniquely identified by a relative record number which can be used to access the area without reference to any other area. The first area in the file always has relative record number one and succeeding areas are numbered in sequence: two, three, etc. Thus the relative record number fulfils a similar role to the subscript of a table.

At any given time, not all of the areas of the file need contain data; therefore a record can be written into the area with relative record number fifty regardless of whether areas one to forty-nine contain data or not. Initially all areas of a relative file can be considered as empty, a special state which needs to be recognized by input/output statements accessing the file.

In order to use relative files it is necessary to extend the repertoire of input/output statements and the following are provided:

READ - read a record from a specified area,
WRITE - write a record into an area,

REWRITE - write a record into an area, overwriting the existing record in that area,
DELETE - delete the contents of the specified area, leaving the area 'empty'.

In all cases the area must be specified by giving its relative record number. All the above statements need to have an INVALID KEY qualifier to specify what happens if an attempt is made to perform an illegal operation. In the case of READ, REWRITE and DELETE, an invalid-key condition arises if the specified area is empty, while for WRITE, an invalid-key condition occurs if the specified area already contains a record.

To illustrate the use of relative files the solution to a simple problem will be outlined. Customers of the Erewhon Building Society with savings accounts have ten digit account numbers; the first three digits identify the type of account, the next three digits indicate the branch at which the account is handled and the last four digits are the customer's number within that branch. Each branch requires a file of customer accounts which can be updated directly by transactions taking place at the front counter of the branch. This can be achieved using a relative file taking the last four digits of the customer's account number as a relative record number.

To describe a relative file it is necessary to use a modified form of the SELECT clause. For example:

```
ENVIRONMENT DIVISION.
. . . . .
INPUT-OUTPUT SECTION.
FILE-CONTROL.
    SELECT CUST-FILE ASSIGN TO <external-file-name>
        ORGANIZATION RELATIVE
        ACCESS MODE RANDOM
        RELATIVE KEY CUST-FILE-KEY.
```

Note that there is no full stop after <external-file-name> because the succeeding lines are part of the SELECT statement for this file. The data-item CUST-FILE-KEY must <u>not</u> be part of a record-description associated with the file-description for CUST-FILE.

The ORGANIZATION clause specifies how records are stored in a file. In the SELECT statement above, ORGANIZATION RELATIVE indicates that the records in CUST-FILE are stored in such a way that each record can be uniquely identified by a relative record number. The ACCESS MODE clause specifies the way in which the file is to be used in a particular program. In the above example, ACCESS MODE RANDOM indicates that the program will access records 'at random', that is, by using the relative record numbers to select individual records for manipulation.

In the DATA DIVISION the file-description for CUST-FILE will look similar to those already encountered in this book; the file organization details are contained in the SELECT clause given above. For example:

```
DATA DIVISION.
FILE SECTION.
FD  CUST-FILE
    LABEL RECORDS STANDARD.
01  CUST-RECORD.
    05  CUST-ACC-NUMBER      PIC 9(10).
    . . . . .
```

The data-item CUST-FILE-KEY, to hold the relative record numbers for the file, will need to be described in the WORKING-STORAGE SECTION, possibly as part of STATE-VECTOR. For example:

```
WORKING-STORAGE SECTION.
01  STATE-VECTOR.
    05  CUST-FILE-KEY        PIC 9999.
    . . . . .
```

Any data-item to be used to hold a relative record number will, like a subscript data-item, need to be of integer numeric type and it must not be edited. The size of this data-item will define the absolute limit of the size of the file; in this case 9999 records.

Moving on to the PROCEDURE DIVISION, the file will need to be opened before it can be used. In order to make full use of a relative file it must be opened for both input and output simultaneously. For example:

```
    OPEN I-O CUST-FILE . . . . .
```

The option 'I-O' of the OPEN statement allows a file to be used for both input and output.

To obtain the record relating to a particular customer, for example to print the current balance, it is necessary to specify the relative record number of the required record and then issue a READ statement. In the example this could be written as:

```
FIND-CUST-RECORD.
    MOVE ACC-NUMBER TO CUST-FILE-KEY
    READ CUST-FILE
        INVALID KEY PERFORM NO-CUST-RECORD.
```

If ACC-NUMBER is a full ten digit account number the MOVE statement above will truncate the most significant digits leaving the four least significant digits in CUST-FILE-KEY. The READ statement should then return the appropriate customer record in the input-area for the file (which will also be the output-area, since the file is opened for I-O.) If no record exists with the given relative record number then the READ statement fails and the procedure NO-CUST-RECORD is executed.

To update a customer record, for example to amend the current account balance, the following procedure could be used:

```
UPDATE-CUST-RECORD.
    MOVE ACC-NUMBER TO CUST-FILE-KEY
    READ CUST-FILE
        INVALID KEY PERFORM NO-CUST-RECORD.
    PERFORM AMEND-BALANCE
    REWRITE CUST-RECORD
        INVALID KEY PERFORM UPDATE-FAILED.
```

The first part of this procedure is the same as FIND-CUST-RECORD, above. If a record is successfully read from the file then the procedure AMEND-BALANCE is used to modify the record and the amended record is written back into the file, using the REWRITE statement. Unless the programmer does something stupid which changes the value of CUST-FILE-KEY between the READ and REWRITE statements the procedure UPDATE-FAILED should never be executed.

A new customer record can be created by using the WRITE statement. For example:

```
ADD-CUSTOMER.
    PERFORM CREATE-NEW-CUST
    MOVE NEW-ACC-NUMBER TO CUST-FILE-KEY
    WRITE CUST-RECORD FROM NEW-CUST-RECORD
        INVALID KEY PERFORM ILLEGAL-CREATE.
```

It is assumed that the procedure CREATE-NEW-CUST builds up a new customer record in NEW-CUST-RECORD. The MOVE statement then puts the relative record number into CUST-FILE-KEY ready for the WRITE statement. The contents of NEW-CUST-RECORD are then written into CUST-FILE at the specified position unless the area is already occupied in which case the procedure ILLEGAL-CREATE is executed.

An existing customer record can be deleted by a procedure of the form:

```
DELETE-CUSTOMER.
    MOVE DEL-ACC-NUMBER TO CUST-FILE-KEY
    DELETE CUST-FILE
        INVALID KEY PERFORM DELETE-NO-CUST.
```

Having specified the relative record number, the corresponding area is marked empty, or if already empty the procedure DELETE-NO-CUST is executed.

Although the example given uses the fact that there is a straightforward correspondence between account numbers and relative record numbers this does not have to be the case. Any keys can be handled where it is possible to map the key values onto the relative record numbers algorithmically. This is similar to the problem of mapping keys onto table subscripts discussed in Section 10.4.

It is possible to read a relative file <u>sequentially</u> in which case the records are read in the order of relative record number with any empty areas being ignored. Suppose the Erewhon Building Society branch requires a listing of all active customer accounts. Then a program could be written which treated the relative file, CUST-FILE, as a serial file by including a SELECT clause of the form:

```
SELECT CUST-FILE ASSIGN TO <external-file-name>
    ORGANIZATION RELATIVE
    ACCESS MODE SEQUENTIAL.
```

The file, CUST-FILE, can now be opened for input and treated exactly like a serial file using a READ statement with an AT END qualifier.

The ORGANIZATION of the file is still specified as RELATIVE, meaning that records are uniquely identified by relative record numbers. However, ACCESS MODE SEQUENTIAL indicates that records will be read or written in the order in which they appear in the file, rather than at random.

11.5 Indexed Files

An indexed file is a file in which each record can be uniquely identified by a key value contained within the record. The system maintains an index or hierarchy of indexes which allows a program to access the record with a given key value. The programmer does not need to be concerned with how this index structure is maintained.

The input/output statements which can be used with an indexed file are the same as those for a relative file: READ, WRITE, REWRITE and DELETE. The INVALID KEY qualifier again needs to be specified to deal with attempts to perform illegal operations on the file. In the case of READ, REWRITE and DELETE, an invalid-key condition occurs if there is no record with the specified key stored in the file, while for WRITE, an invalid-key condition arises if a record with the specified key is already stored in the file.

To illustrate the use of an indexed file an outline solution to the simple problem sketched in Section 11.3 is given. This will allow direct comparison of the use of indexed and relative files.

The SELECT clause for the file will now need to specify that the organization of the file is INDEXED. For example:

```
ENVIRONMENT DIVISION.
. . . . .
INPUT-OUTPUT SECTION.
FILE-CONTROL.
    SELECT CUST-FILE ASSIGN TO <external-file-name>
        ORGANIZATION INDEXED
        ACCESS MODE RANDOM
        RECORD KEY CUST-ACC-NUMBER.
```

Note that the data-item specified as the RECORD KEY must be part of a record-description associated with the file.

The file-description for CUST-FILE can be exactly the same as that for the relative file, that is:

```
DATA DIVISION.
FILE SECTION.
FD  CUST-FILE
    LABEL RECORDS STANDARD.
01  CUST-RECORD.
    05  CUST-ACC-NUMBER     PIC 9(10).
    . . . . .
```

In the PROCEDURE DIVISION the file will need to be opened for both input and output:

```
    OPEN I-O CUST-FILE . . . . .
```

The major difference between indexed and relative occurs in the initialization of data-items prior to the execution of an input or output statement. For the indexed file organization it is the value of the record-key, CUST-ACC-NUMBER, that controls the access to the file. Therefore to obtain the record relating to a particular customer the following procedure could be used:

```
FIND-CUST-RECORD.
    MOVE ACC-NUMBER TO CUST-ACC-NUMBER
    READ CUST-FILE
        INVALID KEY PERFORM NO-CUST-RECORD.
```

The READ statement will attempt to find a record in CUST-FILE with the key value corresponding to the value transferred from ACC-NUMBER to CUST-ACC-NUMBER. If the READ statement is successful than the contents of the record will be copied into the input-area otherwise the procedure NO-CUST-RECORD is executed.

To update an existing record the procedure is the same as that for the relative file except for the initialization of the record-key.

```
UPDATE-CUST-RECORD.
    MOVE ACC-NUMBER TO CUST-ACC-NUMBER
    READ CUST-FILE
        INVALID KEY PERFORM NO-CUST-RECORD.
    PERFORM AMEND-BALANCE
    REWRITE CUST-RECORD
        INVALID KEY PERFORM UPDATE-FAILED.
```

The first part of this procedure is the same as FIND-CUST-RECORD, above. If a record is successfully read from the file then the procedure AMEND-BALANCE is used to modify the record and the amended record is written back into the file, using the REWRITE statement. Unless the programmer changes the value of CUST-ACC-NUMBER, in the input-area, between the READ and REWRITE statements the procedure UPDATE-FAILED should never be executed.

A new customer record can be created by using the WRITE statement. For example:

```
ADD-CUSTOMER.
    PERFORM CREATE-NEW-CUST
    WRITE CUST-RECORD FROM NEW-CUST-RECORD
        INVALID KEY PERFORM ILLEGAL-CREATE.
```

It is assumed that the procedure CREATE-NEW-CUST builds up a new customer record in NEW-CUST-RECORD. This new record, in NEW-CUST-RECORD, should contain an account number in the same format as CUST-ACC-NUMBER so the WRITE . . . FROM statement will implicitly initialize the record-key in the output-area. If a record already exists with this record-key then the WRITE statement will fail and the procedure ILLEGAL-CREATE will be executed.

An existing customer record can be deleted by a procedure of the form:

```
DELETE-CUSTOMER.
    MOVE DEL-ACC-NUMBER TO CUST-ACC-NUMBER
    DELETE CUST-FILE
        INVALID KEY PERFORM DELETE-NO-CUST.
```

If there is no record in the file with the record-key corresponding to the value transferred from DEL-ACC-NUMBER then the procedure DELETE-NO-CUST will be executed.

It is possible to read an indexed file <u>sequentially</u>, in which case the records are read in ascending order of the record-key values.

Suppose the Erewhon Building Society branch requires a listing of all active customer accounts. Then a program could be written which treated the indexed file, CUST-FILE, as a serial file by including a SELECT clause of the form:

```
SELECT CUST-FILE ASSIGN TO <external-file-name>
    ORGANIZATION INDEXED
    ACCESS MODE SEQUENTIAL
    RECORD KEY CUST-ACC-NUMBER.
```

Note that the record-key must still be specified for sequential access because the record-key defines the ordering of the file. The file, CUST-FILE, can now be opened for input and treated exactly like a serial file using a READ statement with an AT END qualifier.

From the programmer's point of view, indexed files are easier to use than relative because the mapping of the key values onto record positions in a file is done by the system and not within a program. The other reason why indexed files are more generally useful is that the record-keys can be of any type and need not be in contiguous ranges of values. Therefore a file can be indexed by an alphabetic key, an alphanumeric key or a random collection of numeric keys, all of which are difficult to map onto the relative record numbers of a relative file.

It would be possible to use a name as an index key to a suppliers' file, for example, provided that each name uniquely identifies a record. The problem with names, particularly personal names, is that it is difficult to guarantee the uniqueness of the key value. Therefore files are commonly accessed by using constructed key values such as customer account numbers or National Insurance numbers which can be guaranteed to identify uniquely an account or a person, respectively.

However, relative files should not be dismissed out of hand. An indexed file has an inherent overhead in both space requirements and the time taken to access a particular record because of the index structure and the need to systematically search the index. Therefore relative files are used where there is a need for fast access to records and the mapping of keys to relative record numbers can be carried out efficiently within a program.

This mapping could be achieved by using methods similar to those discussed in Section 10.4. It is also possible to use 'hashing algorithms', together with a technique for handling collisions between synonyms, where the range of key values is large. Most books on data structures will include sections on hash coding and the problems of collisions between synonyms.

Appendix 1 The COBOL Program Skeleton

The examples and exercises in the first eight chapters of this book are based on a standard program skeleton. This skeleton has been created to hide some of the features of COBOL which are irrelevant to the beginner.

There is a prescribed framework for all COBOL programs given in Appendix 4. The program skeleton given in this appendix goes beyond those rules and imposes an additional structure on beginners' program. Therefore it should be emphasized that this program skeleton is not a structure for all COBOL programs, merely a convenient teaching aid for this book. More advanced programs, using the full power of COBOL, will have different structures within the mandatory framework of the program.

The skeleton given below is based on a simple COBOL program with one serial input file and one serial output file, each with a single associated record.

The objects within angle brackets, '<' and '>', are to be replaced by appropriate names when generating a particular program. Notes are given at the end of this appendix on how to choose these substitutions.

```
       IDENTIFICATION DIVISION.
       PROGRAM-ID. <program-name>.

       ENVIRONMENT DIVISION.
       CONFIGURATION SECTION.
       SOURCE-COMPUTER. <computer-name>.
       OBJECT-COMPUTER. <computer-name>.
      *    <computer-name> should be replaced by the name
      *    of the computer being used to run programs.

       INPUT-OUTPUT SECTION.
       FILE-CONTROL.
           SELECT <input-file-name> ASSIGN TO <system-input>.
           SELECT OUTFILE ASSIGN TO <system-output>.
      *        <system-input> and <system-output> must conform
      *        to the rules for the system being used.

       DATA DIVISION.
       FILE SECTION.
       FD  <input-file-name>
           LABEL RECORDS OMITTED.

      *        Description of the input record
      *        to be inserted here.

       FD  OUTFILE
           LABEL RECORDS OMITTED.
       01  OUT-LINE          PIC X(120).
```

```
WORKING-STORAGE SECTION.
01  STATE-VECTOR.
    05  END-<input-file-name>         PIC X.
        88  END-OF-<input-file-name>    VALUE "E".
*       Description of the output record(s),
*       any headings or temporary variables,
*       to be inserted here.


PROCEDURE DIVISION.
MAIN-PROGRAM.
    PERFORM INIT-STATE
    PERFORM <main-process>
    PERFORM CLOSE-DOWN.
INIT-STATE.
    MOVE SPACE TO END-<input-file-name>
    OPEN INPUT <input-file-name> OUTPUT OUTFILE
    MOVE SPACES TO <record-name>.
CLOSE-DOWN.
    CLOSE <input-file-name> OUTFILE
    STOP RUN.
GET-NEXT-<input-file-name>.
    READ <input-file-name>
        AT END MOVE "E" TO END-<input-file-name>.
PUT-<record-name>.
    WRITE OUT-LINE FROM <record-name>
    MOVE SPACES TO <record-name>.

<main-process>.

*           Main algorithm for the program
*           to be developed from here.
```

Notes

1. The <program-name> identifies the source program and it is a user-defined name (see 3.2). However, the computer system being used may impose some special restrictions on the format of the name.

2. The <computer-name> identifies the computer system being used to compile and execute the program. Its format will obviously vary from system to system.

3. The <system-input> and <system-output> are again particular to a given computer system. These will be the references to the actual files being used for input and output by the program.

4. The references to <input-file-name> should all be replaced by the name chosen by the programmer for the input file.

5. The references to <record-name> should all be replaced by the name of the output record chosen for the program.

6. If the program uses multiple output records containing variable data then each record type should have a PUT-<record-name> paragraph, in

the format given above, defined for it. The <record-name> should also be added at the end of INIT-STATE, so that the last line is of the form:

```
MOVE SPACES TO <record-name-1> <record-name-2>
    . . . <record-name-n>.
```

The use of multiple output records is discussed in Section 5.5.

7. To output a constant line, such as a heading, or a line containing a mixture of constant and variable data the PUT-<record-name> paragraph simplifies to:

```
PUT-<record-name>.
    WRITE OUT-LINE FROM <record-name>.
```

because the contents of <record-name> do not need to be reset for future use. A record containing constant data must <u>not</u> be initialized in INIT-STATE because this will destroy the contents.

   The use of constant lines is discussed in Section 5.6.

Appendix 2 COBOL Program Layout

The format in which COBOL statements should be prepared for input to a compiler is rigidly defined. Any line can be considered as consisting of four parts, summarized in the diagram below.

```
L                         C  A           B                R
| 1| 2| 3| 4| 5| 6| 7| 8| 9|10|11|12|13|14| ...           |
| Sequence Number  |  |   Area A   |   Area B             |

                      Indicator
```

The letters at the top of the diagram define the 'margins', where 'L' is the left-hand margin and 'R' the right-hand margin, defining the limits of the line.

The first six characters of the line are reserved for a sequence number. The seventh character is called the indicator area. Characters eight to eleven are called area A and the remaining characters from the twelfth to the right-hand margin are called area B.

<u>Margin conventions</u>

1. Division headers and section headers must start in area A.

2. Paragraph-names must also start in Area A. The first sentence of the paragraph can follow on the same line or in area B of the next line. All subsequent lines of the paragraph must appear in area B. These lines may be indented from margin B to show the structure of the program.

3. The FD of a file description must start in area A, followed by at least one space, the file-name and the remainder of the description in area B.

4. In a record description the level number 01 must begin in area A and be followed by at least one space and the remainder of the description in area B. All other group-items or elementary-items, with level-numbers greater than 01, must have at least one space following the level-number and should be indented to show the structure of the record.

<u>Separators</u>

The main separator used between 'tokens' of the COBOL language is the space. In this context, a token is an indivisible unit of the program. Anywhere in a program where one space is allowed any number of spaces are allowed.

For example, consider:

```
IF TAXABLE-PAY < 500
```

the reserved-word IF, the data-name TAXABLE-PAY, the comparator '<' and the numeric literal 500 are all tokens of the language and must be separated by one or more spaces. Except in the case of nonnumeric literals (see 'Continuation Lines' below) a break in a statement caused by an end of line is treated as a space separator.

The above example could therefore be rewritten as:

```
IF      TAXABLE-PAY   <         500
```

or even:

```
IF TAXABLE-PAY
    < 500
```

It would not be legal to write:

```
IF TAXABLE<500
```

because there are no separators between TAXABLE-PAY and '<', or between '<' and 500. Rewriting the above example as:

```
IF TAXABLE
-PAY < 500
```

would also be illegal as the data-name TAXABLE-PAY has been split by a separator.

The punctuation marks '.' and ',' may also be used as separators but each of these must be followed by at least one space to separate it from the next token. Note that this refers to the character '.' used as a punctuation mark not as a decimal point in a picture clause or literal.

The only other separators which have been encountered in this book are the left and right parentheses, '(' and ')', which may appear in arithmetic expressions, conditions and subscripted names. Without getting too involved in details, safe rules to follow are:

(a) left parentheses should be preceded by one or more spaces but need not be followed by a space,
(b) right parentheses need not be preceded by spaces but should be followed by one or more spaces, unless followed by a full stop.

Continuation Lines

Any element of the COBOL language can be continued onto one or more continuation lines, which should all be within area B regardless of the positioning of the continued line.

A hyphen in the indicator area indicates that the first non-blank character in area B of the continuation line immediately follows the last non-blank character of the preceding line, excluding any intervening comment lines. The only exception to this rule is nonnumeric constants, which are broken over two or more lines using the following rules.

1. Any line which is to be continued should not contain a closing quotation mark and any spaces at the end of the line are considered

as part of the literal.

2. The continuation line must have a hyphen in the indicator area, area A must be blank and the first non-blank character in area B must be a quotation mark.

3. The first character after the opening quotation mark of the continuation line is assumed to follow immediately after the last character of the preceding line, intervening comment lines excluded.

Since the number of spaces used as a separator is not significant, the continuation of nonnumeric constants is the only case in which a continuation indicator is absolutely necessary.

Comments

Any line with an asterisk in the indicator area is treated as a comment line and ignored for all purposes except program listings.

Appendix 3 Reserved Words

The following list gives the reserved words defined for ANS COBOL 74. Further reserved words are likely to be added for any given implementation of COBOL; therefore the appropriate manual should be consulted.

ACCEPT
ACCESS
ADD
ADVANCING
AFTER
ALL
ALPHABETIC
ALSO
ALTER
ALTERNATE
AND
ARE
AREA
AREAS
ASCENDING
ASSIGN
AT
AUTHOR

BEFORE
BLANK
BLOCK
BOTTOM
BY

CALL
CANCEL
CD
CF
CH
CHARACTER
CHARACTERS
CLOCK-UNITS
CLOSE
COBOL
CODE
CODE-SET
COLLATING
COLUMN
COMMA
COMMUNICATION
COMP
COMPUTATIONAL
COMPUTE
CONFIGURATION
CONTAINS
CONTROL
CONTROLS
COPY
CORR
CORRESPONDING
COUNT
CURRENCY

DATA
DATE
DATE-COMPILED
DATE-WRITTEN
DAY
DE
DEBUG-CONTENTS
DEBUG-ITEM
DEBUG-LINE
DEBUG-NAME
DEBUG-SUB-1
DEBUG-SUB-2
DEBUG-SUB-3
DEBUGGING
DECIMAL-POINT
DECLARATIVES
DELETE
DELIMITED
DELIMITER
DEPENDING
DESCENDING
DESTINATION
DETAIL
DISABLE
DISPLAY
DIVIDE
DIVISION
DOWN
DUPLICATES
DYNAMIC

EGI
ELSE
EMI
ENABLE
END
END-OF-PAGE
ENTER
ENVIRONMENT
EOP
EQUAL
ERROR
ESI
EVERY
EXCEPTION
EXIT
EXTEND

FD
FILE
FILE-CONTROL
FILLER
FINAL
FIRST
FOOTING
FOR
FROM

GENERATE
GIVING
GO
GREATER
GROUP

HEADING
HIGH-VALUE
HIGH-VALUES

I-O
I-O-CONTROL
IDENTIFICATION
IF
IN
INDEX
INDEXED
INDICATE
INITIAL
INITIATE
INPUT
INPUT-OUTPUT
INSPECT
INSTALLATION
INTO
INVALID
IS

JUST
JUSTIFIED

KEY

LABEL
LAST
LEADING
LEFT
LENGTH
LESS
LIMIT
LIMITS
LINAGE
LINAGE-COUNTER
LINE
LINE-COUNTER
LINES
LINKAGE
LOCK
LOW-VALUE
LOW-VALUES

MEMORY
MERGE
MESSAGE
MODE
MODULES
MOVE
MULTIPLE
MULTIPLY

NATIVE
NEGATIVE
NEXT
NO
NOT
NUMBER
NUMERIC

OBJECT-COMPUTER
OCCURS
OF
OFF
OMITTED
ON
OPEN
OPTIONAL
OR
ORGANIZATION
OUTPUT
OVERFLOW

PAGE
PAGE-COUNTER
PERFORM
PF
PH
PIC
PICTURE
PLUS
POINTER
POSITION
POSITIVE
PRINTING
PROCEDURE
PROCEDURES
PROCEED
PROGRAM
PROGRAM-ID

QUEUE
QUOTE
QUOTES

RANDOM
RD
READ
RECEIVE
RECORD
RECORDS
REDEFINES
REEL
REFERENCES
RELATIVE
RELEASE
REMAINDER
REMOVAL
RENAMES
REPLACING
REPORT
REPORTING
REPORTS
RERUN
RESERVE
RESET
RETURN
REVERSED
REWIND
REWRITE
RF
RH
RIGHT
ROUNDED
RUN

SAME
SD
SEARCH
SECTION
SECURITY
SEGMENT
SEGMENT-LIMIT
SELECT
SEND
SENTENCE
SEPARATE
SEQUENCE
SEQUENTIAL
SET
SIGN
SIZE
SORT
SORT-MERGE
SOURCE
SOURCE-COMPUTER
SPACE
SPACES
SPECIAL-NAMES
STANDARD
STANDARD-1
START
STATUS
STOP
STRING
SUB-QUEUE-1
SUB-QUEUE-2
SUB-QUEUE-3
SUBTRACT
SUM
SUPPRESS
SYMBOLIC
SYNC
SYNCHRONIZED

TABLE
TALLYING
TAPE
TERMINAL
TERMINATE
TEXT
THAN
THROUGH
THRU
TIME
TIMES
TO
TOP

TRAILING
TYPE

UNIT
UNSTRING
UNTIL
UP
UPON
USAGE
USE
USING

VALUE
VALUES
VARYING

WHEN
WITH
WORDS
WORKING-STORAGE
WRITE

ZERO
ZEROES
ZEROS

Appendix 4 Summary of COBOL Syntax

The objective of this appendix is to gather together all the constructs of COBOL which have been used in this book and summarize their syntax. In some cases, particularly pictures, a concise summary is very difficult and here the reader is referred back to the relevant section(s) of the main text. In all cases, cross-references are given to the principal discussion of a particular feature in the main text. It should be emphasized that what is presented here is a small subset of COBOL, sufficient for writing the programs given in this book.

The notation used in this syntax summary is that used in the ANS COBOL standard document and also in most COBOL manuals. The underlined words in capitals are keywords which must appear if a particular construct is used. The other words in capitals are optional and may be omitted without changing the meaning of a construct. Words in lower case letters indicate references to other definitions.

Alternatives are indicated by a stack of objects, one of which should be chosen. Square brackets indicate that the enclosed thing is optional but if included will change the meaning of the construct. The ellipsis, '. . .', indicates that the preceding object can be repeated as often as required. Braces (curly brackets) are used to enclose a compulsory item, usually a choice of things or a compound object which may be repeated.

User-defined Name

A user-defined name is a sequence of not more than thirty characters chosen from the set A -> Z, 0 -> 9, and '-' (hyphen); not beginning or ending with a hyphen. It must not be a reserved-word of COBOL (see Appendix 3) and each user-defined name must be uniquely associated with one entity in the program.
See: 3.2.

Literal

A literal is a constant used in a program and can be one of three types:

(a) numeric literal; an integer or decimal value, possibly preceded by a sign,
(b) nonnumeric literal; any sequence of characters enclosed in double quotation marks ("),
(c) figurative literal; SPACE[S], LOW-VALUE[S] and HIGH-VALUE[S].

See: 4.2 (Constants).

Identification Division

```
IDENTIFICATION DIVISION.
PROGRAM-ID. program-name.
[AUTHOR. comment-entry ]
[INSTALLATION. comment-entry ]
[DATE-WRITTEN. comment-entry ]
[DATE-COMPILED. comment-entry ]
[SECURITY. comment-entry ]
```

Where: program-name is a user-defined name, possibly restricted by a particular implementation, and comment-entry is any string of characters from the COBOL character set.
See: 8.1.

Environment Division

```
ENVIRONMENT DIVISION.
CONFIGURATION SECTION.
SOURCE-COMPUTER. source-computer-name.
OBJECT-COMPUTER. object-computer-name.
[SPECIAL-NAMES.
    implementor-name IS mnemonic-name.]
INPUT-OUTPUT SECTION.
FILE-CONTROL.
    file-control-entry . . .
```

Where: source-computer-name, object-computer-name and implementor-name should be replaced by a character string defined by the implementor of the system being used; mnemonic-name is a user-defined name.
See: 8.2.

File-control Entry

```
SELECT file-name ASSIGN TO external-file-name.
```

Where: file-name is a user-defined name and the format of external-file-name is implementor-defined.
See: 8.2 and 9.1.

Data Division

```
DATA DIVISION.
[FILE SECTION.
    file-description-entry . . . ]
[WORKING-STORAGE SECTION.
    record-description-entry . . . ]
[LINKAGE SECTION.
    record-description-entry . . . ]
```

See: 8.3 and 11.2.

File-description Entry

```
FD file-name
                          {STANDARD}
    LABEL RECORDS ARE {OMITTED }.
    record-description-entry . . .
```

Where: file-name is a user-defined name.
See: 8.3 and 9.1.

Record-description Entry

```
01  data-name
    [PIC picture-string] .
```

Where: data-name is a user-defined name and picture-string is a legally-formed string of characters describing a data-item.
Pictures are discussed in: 3.4, 5.1, 5.2 and 5.3.
See: 3.3.

Data-description Entry

```
                {data-name}
level-number {FILLER   }
    [REDEFINES data-name]
    [PIC picture-string]
    [OCCURS integer TIMES]
    [VALUE literal] .
```

Where: level-number is an integer between 02 and 49, data-name is a user-defined name and picture-string is a legally formed string of characters describing a data-item. A VALUE clause can only be associated with a data-description entry in the WORKING-STORAGE SECTION.
Pictures are discussed in: 3.4, 5.1, 5.2 and 5.3.
See: 3.3, 5.4 (VALUE), 6.2 (REDEFINES) and 10.1 (OCCURS).

Condition-name

```
88  condition-name VALUE { literal [THRU literal] } . . . .
```

Where: condition-name is a user-defined name; the condition-name is associated with the immediately preceding elementary-item and each literal must be of the same type as that elementary-item.
See: 6.3.

Subscripted-name

```
              {literal  }   [  {literal  } ]
table-name ( {data-name}   [, {data-name} ] . . . )
```

Where: table-name is the name of a group-item or elementary-item which is the subject of one or more OCCURS clauses. Any literal must be an integer value and data-name must be associated with a data-item of integer type which is neither edited nor subscripted.

See: 10.1 (and following sections of Chapter 10).

Identifier

An identifier is the name used to uniquely reference a data-item. If the data-item is part of a table then the data-name will require subscripting. In general, a data-name may also be indexed or qualified but these concepts are beyond the scope of this book.

Condition

```
                          ( > )    literal
identifier [NOT]          { = }    identifier
                          ( < )

[NOT] condition-name

                          ( NUMERIC    )
identifier [NOT]          ( ALPHABETIC )
```

Complete simple conditions, as given above, may be combined into compound conditions using AND and OR, together with parentheses if required.
See: 4.3 (Simple conditions), 6.2 (class conditions), 6.3 (condition-names) and 6.5 (compound conditions).

Procedure Division

```
PROCEDURE DIVISION [USING identifier . . . ] .
    {paragraph-name. sentence . . . } . . .
```

Where: paragraph-name is a user-defined name and sentence is a sequence of COBOL statements terminated by a full stop.
See: 8.4 and 11.2.

Imperative Sequence

This is a sequence of statements which can be executed without any further conditional structure being introduced. Therefore an IF statement cannot be used as part of an imperative sequence and neither can a READ statement with an AT END qualifier (or an INVALID KEY qualifier). This rule is imposed to avoid ambiguity being introduced into the sequence of statements.

An imperative sequence is normally terminated by a full stop but may be terminated by ELSE if embedded within an IF statement. In practice, most imperative sequences consist of a single statement such as a MOVE statement or a PERFORM statement.

Call Statement

```
CALL program-name [USING identifier . . . ]
```

Where: program-name is a nonnumeric literal.
See: 11.2.

Close Statement

```
CLOSE file-name . . .
```

Where: file-name is a user-defined name, appearing in a file-control entry and a file-description.
See: 8.4 and 9.1.

Compute Statement

```
COMPUTE identifier [ROUNDED] = arithmetic-expression
```

Where: identifier is associated with a data-item of numeric type.
The formulation of arithmetic-expressions is discussed in Section 2.1.
See: 4.2 (Calculate operation) and 5.1 (Rounding).

Display Statement

```
        {literal   }
DISPLAY {identifier} . . . [UPON mnemonic-name]
```

Where: mnemonic-name is a user-defined name which must have been defined in the SPECIAL-NAMES paragraph.
See: 7.2

Exit-program Statement

```
EXIT PROGRAM.
```

Where: this statement must be the *only* statement in a paragraph.
See: 11.2.

Go To Statement

```
GO TO paragraph-name
```

Where: paragraph-name is a user-defined name identifying a paragraph in the PROCEDURE DIVISION.
See: 11.1.

If Statement

```
IF condition statement-sequence [ELSE statement-sequence]
```

Where: statement-sequence is any sequence of one or more COBOL statements.
See: 4.3 (Selection) and 6.4.

Move Statement

```
     {literal   }
MOVE {identifier} TO identifier . . .
```

See: 4.2 (Transfer operation).

Open Statement

```
OPEN INPUT file-name . . .  OUTPUT file-name . . .
```

Where: file-name is a user-defined name appearing in a file-control entry and a file-description.
See: 8.4 and 9.1.

Perform Statement

```
PERFORM paragraph-name
```

Where: paragraph-name is a user-defined name identifying a paragraph in the PROCEDURE DIVISION.
See: 4.2 (Refinement).

Perform-until Statement

```
PERFORM paragraph-name UNTIL condition
```

Where: paragraph-name is a user-defined name identifying a paragraph in the PROCEDURE DIVISION.
See: 4.3 (Repetition).

Perform-varying Statement

```
PERFORM paragraph-name VARYING identifier
          {literal   }    {literal   }
     FROM {identifier} BY {identifier} UNTIL condition
```

Where: paragraph-name is a user-defined name identifying a paragraph in the PROCEDURE DIVISION. Any literal must be of numeric type and identifiers must be associated with data-items of numeric type, which are not edited.
(This statement is most commonly used in conjunction with tables, in which case the literals and identifiers are restricted to integer values.)
See: 10.1 (for loop).

Read Statement

```
READ file-name [INTO identifier] AT END imperative-sequence
```

Where: file-name is a user-defined name appearing in a file-control entry and a file-description. The identifier must specify a data-item which is independent of the file description (normally a record-description in the WORKING-STORAGE SECTION).
See: 8.4, 8.6 and 9.1.

Stop Statement

```
        (literal)
STOP    {RUN    }
```

See: 8.4.

Write Statement

```
WRITE record-name [FROM identifier]
```

Where: record-name is the name of a record-description appearing in a file-description and identifier specifies a data-item independent of that file-description (normally a record-description entry in the WORKING-STORAGE SECTION).
See: 8.4 and 9.1.

Write Statement (Printer)

```
WRITE record-name [FROM identifier]
     {BEFORE}             {integer LINES}
     {AFTER } ADVANCING   {PAGE         }
```

Where: record-name is the name of a record-description appearing in a file-description and identifier specifies a data-item independent of that file-description (normally a record-description entry in the WORKING-STORAGE SECTION).
For one particular output file, it is advisable to use either BEFORE or AFTER consistently rather than mix the two options.
See: 8.5.

Direct-access Files

The use of the direct-access file structures, indexed and relative, requires alternative forms of the file-control entry and the various input/output statements. These are given separately to avoid including too many alternatives in the syntax for the basic forms of the statements given above.

File-control Entry (Relative File)

```
SELECT file-name ASSIGN TO external-file-name
    ORGANIZATION RELATIVE
                 {RANDOM    }
    ACCESS MODE  {SEQUENTIAL}
    [RELATIVE KEY data-name] .
```

Where: file-name and data-name are user-defined names, and the format of external-file-name is implementor-defined. The RELATIVE KEY clause is required for ACCESS MODE RANDOM. The data-name must be associated with a data-item of numeric integer type which must not be contained within a record-description associated with file-name.
See: 11.4.

File-control Entry (Indexed File)

```
SELECT file-name ASSIGN TO external-file-name
    ORGANIZATION INDEXED
                 {RANDOM    }
    ACCESS MODE  {SEQUENTIAL}
    RECORD KEY data-name .
```

Where: file-name and data-name are user-defined names, and the format of external-file-name is implementor-defined. Note that the RECORD KEY clause is required in all cases. The data-name must be associated with a data-item which is described as part of a record-description associated with file-name.
See: 11.5.

Delete Statement

```
DELETE file-name INVALID KEY imperative-sequence
```

Where: file-name is a user-defined name appearing in a file-control entry and a file-description.
See: 11.4 and 11.5.

Open Statement (Direct-access)

```
     {I-O    file-name . . .}
OPEN {OUTPUT file-name . . .} . . .
     {INPUT  file-name . . .}
```

Where: file-name is a user-defined name which must have appeared in a file-control entry and a file-description.
See: 11.4 and 11.5.

Read Statement (Direct-access)

```
READ file-name [INTO identifier]
    INVALID KEY imperative-sequence
```

Where: file-name is a user-defined name appearing in a file-control entry and a file-description. The identifier must specify a data-item which is independent of the file description (normally a record-description in the WORKING-STORAGE SECTION). This format is only valid when the file-control entry specifies ACCESS MODE RANDOM.
See: 11.4 and 11.5.

Rewrite Statement

```
REWRITE record-name [FROM identifier]
    INVALID KEY imperative-sequence
```

Where: record-name is the name of a record-description appearing in a file-description and identifier specifies a data-item independent of that file-description (normally a record-description entry in the WORKING-STORAGE SECTION).

See: 11.4 and 11.5.

Write Statement (Direct-access)

```
WRITE record-name [FROM identifier]
    INVALID KEY imperative-sequence
```

Where: record-name is the name of a record-description appearing in a file-description and identifier specifies a data-item independent of that file-description (normally a record-description entry in the WORKING-STORAGE SECTION). This format is only valid when the file-control entry for the associated file specifies ACCESS MODE RANDOM.
See: 11.4 and 11.5.

Copy Statement

```
COPY library-entry-name
   [ REPLACING  {{literal   } BY {literal   }}  ... ] .
                 {identifier}    {identifier}
```

Where: library-entry-name is a user-defined name identifying a piece of text in a COBOL source library.
See: 11.3.

Appendix 5 Notes for Users of Low-Level ANS COBOL

The American National Standard for COBOL is structured so that a variety of levels of ANS COBOL compilers can be produced depending on the size of computer being used. A minimal ANS COBOL, for example on a microcomputer, will not implement all of the features described in this book. Therefore this appendix is designed to help those readers who may be using such a low-level system.

A5.1. Arithmetic

The COMPUTE statement may not be implemented in all ANS COBOL compilers. In this case the programmer will have to use the basic arithmetic statements: ADD, SUBTRACT, MULTIPLY and DIVIDE. The syntax of these statements is given below:

```
    {literal   }  [literal   ]
ADD {identifier}  [identifier] . . . TO identifier [ROUNDED]

    {literal   }  {literal   }  [literal   ]
ADD {identifier}  {identifier}  [identifier] . . .
     GIVING identifier [ROUNDED]

         {literal   }  [literal   ]
SUBTRACT {identifier}  [identifier] . . . FROM identifier
      [ROUNDED]

         {literal   }  [literal   ]                {literal   }
SUBTRACT {identifier}  [identifier] . . . FROM     {identifier}
     GIVING identifier [ROUNDED]

         {literal   }
MULTIPLY {identifier}  BY identifier [ROUNDED]

         {literal   }       {literal   }
MULTIPLY {identifier}  BY   {identifier}
     GIVING identifier [ROUNDED]

       {literal   }
DIVIDE {identifier}  INTO identifier [ROUNDED]

       {literal   }       {literal   }
DIVIDE {identifier}  INTO {identifier}
     GIVING identifier [ROUNDED]
```

Where: all identifiers must reference data-items of numeric type; an identifier following GIVING may refer to an edited data-item, all other identifiers must refer to unedited data-items, and all literals must be numeric. In the MULTIPLY and DIVIDE without GIVING the result is stored in the rightmost identifier. The ROUNDED option has the same effect on the results as it does in the COMPUTE statement (see 5.1).

If a calculation involves only one operand it can be directly translated into one of the above statements. For example:

```
calculate detail-order-charge =
   carpet-charge + delivery-charge
```

can be translated into:

```
ADD CARPET-CHARGE DELIVERY-CHARGE
    GIVING DETAIL-ORDER-CHARGE
```

Similarly:

```
calculate billing-charge = 1.125 * basic-charge
```

can be translated into:

```
MULTIPLY 1.125 BY BASIC-CHARGE GIVING BILLING-CHARGE
```

To undertake more complex calculations it will be necessary to break them down into two or more simple operations and define data-items to hold intermediate results. For example:

```
calculate basic-charge = phone-rental
   + 0.02 * phone-dialled + 0.03 * phone-op-units
```

could be translated as:

```
MULTIPLY 0.02 BY PHONE-DIALLED GIVING INTER-RESULT
ADD PHONE-RENTAL INTER-RESULT GIVING BASIC-CHARGE
MULTIPLY 0.03 BY PHONE-OP-UNITS GIVING INTER-RESULT
ADD INTER-RESULT TO BASIC-CHARGE
```

where INTER-RESULT is a data-item appended to TEMPORARY-ITEMS, specified in such a way that it can hold any intermediate result.

A5.2 Condition-names

Some low-level ANS COBOL compilers may not implement level-number 88 condition names. Since a condition-name is only a short-hand notation it is always possible to construct an equivalent test structure using simple conditions or nested IF statements.

To implement the condition end-of-<file-name>, without using condition-names, the following technique can be used:

(a) Describe a data-item called END-OF-<file-name> in STATE-VECTOR.

```
e.g.    01  STATE-VECTOR.
            05  END-OF-ORDER-FILE        PIC X.
```

(b) Initialize this data-item to space in INIT-STATE.

```
e.g.    INIT-STATE.
            MOVE SPACE TO END-OF-ORDER-FILE
            . . . . .
```

(c) Set the value of the data-item to "E" at end of file.

e.g.
```
GET-NEXT-ORDER-FILE.
    READ ORDER-FILE
        AT END MOVE "E" TO END-OF-ORDER-FILE.
```

(d) Change any condition of the form end-of-<file-name> to an explicit test for END-OF-<file-name> = "E" and <u>not</u> end-of-<file-name> to END-OF-<file-name> NOT = "E".

e.g.
```
    PERFORM PROCESS-ORDER
        UNTIL END-OF-ORDER-FILE = "E"

    IF END-OF-ORDER-FILE NOT = "E"
```

Booleans can be implemented in an analogous way using explicit tests for "T" and "F" in place of condition-names. For example, to implement the Boolean 'searchover':

```
01  STATE-VECTOR.
    05  SEARCHOVER       PIC X.

    transfer false to searchover
    MOVE "F" TO SEARCHOVER

    transfer true to searchover
    MOVE "T" TO SEARCHOVER

    until searchover do
    PERFORM <paragraph-name>
        UNTIL SEARCHOVER = "T"

    if not searchover then
    IF SEARCHOVER NOT = "T"
or  IF SEARCHOVER = "F"
```

Condition-names associated with multiple values or ranges of values, for example in data validation (see 6.3), will have to be replaced by a series of explicit tests for the values. For example:

```
    05  CUST-TYPE        PIC A.
        88  VALID-CUSTOMER VALUE "C" THRU "H", "X".
. . . . .
    IF VALID-CUSTOMER
        PERFORM CALCULATE-BILL.
```

would have to be replaced by:

```
    05  CUST-TYPE        PIC A.
. . . . .
    IF CUST-TYPE > "B"
        IF CUST-TYPE < "I"
            PERFORM CALCULATE-BILL.
    IF CUST-TYPE = "X"
        PERFORM CALCULATE-BILL.
```

A5.3 Perform-until

Only the straightforward implementation of PERFORM is required in a minimal ANS COBOL compiler therefore PERFORM . . . UNTIL may not be implemented. In this case the <u>until</u> operation will have to be translated using IF and GO TO.

A possible implementation of:

```
until <condition> do
   <procedure>
enduntil
```

is:

```
UNTIL-LOOP-<id>.
    IF NOT <condition>
        PERFORM <loop-body>
        GO TO UNTIL-LOOP-<id>.
. . . . .
<loop-body>.
    <procedure>.
```

Where <id> should be replaced by any suitable identifier to distinguish this loop from all other <u>until</u> loops in the program. For example the first <u>until</u> loop encountered could have <id> = 1, the second <id> = 2, etc.

Perform-thru

Unfortunately the translation outlined above introduces a new problem because the insertion of the extra paragraph-name, UNTIL-LOOP-<id>, changes the flow of control through the program. Consider the following top-level program design.

```
summarize-orders
   get-next-order-file
   until end-of-order-file do
      update-counters
      get-next-order-file
   enduntil
   print-order-summary
```

An attempt could be made to translate this as:

```
PROCEDURE DIVISION.
MAIN-PROGRAM.
    PERFORM INIT-STATE
    PERFORM SUMMARIZE-ORDERS
    PERFORM CLOSE-DOWN.
. . . . .
```

```
SUMMARIZE-ORDERS.
    PERFORM GET-NEXT-ORDER-FILE.
UNTIL-LOOP-1.
    IF NOT END-OF-ORDER-FILE
        PERFORM PROCESS-ORDER-RECORD
        GO TO UNTIL-LOOP-1.
    PERFORM PRINT-ORDER-SUMMARY.
PROCESS-ORDER-RECORD.
    PERFORM UPDATE-COUNTERS
    PERFORM GET-NEXT-ORDER-FILE.
. . . . .
```

The problem with this translation is that PERFORM SUMMARIZE-ORDERS will only execute the named paragraph, SUMMARIZE-ORDERS, and the new paragraph named UNTIL-LOOP-1 will be ignored. The simple way round this problem is to use a variation of the PERFORM statement which allows a sequence of paragraphs to be grouped for execution.

The paragraph MAIN-PROGRAM could be implemented as:

```
PROCEDURE DIVISION.
MAIN-PROGRAM.
    PERFORM INIT-STATE
    PERFORM SUMMARIZE-ORDERS THRU UNTIL-LOOP-1
    PERFORM CLOSE-DOWN.
```

The statement:

```
    PERFORM first-paragraph-name THRU last-paragraph-name
```

means that the statements from the beginning of first-paragraph to the end of last-paragraph are regarded as a single unit by this PERFORM statement. It is recommended that this construct is used only in these special cases as it tends to obscure the meaning of the program unless used carefully.

As a matter of style, it is suggested that an additional paragraph-name is introduced for the continuation of a split paragraph. One convention, used by the author, is to construct a new paragraph-name by appending '-CONT' (continuation) to the original paragraph-name. Therefore the program design for 'summarize-orders' would be translated as:

```
PROCEDURE DIVISION.
MAIN-PROGRAM.
    PERFORM INIT-STATE
    PERFORM SUMMARIZE-ORDERS THRU SUMMARIZE-ORDERS-CONT
    PERFORM CLOSE-DOWN.
. . . . .
SUMMARIZE-ORDERS.
    PERFORM GET-NEXT-ORDER-FILE.
UNTIL-LOOP-1.
    IF NOT END-OF-ORDER-FILE
        PERFORM PROCESS-ORDER-RECORD
        GO TO UNTIL-LOOP-1.
SUMMARIZE-ORDERS-CONT.
    PERFORM PRINT-ORDER-SUMMARY.
```

```
PROCESS-ORDER-RECORD.
    PERFORM UPDATE-COUNTERS
    PERFORM GET-NEXT-ORDER-FILE.
. . . . .
```

If there are no operations following the <u>enduntil</u> then the continuation paragraph is empty and <paragraph-name>-CONT is attached to a null paragraph, that is the next paragraph-name follows immediately. An example of this is given at the end of Section A5.5.

A5.4 Compound Conditions

Many lower-level ANS COBOL compilers do not implement AND and OR to combine simple conditions into compound conditions. Therefore any compound conditions will have to be replaced by nested IF statements and refinements. Nested IF statements are discussed in Section 6.4 and their relationship to compound conditions in Section 6.5. Care must be taken when implementing the <u>else</u> associated with a compound condition. For example:

```
if cust-type = "W" and cust-quantity > 100 then
   discount-routine
else
   full-price-routine
endif
```

could be implemented as:

```
IF CUST-TYPE = "W"
    IF CUST-QUANTITY > 100
        PERFORM DISCOUNT-ROUTINE
    ELSE
        PERFORM FULL-PRICE-ROUTINE
ELSE
    PERFORM FULL-PRICE-ROUTINE.
```

In a minimal (level 1) ANS COBOL system nested IF statements will not be available and therefore the above compound condition would have to translated as:

```
    IF CUST-TYPE = "W"
        PERFORM CHECK-CUST-QUANTITY
    ELSE
        PERFORM FULL-PRICE-ROUTINE.
    . . . . .
CHECK-CUST-QUANTITY.
    IF CUST-QUANTITY > 100
        PERFORM DISCOUNT-ROUTINE
    ELSE
        PERFORM FULL-PRICE-ROUTINE.
```

To implement an <u>until</u> loop controlled by a compound condition will require the construction of an extra data-item to control the loop; this is discussed in Section 6.6 in the context of testability of conditions.

A5.5 Perform-varying

This variant of the PERFORM statement is unlikely to be available in low-level ANS COBOL compilers. A for loop of the form:

```
for <control-data-item> = <initial-value> to <final-value> do
   <procedure>
endfor
```

can be implemented as:

```
        MOVE <initial-value> TO <control-data-item>.
    FOR-LOOP-<id>.
        IF <control-data-item> NOT > <final-value>
            PERFORM <loop-body>
            ADD 1 TO <control-data-item>
            GO TO FOR-LOOP-<id>.
    . . . . .
    <loop-body>.
        <procedure>.
```

Where <id> should be replaced by any suitable identifier to distinguish this loop from all other for loops in the program. For example the first for loop encountered could have <id> = 1, the second <id> = 2, etc.

This implementation uses only verbs which must be available in a minimal implementation of ANS COBOL.

There is a problem with the program structure when the new paragraph-name FOR-LOOP-<id> is introduced - this is discussed in Section A5.3 (see "Perform-thru").

As an example of this translation of the for loop consider the following simplified extract from the case study discussed in Section 10.6.

```
print-table
   print-headings
   for mc-subscript = 1 to mc-limit do
      transfer model-c-code (mc-subscript) to summary-code
      transfer model-c-numbers (mc-subscript) to summary-numbers
      put-summary-line
   endfor
print-headings
   . . . . .
```

This could be translated as:

```
PRINT-TABLE.
    PERFORM PRINT-HEADINGS
    MOVE 1 TO MC-SUBSCRIPT.
```

```
FOR-LOOP-1.
    IF MC-SUBSCRIPT NOT > MC-LIMIT
        PERFORM PRINT-MODEL-DETAILS
        ADD 1 TO MC-SUBSCRIPT
        GO TO FOR-LOOP-1.
PRINT-TABLE-CONT.
PRINT-MODEL-DETAILS.
    MOVE MODEL-C-CODE (MC-SUBSCRIPT) TO SUMMARY-CODE
    MOVE MODEL-C-NUMBERS (MC-SUBSCRIPT) TO SUMMARY-NUMBERS
    PERFORM PUT-SUMMARY-LINE.
PRINT-HEADINGS.
    . . . . .
```

Any reference to PRINT-TABLE will now need to changed, for example:

```
PERFORM PRINT-TABLE
```

will need to become:

```
PERFORM PRINT-TABLE THRU PRINT-TABLE-CONT
```

so that the correct program structure is maintained.

Answers to Selected Exercises

Outline solutions for most of the exercises (but not the programming exercises) are given here. Many of the exercises have alternative, equally satisfactory, answers.

Answers 2

2.1 Assume the input file is called 'employee-file' and the names of the data-items in the input record are:

employee-number	employee's number
employee-month-pay	gross monthly pay
employee-year-allow	annual allowance against tax

A possible program design, similar to that used in Example 2.4, is shown below.

```
employee-tax
   get-next-employee-file
   until end-of-employee-file do
      tax-current-employee
      print-employee-details
      get-next-employee-file
   enduntil

tax-current-employee
   calculate pension-contr = 0.05 * employee-month-pay
   calculate month-allow = employee-year-allow / 12
   calculate taxable-pay =
      employee-month-pay - month-allow - pension-contr
   find-tax
   calculate net-pay =
      employee-month-pay - pension-contr - tax-to-pay

print-employee-details
   transfer employee-number to printer-emp-no
   transfer employee-month-pay to printer-month-pay
   transfer pension-contr to printer-pension-contr
   transfer tax-to-pay to printer-tax-to-pay
   transfer net-pay to printer-net-pay
   put-printer-line

find-tax
   if taxable-pay > 0 then
      calculate tax-to-pay = 0.2 * taxable-pay
   else
      transfer 0 to tax-to-pay
   endif
```

2.2 Assume the input file is called 'census-file' and that the input records contain the data-items:

census-no-people	number of people in household
census-no-rooms	number of living rooms in house

A possible program design, based on that of Example 2.5, is shown below.

```
census-data
   initialize-counters
   get-next-census-file
   until end-of-census-file do
      update-counters
      get-next-census-file
   enduntil
   print-counters

initialize-counters
   transfer 0 to no-of-households
   transfer 0 to households-over-2
   transfer 0 to dense-households

update-counters
   calculate no-of-households = no-of-households + 1
   if census-no-people > 2 then
      calculate households-over-2 = households-over-2 + 1
   endif
   calculate household-ratio =
      census-no-of-people / census-no-of-rooms
   if household-ratio > 1.5 then
      calculate dense-households = dense-households + 1
   endif

print-counters
   calculate summary-perc-over-2 =
      households-over-2 / no-of-households * 100
   calculate summary-perc-dense =
      dense-households /no-of-households * 100
   put-summary-line
```

2.3 Assume the input file is called 'elec-file' and that the data-items are named:

elec-cust-no	customer account number
elec-tariff	tariff code
elec-name-address	customer's name and address
elec-units-used	units consumed in quarter

A possible program design, based on a combination of the previous two designs and similar to the case study in Section 2.5, is given below.

```
electricity-billing
   initialize-totals
   get-next-elec-file
   until end-of-elec-file do
      process-customer
      print-customer-details
      update-counters
      get-next-elec-file
   enduntil
   print-totals

initialize-totals
   transfer 0 to total-units
   transfer 0 to total-charge

process-customer
   if elec-tariff = "D" then
      domestic-tariff
   else
      commercial-tariff
   endif

print-customer-details
   transfer elec-cust-no to detail-cust-no
   transfer elec-tariff to detail-tariff
   transfer elec-name-address to detail-name-address
   transfer elec-units-used to detail-units-used
   transfer amount-charged to detail-amount-charged
   put-detail-line

update-counters
   calculate total-units = total-units + elec-units-used
   calculate total-charge = total-charge + amount-charged

print-totals
   transfer total-units to summary-units
   transfer total-charge to summary-charge
   put-summary-line

domestic-tariff
   if elec-units-used > 100 then
      calculate amount-charged =
         13 + (elec-units-used - 100) * 0.08
   else
      calculate amount-charged = 3 + elec-units-used * 0.01
   endif

commercial-tariff
   if elec-units-used > 200 then
      calculate amount-charged =
         30 + (elec-units-used - 200) * 0.05
   else
      calculate amount-charged = elec-units-used * 0.15
   endif
```

Answers 3

3.1 The following names are valid: (a), (b), (d), (e) and (i). The names (d) and (e) are only valid as procedure-names, while the others are valid as both data-names and procedure-names. The invalid names are: (c) and (g) because they contain illegal characters ('.' and '%' respectively), (f) is a reserved-word, (h) begins with a hyphen and (j) exceeds 30 characters in length.

3.2 Possible data records are:

```
8100123ASTEWART, ALAN BRECK              F03012  023
8016725%MCGREGOR, ROB ROY                BAA001  003
8100001*STEVENSON, ROBERT LOUIS          S--157  120
```

3.3 The record structure should be of the form:

```
01  STOCK-RECORD.
    05  STOCK-NUMBER.
        10  STOCK-NO-MAN.
            15  STOCK-NO-MAN-1      PIC AA.
            15  STOCK-NO-MAN-2      PIC 999.
            15  STOCK-NO-MAN-3      PIC X.
        10  STOCK-NO-SER            PIC 9(8).
    05  STOCK-DESC                  PIC X(30).
    05  STOCK-BIN.
        10  STOCK-BIN-1             PIC AA.
        10  STOCK-BIN-2             PIC 9999.
    05  FILLER                      PIC XXXX.
    05  STOCK-REORDER-LEV           PIC 999.
```

Answers 4

4.1 The output form the program, for the given input data, will now consist of only two lines:

```
A00008  SELECTED - LOW STOCK           0024     LOW STOCK
B00009  SELECTED - LOW STOCK           0004     LOW STOCK
```

This is because PERFORM PUT-DETAILS is now part of the preceding IF structure and therefore PUT-DETAILS will only be executed when STOCK-QUANTITY < 25 is true.

4.2 The translation of the design should be:

```
        PERFORM GET-NEXT-ACCOUNT-FILE
        PERFORM LOOP-FOR-ONE-ACCOUNT
            UNTIL END-OF-ACCOUNT-FILE.
    LOOP-FOR-ONE-ACCOUNT.
        PERFORM PROCESS-ACCOUNT
        PERFORM GET-NEXT-ACCOUNT-FILE.
```

Assuming that the paragraph PROCESS-ACCOUNT does not contain a PERFORM GET-NEXT-ACCOUNT-FILE statement, the incorrect coding will cause an 'infinite loop', repeatedly processing the first record from

ACCOUNT-FILE.

Answers 5

5.1 The input values should be written as follows:

23	002300
27.5	002750
133.42	013342
2,125	212500

5.2 The values calculated will be:

FULL-PRICE	DISCOUNT-GIVEN	FINAL-PRICE
10.00	1.55	8.45
20.50	3.17	17.33
37.25	5.77	31.48
1500.00	32.50	1467.50

Note that in the second and third examples the least significant digits of DISCOUNT-GIVEN are truncated and in the last case the most significant digit has been truncated.

5.3 The following results should be produced:

PIC	87654321	0.756	-253
£££,££9.99	£54,321.00	ƀƀƀƀƀ£0.75	ƀƀƀ£253.00
Z(5)9	654321	ƀƀƀƀƀ0	ƀƀƀ253
£**,***.99	£54,321.00	£******.75	£***253.00
££,££9.99DB	£4,321.00ƀƀ	ƀƀƀƀƀ0.75ƀƀ	ƀƀ£253.00DB
ZZ.ZZ9+	54,321+	ƀƀƀƀƀ0+	ƀƀƀ253-

Answers 6

6.1 (a) Possible descriptions for 'part-model-id' and 'model-stocked' would be:

```
05  PART-MODEL-ID        PIC 99.
    88  MODEL-STOCKED    VALUE
        4 THRU 9, 12 THRU 16, 20, 24.
```

(b) A possible equivalent design fragment would be:

```
if part-model-id > 3 and part-model-id < 10 then
   check-part-available
else
   if part-model-id > 11 and part-model-id < 17 then
      check-part-available
   else
      if part-model-id = 20 then
         check-part-available
      else
         if part-model-id = 24 then
            check-part-available
         endif
      endif
   endif
endif
```

There are many other possible solutions using simple conditions with nested *ifs* and also refinement. Translation of the above design fragment into COBOL is quite straightforward.

6.2 The piece of program shown does not include any full stops therefore all the IFs are linked. When executed with ACCOUNT-TYPE containing the value 'W' the procedure WHOLESALE-ROUTINE will be executed; in all other cases the paragraph PROCESS-AC-TYPE has no effect.

An equivalent program design is:

```
process-ac-type
   if account-type = "W" then
      wholesale-routine
      if account-type = "R" then
         retail-routine
         if (account-type = "W")
               or (account-type not = "R") then
            ac-type-error
         endif
      endif
   endif
```

Note that inserting full stops after WHOLESALE-ROUTINE and RETAIL-ROUTINE, in the piece of COBOL given, will still not produce the correct solution. The third condition must contain an AND rather than an OR, otherwise AC-TYPE-ERROR is always executed.

The best solution is a nested *if* structure of the form:

```
if account-type = "W" then
   wholesale-routine
else
   if account-type = "R" then
      retail-routine
   else
      ac-type-error
   endif
endif
```

The translation to COBOL is quite straightforward.

Answers 7

7.1 In exercise (a) only equivalence partitioning is relevant but in (b) and (c) both equivalence partitioning and boundary-value analysis can be applied.

(a) There will need to be at least five test cases.

discount-rate = 10	: valid
discount-rate = 15	: valid
discount-rate = 20	: valid
discount-rate numeric but not = 10, 15 or 20	: invalid
discount-rate not numeric	: invalid

(b) There will need to be at least five test cases.

hourly-rate = 209	: invalid (boundary)
hourly-rate = 210	: valid (boundary)
hourly-rate = 725	: valid (boundary)
hourly-rate = 726	: invalid (boundary)
hourly-rate not numeric	: invalid

(c) This exercise is similar to Example 7.4. A table could be drawn up as follows.

class	tariff-code	units-consumed	
1	B	not numeric	invalid
2	B	200	valid (boundary)
3	B	201	valid (boundary)
4	B	9999	valid (maximum)
5	H	not numeric	invalid
6	H	100	valid (boundary)
7	H	101	valid (boundary)
8	H	9999	valid (maximum)
9	not B or H	-	invalid

7.2 Test data to exercise the piece of program could be:

CUST-TYPE	SPECIAL-TERMS	CUST-QUANTITY	expected result
D	-	-	DEALER-DISCOUNT
T	-	-	TRADE-DISCOUNT
X	true	-	TRADE-DISCOUNT
X	false	51	QUANTITY-DISCOUNT
X	false	50	none

A value of CUST-TYPE other than 'D' or 'T' is indicated by 'X' and '-' indicates that any valid value can be used for this data-item. The procedures expected to be executed are shown on the right; all cases should execute PRODUCE-INVOICE.

7.3 The test data should be of the form:

SALES-QUANTITY	BULK-DISCOUNT-LEVEL	TRADE-CUSTOMER	outcome
25	50	false	DISCOUNT-10
25	50	true	DISCOUNT-5
75	50	-	none

Any appropriate values of SALES-QUANTITY and BULK-DISCOUNT-LEVEL can be used to make the relevant condition both true and false.

Using the above test data to desk check the program design will show that these three test cases should have produced the following outcomes: none, discount-5 and discount-10; therefore the translation is incorrect.

Answers 8

8.1 Adding a page number at the top of each output page is quite straightforward. An extra data-item can be added to PAGE-HEADING, for example:

```
05  PAGE-NO      PIC ZZ9.
```

and a page counter can be appended to STATE-VECTOR, for example:

```
05  CURRENT-PAGE         PIC 999  VALUE 1.
```

Each time a PAGE-HEADING is to be printed the value of CURRENT-PAGE is transferred to PAGE-NO and CURRENT-PAGE incremented by one, ready for the next page. For example:

```
PUT-PAGE-HEADING.
    MOVE CURRENT-PAGE TO PAGE-NO
    WRITE OUT-LINE FROM PAGE-HEADING
        AFTER ADVANCING PAGE
    COMPUTE CURRENT-PAGE = CURRENT-PAGE + 1.
```

Alternatively, CURRENT-PAGE could be initialized to zero in INIT-STATE and incremented by one before transferring its value to PAGE-NO.

Printing a page number at the bottom of the page is more difficult. It means counting the number of lines printed so far and then advancing the appropriate number of lines to the bottom of the current page before writing the page number. (There is, unfortunately, no AFTER ADVANCING BOTTOM-OF-PAGE option.) The printing of the page number will need to be added at the end of PROCESS-BATCH to avoid problems with the numbering of the last page.

8.2 What is required here is a means of distinguishing between a batch finishing with a type four record and one terminated, unexpectedly, by either the type one record for the next batch or the end of the input file. It would be possible to add another Boolean data-item to distinguish a complete batch from one which terminated without a type four record.

Alternatively, a three-state state-variable can be used. Suppose that 'batch-state' can take three values: batch being processed, represented by a space; type four record found - 'batch-complete', represented by 'C'; and batch ended without a type four record - 'batch-end', represented by 'E'.

The program design can then be modified as follows:

```
process-batch
   print-headings
   store-account-details
   transfer space to batch-state
   until batch-complete or batch-end do
      get-next-account-file
      deal-with-current-record
   enduntil
   tidy-up-batch

deal-with-current-record
   if account-rec-type = 4 then
      check-for-end-of-batch
   else
      if end-of-account-file then
         transfer "E" to batch-state
      else
         if account-rec-type = 1 then
            transfer "E" to batch-state
         else
            process-detail-record
         endif
      endif
   endif

check-for-end-of-batch
   if account-number = current-account-number then
      transfer "C" to batch-state
   else
      error-invalid-account-number
   endif

tidy-up-batch
   if batch-end then
      error-type-four-missing
   else
      compare-totals
   endif
   print-amount-due

error-type-four-missing
   display "type 4 record missing for: ", current-account-number

compare-totals
   if account-t-balance not = current-balance then
      display "discrepancy in balances for: ",
         current-account-number
      display "trailer = ", account-t-balance,
         " computed = ", current-balance
   endif
```

Where 'account-t-balance' is the balance given in the trailer record.
In COBOL, the additional record could be described as:

```
01  TRAILER-RECORD.
    05  FILLER              PIC 9.
    05  FILLER              PIC X(6).
    05  ACCOUNT-T-BALANCE   PIC S999V99.
```

The translation into COBOL also involves describing the three-state state-variable 'batch-state' as follows:

```
05  BATCH-STATE         PIC X.
    88  BATCH-COMPLETE  VALUE "C".
    88  BATCH-END       VALUE "E".
```

The remainder of the translation into COBOL should be quite straightforward.

8.3 The program will not terminate correctly because once a file is in the at-end condition the input-area for the file is no longer available to the program. Therefore the statement

```
MOVE 999999 TO CUSTOMER-ID
```

should cause the program to fail with an execution error.

Answers 9

9.1 The first step is change the description of 'current-acc-number' so that its first two digits can be tested separately. For example:

```
current-acc-number
   current-acc-no-12        first 2 digits of account number
   current-acc-no-rest      remaining 6 digits of account number
```

In addition, a temporary data-item to hold the first two digits of the last account number can be described:

```
temporary-items
   last-acc-no-12           first 2 digits of last account number
```

This data-item can be initialized after setting up 'current-acc-number' at the beginning of the program:

```
. . . . .
find-current-acc-number
transfer current-acc-no-12 to last-acc-no-12
until current-acc-number = 99999999 do
. . . . .
```

To print the necessary page headings the refinement 'start-group' is modified to:

```
start-group
   if current-acc-no-12 not = last-acc-no-12 then
      put-summary-page-heading (after new page)
      put-summary-col-headings (after two blank lines)
      transfer current-acc-no-12 to last-acc-no-12
      endif
      . . . . .
```

It is possible to modify the first attempt algorithm but the test for change of digits must be made at a high level in the design or the changes are unnecessarily complex.

9.3 There are only three changes required in the balanced line algorithm to deal with descending order of key values. The getin-next-<input-file-name> must attempt to read a record from <input-file-name> and if no record is available set the record key to an impossibly low value. The main control loop must continue until this low value is encountered, that is:

```
balanced-line
   getin-next-transactions
   getin-next-old-master
   find-current-key
   until current-key = <low-value> do
      process-group-of-current-key
      find-current-key
   enduntil
```

The procedure to find the current key must be modified to find the highest key value, therefore the amended version is:

```
find-current-key
   if trans-key > old-master-key then
      transfer trans-key to current-key
   else
      transfer old-master-key to current-key
   endif
```

The implementation of getin-next-<input-file-name> needs to be modified to:

```
GETIN-NEXT-<input-file-name>.
     READ <input-file-name> INTO <store-record-name>
         AT END MOVE <low-value> TO <store-record-key>.
```

If <store-record-key> is of alphanumeric type then the figurative constant LOW-VALUES may be used as <low-value>.

The first attempt algorithm can be modified by complementing the comparators in the first two tests in the main control loop, as shown below.

```
until end-of-old-master or end-of-transactions do
   if trans-key < old-master-key then
      copy-old-new
   else
      if trans-key > old-master-key then
         should-be-new-record
         . . . . .
```

Answers 10

10.1 The maximum numbers of a given model which can be sold are governed by the picture of MODEL-C-NUMBERS; the current limit is therefore 99 of any given model. The size of MODEL-C-GROSS and MODEL-C-PROFIT are also dependent on the numbers of a particular model sold as they are the product of MODEL-C-NUMBERS with VEHICLE-GROSS and VEHICLE-PROFIT, respectively.

If the number of model codes in use increases to 150 then this indicates that 'model-table' should be expanded so that 'model-counter' is repeated 150 times. The other implications of this change are in the COBOL program, where MC-SUBSCRIPT and MC-LIMIT will both have to be increased to PIC 999, to accommodate subscript values up to 150.

10.2 (a) The simplest solution, but not necessarily the most efficient is:

```
for cr-subscript = 1 to number-of-subscripts do
   if currency-r-code (cr-subscript) = "GDM" then
      transfer 4.21 to currency-r-exchange (cr-subscript)
   endif
endfor
```

The weakness of this solution is that it does not indicate whether the update was successful. A better solution would be:

```
transfer false to update-successful
for cr-subscript = 1 to number-of-subscripts do
   if currency-r-code (cr-subscript) = "GDM" then
      transfer 4.21 to currency-r-exchange (cr-subscript)
      transfer true to update-successful
   endif
endfor
if not update-successful then
   display "failed to find GDM in table"
endif
```

In practice, of course, the currency code to be updated and the corresponding exchange rate would be supplied in data-items rather than as constants.

It is also possible to formulate an alternative solution which stops searching once the required element of the table has been found.

10.2 (b) The solution to this exercise is similar to (a), above. A straightforward solution is:

```
transfer false to currency-found
for cr-subscript = 1 to number-of-subscripts do
   if currency-r-code (cr-subscript) = "FFR" then
      calculate exchange-amount =
         amount-required * currency-r-exchange (cr-subscript)
      transfer true to currency-found
   endif
endfor
if not currency-found then
   display "failed to find FFR in table"
endif
```

10.2 (c) This one does not require a for loop.

```
calculate number-of-currencies = number-of-currencies + 1
transfer "NGU" to currency-r-code (number-of-currencies)
transfer 3.88 to currency-r-exchange (number-of-currencies)
```

This solution does not allow for table overflow and a safer solution would be:

```
if number-of-currencies < 40 then
   calculate number-of-currencies = number-of-currencies + 1
   transfer "NGU" to currency-r-code (number-of-currencies)
   transfer 3.88 to currency-r-exchange (number-of-currencies)
else
   display "overflow in currency table"
   close-down
endif
```

Data-items required are:

```
        05  CR-SUBSCRIPT        PIC 99.
```

which can be added to CURRENCY-TABLE, and

```
        05  EXCHANGE-AMOUNT     PIC 9(8)V99.
```

which might be added to TEMPORARY-ITEMS or alternatively might be described as edited and be part of an output record. The Booleans used in (a) and (b) are:

```
    05  UPDATE-FLAG      PIC X.
        88  UPDATE-SUCCESSFUL   VALUE "T".
    05  FOUND-FLAG       PIC X.
        88  CURRENCY-FOUND  VALUE "T".
```

these should be added to STATE-VECTOR.

Index